English for New Americans

ENGLISH for
NEW AMERICANS

Everyday Life
Work and School
Health, Home, and Community

WRITTEN BY
Carol Piñeiro, Ed.D.
Boston University

EDITED BY
Ana Stojanović, M.A.

LIVING LANGUAGE®

Published in the United States by Living Language, an imprint of Random House, Inc.

www.livinglanguage.com

Editor: Christopher Warnasch
Production Editor: Carolyn Roth
Production Manager: Tom Marshall
Interior Design: Sophie Chin
Illustrations: Christopher Medellín and Josef Medellín

ISBN: 978-1-4000-0658-8

Library of Congress Cataloging-in-Publication Data available upon request.

This book is available at special discounts for bulk purchases for sales promotions or premiums. Special editions, including personalized covers, excerpts of existing books, and corporate imprints, can be created in large quantities for special needs. For more information, write to Special Markets/Premium Sales, 1745 Broadway, MD 6-2, New York, New York 10019 or e-mail specialmarkets@randomhouse.com.

PRINTED IN THE UNITED STATES OF AMERICA

10 9 8 7 6 5 4

To my mother, Fredesvinda Ammay Houser, who dedicated her life to teaching, and my mother-in-law, Dolores Parada de Piñeiro, who would have been a teacher had circumstances allowed, and finally to my daughter, Aliana Houser Piñeiro, whose love and humor have helped me through this project.

Acknowledgements

Thanks to the Living Language team: Tom Russell, Christopher Warnasch, Nicole Benhabib, Suzanne McQuade, Shaina Malkin, Elham Shabahat, Alison Skrabek, Linda Schmidt, Carolyn Roth, Tom Marshall, and Sophie Chin. Special thanks to the staff of VPG: Al Browne, Doug Latham, Raquel Ortiz, Sabrina Aviles, Andrei Campeanu, and Alex Taylor.

Contents

English for New Americans

Introduction

Welcome to *English for New Americans,* from Living Language. *English for New Americans* will greatly improve your ability to speak and understand "real" American English. The complete course consists of this workbook, three 60-minute DVDs, and three 60-minute audio CDs.

The *English for New Americans* program uses an immersion approach, so you'll be using English from the start, just as you would in real life. The program provides you with the tools you'll need—vocabulary, phrases, and basic grammar—to help you communicate in typical situations in the United States. We recommend that you also buy a good dictionary for reference. There are three parts in this program: Everyday Life; Work and School; and Health, Home, and Community.

How to Use the Program

The *English for New Americans* 1-2-3 method makes the program very easy to use.

1. WATCH A UNIT ON THE DVD.
Put the DVD into your DVD player, sit back, and watch a unit straight through. Don't worry if you don't understand everything the first time around. You'll have the chance to watch again. Pay attention to facial expressions, body language, and the surroundings as you watch. You might be surprised at just how much you already understand! After the first viewing, you may want to write down a brief summary of what you think happened in the *Watch and Listen* section. When you're done, rewind to the beginning of the unit.

2. WATCH AGAIN. READ AND WRITE IN THE WORKBOOK.
Watch the same unit again. When you see the ▶️ symbol on screen, stop the DVD and go to the workbook. Complete the exercises in order until you reach the ▣ symbol. Then continue watching the DVD again until you reach the next ▶️ symbol. In each unit, you will be asked to complete exercises following the *See It, Hear It, Say It* section, following the *Watch and Listen* section, and again following the *Real People…Real Language* section. Remember: whenever you see this: ▶️ , go to the workbook; when you see the ▣ symbol in the workbook, go back to the DVD.

After you've completed all the exercises in the workbook, watch the video unit one more time. Compare how much you are able to understand this time with the first viewing! Look at the summary you wrote—how much were you able to understand? As the program continues, you'll find that you're making real progress.

3. LISTEN AND SPEAK.

Once you've studied with the video and completed the exercises in the workbook, you can practice what you've learned using the audio CD. Just put it into your CD player and listen and repeat wherever it's convenient—at home, on your way to work, while doing housework, or whenever you have a spare ten minutes.

Focus on the sounds of the language. Don't worry if your accent isn't perfect. The more you practice, the more it will improve. In the United States, people speak with a wide variety of accents, but everyone is still able to communicate. As you will see on the video, Jorge, Elena, Ming, and Sasha all have foreign accents, but they are able to get their messages across, and that's what counts!

Materials

• THREE 60-MINUTE DVDs

In the *English for New Americans* video series, you'll meet Simon and Raquel, a couple who volunteers at an International Center, assisting and advising new immigrants as they adjust to life in the United States. You will also get to know Jorge and Elena, a married couple from Mexico; Sasha, a Russian house-painter; and Ming, a waitress from Hong Kong with ambitions of opening her own restaurant. Why don't you join them? Simon and Raquel will be *your* guides as well as theirs.

Each DVD comprises seven units, each dealing with a practical situation. Each unit consists of three sections:

See It, Hear It, Say It
In this section you will learn key vocabulary relating to the topic of the unit. You will hear how to pronounce the word, see what it means, and see how it's spelled in English. Repeat each new word that you learn.

Watch and Listen
This section is the heart of each unit. You'll see and hear language relating to the topic of the unit. At the end of the section, you'll hear a brief review of a few important phrases.

Real People...Real Language
This section features interviews with real people who will tell you about their lives in the United States. This is your chance to hear and practice real language. Each section in the unit builds on the preceding one, and the language becomes

more challenging, so you'll see progress in every unit! What's more, you'll hear English as it's really spoken, so you'll be able to understand regional or foreign accents and use what you learn in daily life.

• WORKBOOK

The workbook is divided into three main parts: Everyday Life; Work and School; and Health, Home, and Community. In it, you'll find exercises to help you build your vocabulary and learn the basic rules of English and how to apply them. You'll also see brief explanations of key concepts. You might be asked to do some of the following:

☞ name an object or person you saw on the video
☞ fill in the correct form of a verb
☞ answer questions with "yes" or "no"
☞ choose the correct answer from several options
☞ match the beginning of a sentence with an ending, or match a question with its answer
☞ fill in missing information

The first one or two questions in each exercise are completed for you, showing you what to do. You can find all the answers at the back of the book in the Answer Key.

At the end of each unit in the workbook, you'll find a complete transcript of the *Watch and Listen* segments from the video. In addition, you can find all of the words used in the program in the Word List at the end of each part, as well as a transcript of the audio from the audio CDs.

• THREE 60-MINUTE AUDIO CDS

Once you've watched the video and completed the exercises in the workbook, you can use the CDs from each part to review and practice what you learned in each unit. Each unit on the CD consists of three sections: First you will review key vocabulary and phrases that were used on the video and in the workbook. Just listen and repeat after the native speakers in the pauses provided. Next, you'll hear an excerpt from the scene you saw on the video, and again you'll have a chance to repeat the phrases yourself. Finally, you'll be asked to respond to questions and make sentences on your own. Again, the language you use will build from one section to the next, until, by the end, you'll be speaking on your own!

Now, let's get started...

Everyday Life

Unit 1
At the International Center: Introductions

A. Introductions

Write the word.

1. Hello.

2. How _____**are**_____ you?

3. _____, thanks.

4. And _____?

5. _____ is Ming.

6. Nice to _____ you.

7. This _____ Jorge.

8. _____ pleasure.

B. Countries

Write the country.

1. Hong Kong, _____**China**_____

2. Moscow, _____

3. New York, _____

4. Mexico City, _____

C. Professions

Where do they work?

a.

1. TEACHER

b.

2. PAINTER

c.

3. CASHIER

d.

4. WAITRESS

5. ENGINEER

e.

D. Verbs: Present Tense—*To Be*

Subject Pronouns

SINGULAR   PLURAL

 I   we

 you   you

 he

 she   they

 it

SINGULAR		PLURAL	
I	am	we	are
you	are	you	are
he	is	they	are
she	is	they	are
it	is	they	are

yesterday   today   tomorrow

PRESENT

Write the verbs in the sentences.

1. Simon _____is_____ at the International Center.

2. Jorge and Elena _____ from Mexico.

3. Raquel _____ Simon's wife.

4. Jorge _____ Elena's husband.

5. Ming _____ a waitress.

6. Sasha _____ from Russia.

7. Raquel and Jorge _____ hungry.

8. I _____ hungry, too.

9. We _____ at home.

10. You _____ a teacher.

E. Contractions

I am = I'm	we are = we're
you are = you're	you are = you're
he is = he's	
she is = she's	they are = they're
it is = it's	

Write the contractions.

1. you are = __you're__

2. they are = _____

3. it is = _____

4. I am = _____

5. we are = _____

6. he is = _____

F. Negatives

Simon is a teacher. He **is not** a painter.

Raquel is a social worker. She **is not** an engineer.

I am not	we are not
you are not	you are not
he is not	
she is not	they are not
it is not	

Write the negative form of the verb.

1. I __am not__ at the International Center.

2. Simon and Raquel __are not__ at home.

3. Ming _____ an engineer.

4. Elena _____ hungry.

5. Sasha _____ from Mexico.

6. Jorge _____ a teacher.

7. You _____ a social worker.

8. Elena and Jorge _____ from Russia.

9. We _____ on vacation.

10. The food _____ on the table.

G. Negative Contractions

I'm not	**we're not / we aren't**
you're not / you aren't	**you're not / you aren't**
he's not / he isn't	
she's not / she isn't	**they're not / they aren't**
it's not / it isn't	

Write the contractions.

1. he is not =   **he's not/he isn't**

2. they are not = _____

3. we are not = _____

4. I am not = _____

5. you are not = _____

6. she is not = _____

H. Questions and Yes/No Answers

Jorge is an engineer. Is Jorge an engineer? Yes, he is.

Elena is a cashier. Is Elena a waitress? No, she is not.

Write a "yes" or "no" short answer after the question.

1. Is Sasha from the Dominican Republic? **No, he is not.**

2. Is he from Russia? **Yes, he is.**

3. Is Raquel from the Dominican Republic? **Yes,**

4. Are you from the United States? **No,**

5. Are Jorge and Elena from the United States? **No,** _____

Change the sentence to a question.

6. Simon is from the United States.

   Is Simon from the United States?

7. You are from Hong Kong.

   _____

8. Sasha and Ming are at the International Center.

   _____

9. Elena and Jorge are hungry.

   _____

10. The food is on the table.

   _____

I. Question Words

Who?   What?   Where?

*Write **Who, What,** or **Where** in the question.*

1. _____**Who**_____ is at the International Center? —Simon and
   Raquel are.

2. _____ is with Simon and Raquel? —Jorge, Elena, Sasha,
   and Ming are.

3. _____ is on the table? —The food is.

4. _____ is with you? —My friends are.

5. _____ are the children? —In school.

6. _____ is Sasha? —A painter.

7. _____ are you? —At home.

8. _____ are you? —A student.

J. Short Answers

Circle the correct short answer to the question.

1. **Who** is from China?   (Ming is.)   Elena is.

2. **Where** are Jorge and Elena from? From Colombia. From Mexico.

3. **Who** is from Russia?   Raquel is.   Sasha is.

4. **Where** is Raquel from?   From the U.S.   From the D.R.

5. **Who** is from the United States? Sasha is.   Simon is.

K. Country/Nationality/Language

I am from <u>Brazil</u>.   I am <u>Brazilian</u>.   I speak <u>Portuguese</u>.
   (country)   (nationality)   (language)

Fill in the chart with a country, nationality, or language.

	Country	Nationality	Language
1.	Brazil	Brazilian	**Portuguese**
2.	Dominican Republic		Spanish
3.		Chinese	Chinese
4.	Haiti	Haitian	French
5.	Japan	Japanese	Japanese

6.	Korea	Korean	Korean
7.	Mexico		Spanish
8.	Russia		Russian
9.	United States		English
10.	Vietnam	Vietnamese	Vietnamese

L. People/Countries

Write a country, nationality, or language in the sentence.

1. Raquel is from the **Dominican Republic**. She's Dominican.

2. Ming is from China. She's _____.

3. Elena and Jorge are from _____. They're Mexican.

4. Sasha is from Russia. He's _____.

5. Simon is from the _____. He's American.

6. Raquel, Jorge, and Elena speak English and _____.

7. Sasha speaks English and _____.

8. Ming speaks English and _____.

9. Simon speaks only _____!

M. Dialogue

Read the dialogue and fill in the missing words.

1. SIMON: Hi! My name is **Simon**.

2. JORGE: Nice to meet _____.

   This _____ Elena.

3. ELENA: Pleased to _____ you.

4. SIMON: _____ pleasure.

5. RAQUEL: I'd like to introduce _____ to Ming.

6. MING: _____ to meet you.

7. SIMON: How are _____ ?

8. RAQUEL: And _____ is Sasha.

9. JORGE: Nice to _____ you.

10. SASHA: My _____ .

11. JORGE: _____ you hungry?

_____ am. Let's eat!

N. Professions and Workplaces

Make a word from the letters for a person who works in this place.

1. (CREETAH)

A **teacher** works in a school.

3. (SATISREW)

A _____ works in a restaurant.

2. (RESHICA)

A _____ works in a store.

4. (GERNINEE)

An _____ works for a company.

O. Real People...Real Language

Circle the word you hear.

1. Paul   (computer)   collector
2. Jen   student   secretary
3. Shin   Thailand   Taiwan
4. Eleanor   consultant   college
5. Consuelo   American   Mexican
6. Anna   Ukraine   Uruguay
7. Yao Li   Tai Chi   Taipei
8. Manuel   Colorado   Colombia
9. Liz   mother   math teacher
10. Sandra   Port au Prince   Puerto Rico
11. Susan   Jamaica   Georgia
12. Ken   technology   telephone

VIDEO TRANSCRIPT

Watch and Listen

Simon: Today we're having a party at the International Center. We're going to meet some new people and introduce ourselves. Come and join us!... Jorge! Hello, how are you?

Jorge: Fine, thank you. And you?

Simon: Very well, thank you.

Jorge: I'd like to introduce my wife, Elena.

Simon: Pleased to meet you.

Elena: My pleasure.

Simon: And this is my lovely wife, Raquel.

Jorge: Nice to meet you.

Elena: Nice to meet you.

Raquel: I'd like you to meet Ming.

Simon: Pleased to meet you, Ming.

Ming: How do you do?

Raquel: Ming is from Hong Kong. She's a waitress.

Simon: Oh, really? Where?

Ming: In the Golden Garden Restaurant.

Simon: We'll have to go there for dinner sometime.

Raquel: That's a good idea. And this is Sasha.

Simon: How are you?

Sasha: Nice to meet you.

Simon: Where are you from, Sasha?

Sasha: I'm from Russia.

Simon: And what do you do?

Sasha: I'm a painter—I paint houses.

Simon: That's a very useful profession!

Sasha: And what do you do?

Raquel: Well, I'm a social worker and Simon is an English teacher.

Simon: And, Jorge, what about you?

Jorge: I'm an engineer.

Raquel: And where are you from?

Elena: We're from Mexico.

Simon: Chinese, Russian, Mexican. This truly is the International Center.

Elena: And what about you?

Raquel: Simon is an American, and I'm Dominican. We met on vacation.

Ming: Oh, that sounds romantic!

Simon: It was. So, is anybody hungry?

Raquel: Yes—let's eat!

Jorge: Yes, let's eat!

Simon: While they're eating, let's review some useful phrases you've just heard.

To introduce yourself, say:

> **Hi, I'm...**   or
>
> **My name is...**

To introduce someone else, say:

> **I'd like you to meet...** or
>
> **This is...**

To answer, you say:

> **Nice to meet you.**   or
>
> **My pleasure.**

Now let's meet some more people.

Unit 2
A City Tour:
The Time and Date

A. Days, Months, and Seasons

Write the days on the calendar.

1.

JANUARY						
Sunday						
1	2	3	4	5	6	7
8	9	10	11	12	13	14
15	16	17	18	19	20	21
22	23	24	25	26	27	28
29	30	31				

Write the months of the year after the seasons.

2. SPRING _____March_____

4. FALL _____September_____

3. SUMMER _____June_____

5. WINTER _____December_____

B. Verbs: Present Continuous—*To Be* + ___*ing*

work + ing = working   come + ing = coming

go + ing = going   write + ing = writing

I	am ___ing	we	are ___ing
you	are ___ing	you	are ___ing
he	is ___ing	they	are ___ing
she	is ___ing		
it	is ___ing		

Contractions: I am = I'm; you are = you're; etc.

yesterday   today   tomorrow

present continuous:
now
at the moment

Write the verbs in the sentences.

1. Raquel ____**is waiting**____ at the International Center. (wait)

2. Ming ____**is coming**____ on the tour. (come)

3. They _____ about the weekend. (talk)

4. Raquel _____ Ming the time. (ask)

5. Ming _____ at her watch. (look)

6. Ming _____ Raquel the time. (tell)

7. Sasha _____ to the center. (walk)

8. They _____ to the library. (go)

9. We _____ the verbs. (write)

10. I _____ this exercise. (finish)

C. Negatives

I	am not __ ing	we	are not __ ing
you	are not __ ing	you	are not __ ing
he	is not __ ing		
she	is not __ ing	they	are not __ ing
it	is not __ ing		

Write the negative form of the verb.

1. Simon ____**is not going**____ on the tour. (go)

2. Sasha _____ at the International Center. (wait)

3. Ming and Raquel _____. (shop*)

4. Jorge _____ a birthday party. (have)

5. Elena _____ to Raquel. (talk)

6. My friends _____ on the bus. (sit*)

7. I _____ now. (get* up)

8. You _____ dinner now. (eat)

9. We _____ TV. (watch)

10. The cat _____ on the bed. (sleep)

* Notice: shop + ing = sho<u>pp</u>ing; sit + ing = si<u>tt</u>ing; get + ing = ge<u>tt</u>ing

D. Yes/No Answers

Write a "yes" or "no" short answer after the question.

1. Is Raquel waiting for some people? __**Yes, she is.**__

2. Is Jorge getting up? __**No, he isn't.**__

3. Is Ming's birthday this week? __**Yes,**__

4. Are Sasha and Ming going on the tour? **Yes,** _____

5. Is it a beautiful day? **Yes,** _____

6. Are Jorge and Elena at the center? **No,** _____

7. Is it almost ten o'clock? **Yes,** _____

8. Are Ming's weekends fun? **Yes,** _____

9. Is Sasha late? **No,** _____

10. Is the library open? **Yes,** _____

E. Question Words

When?   Which?

*Write **When** or **Which** in the questions.*

1. ___**When**___ is your birthday? —In June.

2. _____ season is your favorite? —Fall is.

3. _____ are you going to bed? —At 11:00.

4. _____ day is today? —It's Saturday.

5. _____ is the baseball game? —At 7:00.

6. _____ is your summer vacation? —In August.

7. _____ are they going on the tour? —At 10:00.

8. _____ days are you working? —On Monday and Friday.

9. _____ is the movie showing? —This weekend.

F. Prepositions of Time

in	January the summer the morning / the afternoon / the evening
on	Monday / Tuesday afternoon June second
at	9:00 / noon night

*Write **in**, **on**, or **at** in the sentences.*

1. Sasha is going to a movie ____at____ 3:30 ____in____ the afternoon.

2. I'm visiting my family _____ December.

3. Raquel is working at the center _____ Tuesday and Thursday.

4. We are in the cafeteria _____ noon.

5. They are getting married _____ July 6th (sixth).

6. Ming is finishing work _____ 10:30 _____ night.

7. You are going on vacation _____ July.

8. Jorge and Elena are going to a restaurant _____ Friday.

9. The weather is beautiful in this part of the country _____ the fall.

10. Simon's birthday is _____ October 17th (seventeenth).

G. Dialogue

Choose the missing words.

SIMON: Hi! I'm ____sorry____ I'm late.
                1. (sorry/happy)

RAQUEL: That's all _____ . Jorge and Elena are
2. (right/wrong)

meeting us at the movie theater _____ 7:00.
3. (in/at)

We have half an hour.

SIMON: Oh good. _____ a nice dress!
4. (Who/What)

RAQUEL: Thank _____ . I went shopping today.
5. (me/you)

SIMON: What _____ we doing this weekend?
6. (are/is)

RAQUEL: I don't know.

SIMON: _____ go for a drive in the country
7. (Let's/What's)

_____ Sunday afternoon.
8. (at/on)

RAQUEL: That's a great idea! The trees are beautiful in the

_____ .
9. (winter/fall)

H. Number Practice

Practice saying these numbers.

1 one	11 eleven	21 twenty-one	40	forty
2 two	12 twelve	22 twenty-two	50	fifty
3 three	13 thirteen	23 twenty-three	60	sixty
4 four	14 fourteen	24 twenty-four	70	seventy
5 five	15 fifteen	25 twenty-five	80	eighty
6 six	16 sixteen	26 twenty-six	90	ninety
7 seven	17 seventeen	27 twenty-seven	100	one hundred
8 eight	18 eighteen	28 twenty-eight	101	one hundred and one
9 nine	19 nineteen	29 twenty-nine	200	two hundred
10 ten	20 twenty	30 thirty	1,000	one thousand

Note: A.M. = *12:00 midnight – 12:00 noon = 00:00 – 11:59*
P.M. = *12:00 noon – 12:00 midnight = 12:00 – 23:59*

I. Telling Time

Write the time in numbers.

What time is it?

1. __1:10__   2. _____   3. _____   4. _____

What's the time?

5. _____   6. _____   7. _____   8. _____

Do you have the time?

9. _____   10. _____   11. _____   12. _____

Write the time in letters.

1. __It's one-ten.__   7. _____

2. __It's two-twenty-five.__   8. _____

3. _____   9. _____

4. _____   10. _____

5. _____   11. _____

6. _____   12. _____

J. What's the Date?

JANUARY						
SUNDAY	MONDAY	TUESDAY	WEDNESDAY	THURSDAY	FRIDAY	SATURDAY
1	2	3	4	5	6	7
8	9	10	11	12	13	14
15	16	17	18	19	20	21
22	23	24	25	26	27	28
29	30	31				

Write the day in the sentences.

1. January **fifth** is a _____ Thursday _____.

2. January **tenth** is a _____.

3. January **eighteenth** is a _____.

4. January **twenty-seventh** is a _____.

5. January **thirtieth** is a _____.

K. Real People...Real Language

1. What time do you go to work?

Check the time you hear.

a. 8:00 _____   8:30 _____ ✔

b. 7:00 _____   7:30 _____

c. 8:00 _____   8:15 _____

d. 7:00 _____   11:00 _____

e. 7:00 _____   11:00 _____

29

f. 6:00 _____   8:00 _____

g. 5:00 _____   9:00 _____

2. When is your birthday? Do you have a party?

Draw a line from the date to the party.

a. October 7th   no party

b. July 3rd   dinner in a restaurant

c. June   stopped having parties

d. October 24th   dinner and phone calls

e. November 9th   party with family and friends

3. What's your favorite season?

Write the season.

a. _____**summer**_____ baseball

b. _____ snowboarding

c. _____ love the heat and swimming

d. _____ change of colors and riding

e. _____ not too hot, not too cold

f. _____ enjoy being outside

g. _____ sailing and golf

VIDEO TRANSCRIPT

Watch and Listen

Raquel: Okay, as soon as everyone gets here, we'll get started.

Ming: Hi, Raquel! Am I the first one here?

Raquel: Yes, you are. How was your weekend?

Ming: It was nice. On Saturday I went shopping, and on Sunday I went to a movie.

Raquel: Sounds like a fun weekend!

Ming: How about you?

Raquel: Saturday we went to a baseball game, and Sunday was Simon's birthday.

Ming: Really? My birthday is October 20th.

Raquel: That's Wednesday. Happy birthday!

Ming: Thank you.

Raquel: What time is it?

Ming: It's 9:45.

Raquel: It's still early.

Ming: Who else is coming?

Raquel: Sasha and maybe some others.

Ming: What a beautiful day for a tour!

Raquel: Yeah, fall is beautiful in this part of the country…Where is everyone?

Sasha: What time is it? Am I late?

Raquel: No, it's almost ten o'clock. You're just in time.

Sasha: Good. I got up late this morning.

Raquel: Sasha, you remember Ming.

Sasha: Yes, we met last week.

Ming: We met at the party here.

Raquel: That's right. Well, let's get started. We'll start with the city library. They open at ten o'clock...But before we go, here are some phrases to remember from this lesson.

If you are sorry about something, you can say:

I'm sorry I'm late.   or

I didn't mean to miss your party.

People might reply:

That's all right.   or

Don't worry about it.

If you are surprised or pleased about something, you can say:

What a nice car!   or

What cute kids!

Now, let's listen to some people talk about their schedules: at what times they do things, on which days, and during which months.

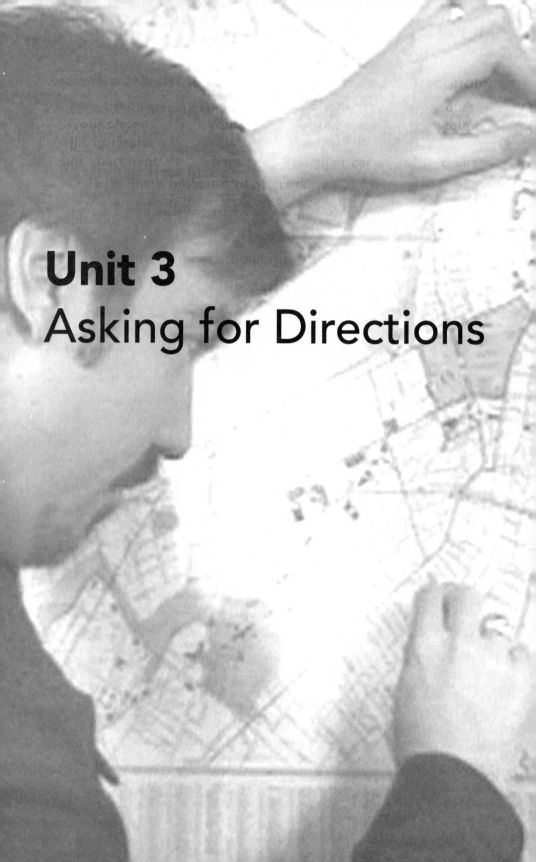

Unit 3
Asking for Directions

A. What is it?

Write the missing word on the line.

1. BUS **STOP**

2. MAIL _____

3. _____ OFFICE

4. _____ THEATER

B. Odd One Out

Cross out the word that does not belong.

1. get on   bus   get off   bus stop   ~~letter~~

2. subway   stamp   machine   token   train

3. movie   turn left go straight   turn right   cross the street

4. letter   stamp   theater   mailbox   post office

C. Opposites

Write the opposite word on the line.

1. Turn left.   ≠   Turn _____ **right** _____.

2. Get on.   ≠   Get _____.

3. It's near.   ≠   It's _____.

4. It's here.   ≠   It's _____.

D. Verbs: Simple Present

SINGULAR		PLURAL	
I	sit	we	sit
you	sit	you	sit
he/she/it	sits	they	sit

yesterday   today   tomorrow

PRESENT

always
usually
sometimes
never

Also use the simple present tense with these words:

	day		Mondays		March
every	week	on	weekends	in	winter
	year		my birthday		the morning

Write the verbs in the sentences.

1. Simon ____**sits**____ at the information desk every week. (sit)

2. He _____ questions. (answer)

3. Elena _____ Simon for directions. (ask)

4. She _____ to go to the supermarket. (want)

5. Jorge _____ some stamps. (need)

6. He _____ the bus to the post office. (take)

7. Elena and Jorge _____ near the International Center. (live)

8. We _____ in a restaurant once a week. (eat)

9. You _____ English well. (speak)

10. I _____ every day. (study)

E. Negatives

I	do not speak	we	do not speak
you	do not speak	you	do not speak
he / she / it	does not speak	they	do not speak

Contractions: I do not = I don't; he does not = he doesn't; etc.

Write the negative form of the verb.

1. Jorge ___**doesn't speak**___ Russian. (speak)

2. Elena _____ a car. (drive)

3. Ming _____ in a bank. (work)

4. Simon and Raquel _____ to work by train. (go)

5. Sasha _____ pictures. (paint)

6. I _____ your friends. (know)

7. You _____ tea for breakfast. (drink)

8. We _____ medicine at that pharmacy. (buy)

9. They _____ movies during the week. (watch)

10. The cat _____ meat, only fish. (eat)

F. Yes/No Answers

Write a "yes" or "no" short answer after the question.

1. Does Simon work at the International Center? **Yes, he does.**

2. Do Elena and Jorge speak Chinese? **No, they don't.**

3. Do you like coffee? **Yes,** _____

4. Does Ming work in a pharmacy? **No,** _____

5. Do I watch TV every day? **No,** _____

6. Does the dog sleep on the sofa? **Yes,** _____

7. Does Jorge go to the supermarket with Elena?
   Yes, _____

8. Do you buy stamps at the post office? **Yes,** _____

9. Do your friends visit you? **No,** _____

10. Do I write the answers to the questions? **Yes,** _____

G. Short Answers

Circle the correct answer.

1. Who asks Simon about the supermarket? Ming does.

   Elena does.

2. Where is the ATM?   Near the supermarket.

                                          Near the post office.

3. Who takes the bus to the post office? Jorge does.

                                          Sasha does.

4. How far does Elena walk?   Four blocks.

                                          Two blocks.

5. Who goes on tour with the students?   Simon does.

                                          Raquel does.

6. Who writes the answers in the book?   I do.

                                          Elena does.

7. How much does the bus cost?   It costs $1.50.

                                          It costs $2.50.

8. How many stops does Jorge go?   Six stops.

                                             Four stops.

9. Where is the post office?   Near the bank.

                                             Near the pharmacy.

10. Who works in a restaurant?   Ming does.

                                             Raquel does.

H. Questions

Who?   Where?

How much?      How many?

*Write **Who, Where, How much,** or **How many** in the question.*

1. ____**Where**____ is the movie theater? —On the corner.

2. _____ are the stores? —They're over there.

3. _____ gives directions? —Simon does.

4. _____ is a subway token? —It's $2.00.

5 _____ goes to work by bus? —Jorge does.

6 _____ stops do you go? —Only two stops.

7. _____ is an airmail stamp? —It's $1.00.

8. _____ paints houses? —Sasha does.

9. _____ blocks do you walk? —Eight blocks.

10. _____ do you live? —Across the street.

I. Plurals

a stamp   stamps

a letter    letters

Give the plurals.

	Singular (=1)	Plural (>1)
1.	bank	**banks**
2.	block	
3.	letter	
4.	map	
5.	stop	
6.	train	

J. There is... /There are...

There is	a token machine in the subway.
	a bus stop on the corner.
	a hospital over there.

There are	tokens in the machine.
	people on the bus.
	visitors in the hospital.

*Write **There is** or **There are** in the sentences.*

1. _____**There are**_____ many people on the train.

2. _____**There is**_____ a real estate office over there.

3. _____ a movie theater on the corner.

4. _____ some letters in the mailbox.

5. _____ many cars on the street.

6. _____ a supermarket two blocks away.

K. Prepositions of Place: *In/On/At*

in	on	at

in	the supermarket / the city / New York
on	the wall / the corner / Main Street / the bus / the train
at	the desk / the bus stop / 715 Maple Avenue

Circle the correct preposition.

1. The information desk is **on** / **in** the International Center.

2. Simon is **at** / **on** the information desk.

3. The map is **on** / **at** the wall.

4. Jorge is standing **in** / **at** the map.

5. The ATM is **at** / **in** the supermarket.

6. The food is **in** / **on** the supermarket.

7. The stamps are **in** / **on** the letter.

8. The mailbox is **on** / **in** the corner.

9. The bus is **in** / **at** the bus stop.

10. The convenience store is **on** / **in** Oak Street.

L. Dialogue

Read the dialogue and write the missing words.

ELENA: Jorge, are you going to the ____**post**____ office?
1. (post/tax)

JORGE: Yes, I'm taking the _____.
2. (car/bus)

ELENA: _____ is the bus stop?
3. (Who/Where)

JORGE: Near the International _____.
4. (Center/market)

ELENA: Oh, _____ going there, too. I have to
5. (she's/I'm)

ask Simon about the _____.
6. (bank/supermarket)

JORGE: Are _____ ready?
7. (they/you)

ELENA: Yes, _____ you?
8. (are/is)

JORGE: Yes, I _____. Let's _____
9. (am/are)   10. (talk/go)
together.

ELENA: Okay. Let's go.

M. Real People... Real Language

1. Is there a movie theater near your house?

Write the numbers you hear.

a. _____ minute walk, _____ blocks...

b. No movie theater...

c. _____ miles away.

d. A _____ minute drive.

2. Is there a convenience store near your house?

Write the numbers you hear.

a. _____ minute walk away.

b. _____ blocks away.

c. _____ block away.

d. Across the street.

e. _____ block away.

3. Is there a pharmacy near your house?

Do they walk or drive?

a. _____✔_____ walk _____ drive

b. _____ walk _____ drive

c. _____ walk _____ drive

d. _____ walk _____ drive

e. _____ walk _____ drive

VIDEO TRANSCRIPT

Watch and Listen

Simon: Today I'm volunteering at the information desk at the International Center. People usually ask me for directions. Why don't you come and join me?...Hi, Elena! What can I do for you today?

Elena: Can you tell me where the supermarket is?

Simon: It's not far from here.

Elena: Oh, that's good.

Simon: You go outside, you turn left.

Elena: Yes...

Simon: You just walk down the street two blocks.

Elena: Two blocks...

Simon: Then you cross the street, and it's right there on the corner.

Elena: That's really near. Is there an ATM there?

Simon: Yes, it's right out front. Here, you can use this map if you like.

Elena: Thanks a lot.

Simon: You're most welcome.

Elena: Go outside and turn left, walk two blocks, cross the street, and the supermarket is on the corner. That's really near.

Simon: Hey, Jorge! Elena just went to the supermarket.

Jorge: Yes. We have a lot of things to do today. Is there a post office around here?

Simon: There's a mailbox down the street.

Jorge: No, but I need to buy stamps.

Simon: In that case, you'll have to take the bus to the post office.

Jorge: Where's the bus stop?

Simon: You go outside, turn right, and it's at the end of the block.

Jorge: How much does it cost?

Simon: $1.50 in exact change.

Jorge: And how many stops do I go?

Simon: I think it's about four. You get off at the pharmacy.

Jorge: So the post office is near the pharmacy.

Simon: Right, you'll see it when you get there.

Jorge: Thanks, Simon.

Simon: Don't mention it.

Jorge: Go outside, turn right, take the bus at the end of the block, go four stops, and get off at the pharmacy. Got it!

Simon: While Jorge works out my directions, let's review some phrases to help you find your way around town.

To ask where something is, you say:

Where's the movie theater?   or

Can you tell me where the hospital is?   or

Are there any banks around here?

In response, you might hear:

It's **over there.**   or

It's **right here.**   or

It's **across the street.**

Now let's listen to some people give directions.

Unit 4
Shopping for Food

A. Odd One Out

Cross out the food that is a different color:

1. red: apples / strawberries / ba~~nanas~~ / tomatoes

2. yellow: butter / carrots / bananas

3. white: onions / rice / soup / milk

4. brown: potatoes / juice / bread / eggs

5. orange: carrots / oranges / juice / sauce

B. What is it?

Write the missing letters.

1. Fruit:

   A __P__ __P__ __L__ __E__ S

   O _ _ _ _ _ S

   B _ _ _ _ _ S

   S _ _ _ _ B _ _ _ _ _ S

2. Vegetables:

   P _ _ _ _ _ _ S

   O _ _ _ _ S

   C _ _ _ _ _ S

   T _ _ _ _ _ _ S

3. Dairy:

   M _ _ K

   E _ _ S

   B _ _ _ _ R

4. Canned goods: S __ __ P

                    S __ __ __ E

C. Verbs: Future with *Going To*

I	am going to __	we	are going to __
you	are going to __	you	are going to __
he / she / it	is going to __	they	are going to __

yesterday   today   tomorrow

future:
tomorrow
next week
next month
next year

Write the verbs in the sentences.

1. Raquel, Ming, and Elena ___**are going to go**___ to the supermarket. (go)

2. Raquel _____ two pounds of apples. (buy)

3. Ming _____ a half gallon of juice. (get)

4. Elena _____ a box of spaghetti. (look for)

5. Later, they _____ lunch at Elena's house. (have)

6. I _____ a movie tonight. (see)

7. You _____ to school tomorrow. (drive)

8. It _____ next week. (snow)

9. We _____ a vacation in July. (take)

10. Jorge _____ a new apartment soon. (rent)

D. Negatives

I	am not going to ___	we	are not going to ___
you	are not going to ___	you	are not going to ___
he/she/it	is not going to ___	they	are not going to ___

Contractions: I am = I'm; you are = you're; he is = he's
     or: are not = aren't; is not = isn't

Write the subject pronoun and the negative form of the verb.

1. __**They aren't going to**__ go to the movie theater.
   (Raquel, Ming, and Elena)

2. _____ get any bananas. (Raquel)

3. _____ buy much juice. (Ming)

4. _____ eat many oranges. (Elena)

5. _____ have pizza for lunch. (they)

6. _____ paint next weekend. (Sasha)

7. _____ take the bus to the
   bank. (you)

8. _____ buy any fruit at the
   market. (I)

9. _____ drink any milk. (the dog)

10. _____ mail the letters today. (we)

E. Yes/No Answers

Circle the correct answer.

1. Is Raquel going to buy a pint of strawberries? Yes, she is.

   No, she isn't.

2. Is Ming going to get a bunch of bananas?   Yes, she is.

   No, she isn't.

3. Is Elena going to buy a bag of potatoes?   Yes, she is.

   No, she isn't.

4. Are they going to use coupons at the   Yes, they are.
   checkout counter?   No, they aren't.

5. Is Jorge going to make lasagna?   Yes, he is.

   No, he isn't.

6. Are Sasha and Simon going to eat   Yes, they are.
   lunch at Elena's house?   No, they aren't.

F. Short Answers

Choose the correct answer, a–j.

1. How many pounds of apples   a. A five-pound bag.
   is Raquel going to buy?

2. How much are apples?   b. Some tomatoes.

3. What kind of fruit would Ming like?   c. A dozen.

4. How many oranges does Elena need?   d. Two pounds.

5. How many potatoes is Raquel going   e. A few.
   to get?

6. How much are the onions?   f. A quart.

7. What is Elena going to buy for the salad? g. Orange juice.

8. How many eggs does Raquel need? h. $1.29 a pound.

9. What kind of juice is Ming going to buy? i. Bananas.

10. How much milk would Elena like? j. $.99 a pound.

G. Questions

How much?

How many?

*Write **How much** or **How many** in the questions.*

1. ___**How much**___ juice is Ming going to buy?

2. _____ eggs is Raquel going to get?

3. _____ lasagna is Elena going to make?

4. _____ rooms is Sasha going to paint?

5. _____ classes is Simon going to teach?

6. _____ money is Jorge going to make?

7. _____ places are the students going to tour?

8. _____ cookies are you going to eat?

9. _____ milk is the cat going to drink?

10. _____ soup are the children going to eat?

H. Singular/Plural Nouns

Write the plural next to the singular.

	Singular (=1)	Plural (>1)
1.	apple	**apples**
2.	banana	
3.	carrot	
4.	egg	
5.	onion	
6.	potato	**potatoes†**
7.	tomato	
8.	strawberry	**strawberries***
9.	raspberry	
10.	cherry	

* Remember: <u>y</u> → <u>ie</u> before <u>s</u>.   † Remember: after <u>o</u> or <u>u</u>, add <u>es</u>.

I. Money

dollar   quarter   dime   nickel   penny

How much money did they spend?

Raquel	
• apples	$2.58
• potatoes	$1.99
• eggs	$1.39
• bread	$1.59
• soup	$ .99
Total	$8.54
Cash	$10.00
Change	$1.46

Ming	
• bananas	$ .89
• onions	$ .99
• juice	$1.49
• rice	$2.99
Total	
Cash	$10.00
Change	

Elena	
• oranges	$2.99
• tomatoes	$2.49
• milk	$1.79
• spaghetti	$ .85
• tomato sauce	$1.09
Total	
Cash	$10.00
Change	

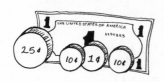

= $ _____
Raquel's change

= $ _____
Elena's change

= $ _____
Ming's change

J. Count and Noncount Nouns

How many?		How much?	
a	tomato	_____	rice
some a few a lot of many	tomatoes	some a little a lot of much	rice
no not many	tomatoes	no not much	rice

Write the food from Raquel's, Ming's, and Elena's lists.

1. some / a few / a lot / many:

apples

potatoes

eggs

_____

_____

_____

2. some / a little / a lot of / much:

bread

soup

_____

_____

_____

_____

K. Recipe: Jorge's Tacos

Unscramble the words in Jorge's recipe.

a pound of ground **BEEF** **SALT** , pepper, spices
          FEBE   LAST

some _____ a little grated _____
      CLUTEET   HEESEC

a _____ a jar of _____
    TOOTAM   LASAS

a few _____ shells a pint of sour _____
     COAT   RAMEC

- Cook the ground beef in a frying pan with salt, pepper, and spices.
- Cut the lettuce and tomato.
- Warm the taco shells in the oven.
- When the ground beef is done, put it in the taco.
- Put the cheese, sour cream, and salsa on top.
- Add the lettuce and tomato.
- Enjoy your taco!

L. Dialogue

SIMON: Do _____ ever cook, Jorge?
            1. (you/he)

JORGE: Of course. I'm going to _____ tonight.
                           2. (wash/cook)

SIMON: Oh, really? _____ are you going to make?
                  3. (Who / What)

JORGE: Something easy, like _____ .
                       4. (lasagna/tacos)

SIMON: What do you _____ to make tacos?
                  5. (need/eat)

JORGE: You need taco shells, ground beef, lettuce, tomatoes,

    _____ , and salsa.
        6. (milk/cheese)

SIMON: And _____ you have all those things?
              7. (do / are)

JORGE: I have everything except the salsa. I need to get

    _____ .
      8. (any/some)

SIMON: I'd like to try making tacos _____ .
                          9. (tonight/next year)

JORGE: If you _____ help, just call me.
             10. (need/have)

SIMON: Okay. I want to surprise Raquel with

_____ tonight.
11. (breakfast/dinner)

JORGE: If I see _____, I won't say anything.
12. (her/him)

M. Containers

Can you think of any more?

1. **a bag of**
   oranges
   potatoes
   onions
   _____

2. **a bottle of**
   ketchup
   wine
   milk
   soy sauce
   _____

3. **a box of**
   spaghetti
   noodles
   cake mix
   _____

4. **a bunch of**
   grapes
   carrots
   bananas
   _____

5. **a can of**
   soup
   tomato sauce
   peas
   pineapple
   _____

6. **a carton of**
   juice
   milk
   eggnog
   _____

7. **a head of**
   lettuce
   cabbage
   garlic
   _____

8. **a jar of**
   jelly
   peanut butter
   pickles
   olives
   _____
   _____

9. **a roll of**
   toilet paper
   paper towels
   film

   _____
   _____

10. **a tube of**
    toothpaste
    shaving cream
    bath gel

    _____
    _____

Now write your shopping list here.

_____	_____
_____	_____
_____	_____
_____	_____
_____	_____
_____	_____
_____	_____

N. Real People...Real Language

1. How often do you go food shopping?

Underline the word they say.

a. Once or twice a week/ **month**

b. Once a week/month

c. Never/hardly ever

d. Once every two/three weeks

2. What do you buy?

Cross out the food they don't buy.

a. fruit / sandwich meat / ch~~ee~~se / butter / meat / vegetables

b. canned goods / eggs / fruits / vegetables / juices

c. bread / meat / cheese / rice / vegetables

3. What's your favorite dish and what's in it?

Write the missing word in the recipe.

a. Pizza: crust, sauce, **onions**, mushrooms, peppers

b. Sancocho: chicken, beef, yams, potatoes, _____, plantains

c. Arroz con pollo: chicken, _____, peas, tomatoes, onions, spices

d. Lubyeh: lamb, string beans, tomato _____

4. Do you do all your food shopping in one store?

Put a check by the number.

a. _____ 1 ✔ 2 _____ 3

b. _____ 1 _____ 2 _____ 3

c. _____ 1 _____ 2 _____ 3

5. How much do you spend on food each week?

Underline the money they spend.

a. <u>$80 to $100</u> / $100 to $180 every two weeks

b. $50 / $150 a week

c. $50 / $150 a week

d. $100 / $200 a week

VIDEO TRANSCRIPT

Watch and Listen

Raquel: Elena, Ming, and I are going shopping for food. Why don't you join us?

Ming: Raquel, what are you going to get?

Raquel: I need some apples. How much are they?

Elena: These are $1.29 a pound.

Raquel: I'm going to get two pounds.

Ming: I think I prefer bananas.

Elena: And I'm going to get some oranges.

Raquel: How about the vegetables? I need a five-pound bag of potatoes.

Ming: Onions are on sale—only $.99.

Elena: Jorge loves salad. I'm going to get lots of tomatoes.

Raquel: Ming, can you hand me a dozen eggs?

Ming: Sure. Here you are. I'd like a little juice.

Elena: Could I have a quart of milk? Thank you, Ming.

Ming: Sure, no problem.

Elena: A box of spaghetti and a jar of tomato sauce... (*Looking at their lists*)

Ming: Some rice...

Raquel: A loaf of bread and a can of soup...

Raquel: You know what? Shopping makes me hungry. How about lunch?

Elena: Come to my house. I'm going to make lasagna.

Raquel: That sounds great, Elena!

Ming: But only if you let us help you.

Raquel: While we're having lunch, here are a few useful phrases to remember when you go shopping.

When you need something, you can say:

I need some bread and milk.   or

She'd like a pound of cheese.   or

Can we have a few apples?

When you need to do something, you say:

> **You need to** go shopping.   or
>
> **He'd like to** eat some grapes.   or
>
> **They have to** buy some rice.

Another thing to remember when you go shopping for food is that you can save money if you use coupons at the checkout counter. Now, let's listen to some other people talk about going shopping.

Unit 5
Finding an Apartment

A. Odd One Out

Cross out the furniture or furnishing that is not in each room.

table
chairs
stove
refrigerator
~~bed~~
sink

1. KITCHEN   dishwasher

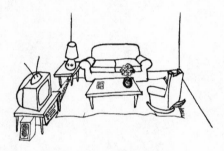

sofa
coffee table
lamp
rocking chair
stereo
TV

2. LIVING ROOM   shower

bed
dresser
mirror
night table
desk
chair
closet

3. BEDROOM   oven

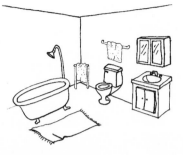

sink
toilet
microwave
bathtub
cabinet

4. BATHROOM

B. Verbs: Present Tense—*Can/Can't*

He **can lift** the suitcase.   She **can't lift** the suitcase.

I	can / can't	we	can / can't
you	can / can't	you	can / can't
he/she/it	can / can't	they	can / can't

Contraction: cannot = can't

yesterday	today	tomorrow
	PRESENT	

*Write **can** or **can't** in the sentences.*

1. Simon _____**can**_____ speak English.

2. He _____**can't**_____ speak Russian.

3. Sasha _____ paint houses.

61

4. He _____ do social work.

5. Ming _____ paint houses.

6. She _____ cook Chinese food.

Questions: Can Jorge cook Chinese food?   No, he can't.

*Write **Can** in the questions. Write "yes" or "no" short answers.*

7. ____**Can**____ Jorge cook Chinese food?   **No, he can't.**

8. _____ he cook Mexican food?   _____

9. _____ Elena work as a cashier?   _____

10. _____ she work as an engineer?   _____

C. Verbs: Past Tense—Could/Couldn't

I	could / couldn't	we	could / couldn't
you	could / couldn't	you	could / couldn't
he / she / it	could / couldn't	they	could / couldn't

yesterday   today   tomorrow

⬅️ ➡️

past

*Write **could** or **couldn't** in the sentences.*

1. Last Sunday, Simon ____**could**____ find some cheap apartments in the newspaper.

2. Jorge ____**couldn't**____ rent an expensive apartment.

3. The real estate agent _____ show them three apartments.

4. Jorge _____ choose an apartment without Elena.

5. Elena _____ see the apartments on Monday.

6. They _____ rent the apartment on Beals Boulevard.

Questions: Could Jorge and Elena buy a pet?   No, they couldn't.

*Write **Could** in the questions. Write "yes" or "no" short answers.*

7. ___**Could**___ they have a pet in their new apartment?

No, they couldn't.

8. _____ Simon and Raquel help them move in?

Yes, _____

9. _____ Sasha help them paint their apartment?

Yes, _____

10. _____ Ming help them move?

No, _____

D. Can/Can't or Could/Couldn't

Circle the correct verb in the sentence.

1. I can / can't speak English well.

2. Simon could / couldn't go to the real estate office with Jorge.

3. Jorge and Elena could / couldn't find an apartment with parking and laundry.

4. Raquel can / can't speak Chinese.

5. Ming could / couldn't help paint the apartment.

6. Elena can / can't make lasagna.

7. She could / couldn't have a cat or a dog in the new apartment.

8. Sasha could / couldn't paint his friend's apartment.

E. Short Answers

Write a short answer after the question.

1. Can you speak Russian? **Yes, I can.**
2. Could Jorge speak English ten years ago? **No, he couldn't.**
3. Can dogs run fast? **Yes,**
4. Could Raquel go shopping with Ming and Elena?
   Yes,
5. Can you understand the video? **Yes,**
6. Could Jorge pay for the apartment on Owens Avenue?
   No,
7. Can we use coupons at the checkout counter?
   Yes,
8. Could you write in English last year? **No,**
9. Can they find a job in the classified ads? **No,**
10. Could Ming go on the tour with Raquel and Sasha?
    Yes,

F. Adjectives: Opposites

cheap	≠	expensive
easy	≠	difficult
fast	≠	slow
funny	≠	serious
interesting	≠	boring
large/big	≠	small/little
light	≠	heavy
new	≠	old
pretty	≠	ugly
same	≠	different
short	≠	tall

Circle the words that are correct.

1. The apartment on Owens Avenue is...

   (new)   ugly   (large)   (expensive)

2. The apartment on Stanford Street is...

   old   small   pretty   different

3. The apartment on Beals Boulevard is...

   large   cheap   interesting   old

G. Adjectives: Comparative and Superlative

Superlative	Comparative	Adjective	Comparative	Superlative
-est	-er		-er	-est
least	less		more	most

Use the **comparative** when comparing **two** things or people.
Use the **superlative** when comparing **three or more** things or people.

Jorge is taller than Ming.

Sasha is taller than Jorge.

Sasha is the tallest of the three.

Fill in the chart with the comparative and superlative forms.

	ADJECTIVE	COMPARATIVE (+/-)	SUPERLATIVE (+++/- - -)
1.	large*	larger*	largest*
2.	small	smaller	smallest
3.	new		
4.	old		
5.	heavy†	heavier	heaviest
6.	pretty†		
7.	easy†		
8.	expensive $\$\$$	more expensive $\$\$\$$	most expensive $\$\$\$\$$
9.	interesting		
10.	difficult $E = mc^2$	less difficult $2x + y = 7$	least difficult $2 \times 3 = 6$
11.	serious		

*e + er = er; e + est = est †y + er = ier; y + est = iest

H. More Comparatives and Superlatives

Jorge looked at these three apartments:

- **Owens Avenue:** $950   new   large   modern
- **Stanford Street:** $900   old   small   nice
- **Beals Boulevard:** $850   old   large   interesting

Write the comparative or superlative in the sentences.

1. The apartment on Stanford Street is _____ older _____
   than the one*on Owens Avenue. (old)

2. The one on Owens Avenue is _____ than the one on Stanford Street. (new)

3. The one on Beals Boulevard is _____ than the one on Stanford Street. (large)

4. The one on Owens Avenue is **more expensive** than the one on Beals Boulevard. (expensive)

5. The one on Beals Boulevard is _____ than the one on Owens Avenue. (interesting)

6. The one on Owens Avenue is _____ than the one on Stanford Street. (modern)

7. The one on Owens Avenue is the **newest** of the three. (new)

8. The one on Beals Boulevard is the _____ of the three. (cheap)

9. The one on Owens Avenue is the **most expensive** of the three. (expensive)

10. The one on Beals Boulevard is the _____ of the three. (interesting)

*one = apartment

I. Questions: *Which/Which one*

> The **apartment** on Owens Avenue is new.
> The **one** on Beals Boulevard is old.
>
> **Which apartment** is the most expensive?
> The **one** on Owens Avenue.
>
> **Which one** is the least expensive?
> The **one** on Beals Boulevard.

*Write **Which** or **Which one** in the question.*

1. _____**Which**_____ apartment is the most expensive?

2. _____**Which one**_____ is the cheapest?

3. _____ house is more interesting?

4. _____ is older?

5. _____ sofa is the newest?

6. _____ is the largest?

7. _____ is the heaviest?

8. _____ car is faster?

9. _____ is prettier?

10. _____ is easier to drive?

J. Dialogue

Read the dialogue and write the missing words.

JORGE: Elena! Simon, and I found a _____**nice**_____ apartment!
1. (nice/ugly)

ELENA: Oh, really? _____ is it?
2. (What/Where)

JORGE: It's _____ the International Center on Beals
3. (near / far)
Boulevard.

ELENA: That's a great location. How _____ is it?
4. (much/many)

JORGE: It's not too _____—$850 a month.
5. (large/expensive)

ELENA: How _____ bedrooms?
6. (much/ many)

JORGE: It has a _____ one and a small one. Or one
7. (large/cheap)
could be an office.

ELENA: Sounds great! When _____ I see it?
8. (can/can't)

JORGE: Anytime _____ want.
9. (she/you)

ELENA: Let's make an appointment for _____.
10. (yesterday / tomorrow)

JORGE: Okay. I think you're going to _____ it.
11. (like / buy)

ELENA: I _____ wait to see it!
12. (can / can't)

K. Newspapers: Classified Ads

Look at these classified ads and fill in the chart.

Apt. 1: 1 bdrm. w/prking, lndry, h+hw included. Only $800/mo. Deposit req. Call 555-6734 eve.

Apt. 3: 2 bdrm w/2 bthrm, h+hw, A/C, dish.+disp, wash+dryer, gar., $1,200/mo. Call 555-4000 days.

Apt. 2: 3 bdrms, 1 1/2 bthrm, h+hw, only $1,500. Call mgr. at 555-4872.

Apt. 4: 4 bdrm, 2 bthrm, 2 pking sp. A/C, lndry, h+hw, $2,000. 555-1032

	APT. 1	APT. 2	APT. 3	APT. 4
Bedrooms	1			
Bathrooms	1			
Parking	Yes			
Laundry	Yes			
Heat & hot water	Yes			
Rent/month	$800			

L. Real People...Real Language

1. What part of the city do you live in?

Check the words you hear.

69

a. ✔——— Mission Hill ——— Mission Hall

b. ——— Hyde Pub ——— Hyde Park

c. ——— West Roxbury ——— East Roxbury

d. ——— South Cambridge ——— North Cambridge

2. How did you find your apartment?

Circle the words you hear.

a. Through a friend / (realtor.)

b. Through a friend / realtor.

c. Through my doctor / dentist.

d. Walking / driving up and down the streets.

e. Through a real estate agent / newspaper.

3. What is your apartment or house like?

Circle the number of bedrooms.

a.   1   (2)   3   4

b.   1   2   3   4

c.   1   2   3   4

d.   1   2   3   4

e.   1   2   3   4

4. Is your rent very high?

Check the numbers you hear.

a. ✔——— $575 ——— $757

b. ——— $300 ——— $600

c. ——— $2,500 ——— $1,500

d. _____ low   _____ high

e. _____ $400   _____ $800

5. Would you like to move to a different area?

Circle the answer you hear.

a.   (yes)   no

b.   yes   no

c.   yes   no

d.   yes   no

e.   yes   no

VIDEO TRANSCRIPT

Watch and Listen

Simon: Do you see any apartments you like, Jorge?

Jorge: A few.

Simon: Where are they?

Jorge: Not far from here.

Simon: Are they expensive?

Jorge: Well, the two-bedrooms are expensive, but the one-bedrooms are cheaper.

Simon: Which would you like?

Jorge: We'd like a two-bedroom, but we can also take a one-bedroom.

Simon: Let's call and ask to see them.

Jorge: Okay, can I use the phone here?

Simon: Go right ahead.

Jorge: Yes. Hi, I'm interested in a few of the apartments listed in the paper... This afternoon would be great.... Two o'clock? Perfect...My name is Jorge Gonzalez...Okay. See you at two. Thank you.

At the real estate office.

Jorge: Hi. I have an appointment at two.

Simon: We'd like to look at some apartments.

Agent: You must be Jorge. Come in. Sit down. So, what are you looking for?

Jorge: A one- or two-bedroom, not too expensive, with laundry and parking.

Agent: No problem. Let's see... There are three apartments I could show you: on Stanford Street, on Owens Avenue, and on Beals Boulevard.

Jorge: How much is the rent?

Agent: They're all under $1,000—with heat and hot water included.

Simon: Could you tell us more about them?

Agent: The one on Owens Avenue is brand new.

Jorge: What about the one on Stanford Street?

Agent: It's nice, but it's old.

Jorge: And the one on Beals Boulevard?

Agent: It's pretty big and not too expensive.

Simon: Why don't we look at that one first?

Agent: All right. Come fill out an application, and I'll get the keys.

Simon: While Jorge is filling out an application, here are some phrases to remember.

When making a request, you say:

Can I use the phone?   or

Could we see some apartments today?   or

Can you show us the kitchen?   or

Could you tell us the address?

When suggesting something, you say:

Let's call and make an appointment.   or

Let's take the subway to the agency.   or

Why don't we look at the big one first?   or

Why don't you sign the contract tomorrow?

Now let's listen to people talk about their apartments.

Unit 6
Opening a Bank Account

A. Vocabulary Practice

Write the letters in the words.

1. SAVE: ___**sav**___ ings account

   to ___**save**___ money

2. CARD: ATM _____

   credit _____

3. CHECK: _____ ing account

   pay _____

   travelers _____ s

Fill in the vowels.

4. put into your account

D _E_ P _O_ s _I_ T

5. take out of your account

W _ T H D R _ W

6. bank worker

T _ LL _ R

7. money in bills and coins

C _ S H

B. Verbs: Future with *Will/Won't*

I	will / won't	we	will / won't
you	will / won't	you	will / won't
he / she / it	will / won't	they	will / won't

Contractions: will not = won't

yesterday   today   tomorrow

future:
tomorrow
next
week/month/year
in a week/month/year

*Write **will** or **won't** in the sentences.*

1. Jorge and Elena _____**will**_____ deposit $1,000 today.

2. They _____**won't**_____ pay a fee if their balance is $1,500.

3. The bank _____ send their ATM cards next week.

4. They _____ get their checks next week, too.

5. Jorge's company _____ deposit his paycheck directly.

6. They _____ apply for a credit card today.

7. The bank teller _____ take care of their application.

8. They _____ send money back to Mexico.

9. They _____ buy a car now.

10. The bank _____ lend them money to buy the car.

C. Yes/No Answers

Write a "yes" or "no" short answer after the question.

1. Will Jorge and Elena open individual accounts?
   No, they won't.

2. Will they open a joint account? __Yes, they will.__

3. Will they both deposit money? __Yes,_____

4. Will they use the ATM? __Yes,_____

5. Will they buy a car this month? __No,_____

6. Will you buy a car in a few months? __Yes,_____

7. Will the weather be nice tomorrow? __No,_____

8. Will we go to the supermarket next week? __Yes,_____

9. Will the bank give you traveler's checks? __Yes,_____

10. Will you get a credit card next year? __No,_____

D. Questions

Draw a line from the question to the answer.

1. What will Jorge and Elena do today? a. A bank teller.

2. Who will they speak with? b. A joint account.

3. What kind of account will they open? c. A thousand dollars.

4. How much will they deposit today? d. By wire transfer.

5. When will their checks arrive? e. In a few months.

6. Will they apply for a credit card today? f. Next week.

7. How will they send money to Mexico? g. No, they won't.

8. Why will they apply for a loan? h. Open a bank account.

9. Will they apply for the loan today? i. To buy a car.

10. When will they buy a car? j. Yes, they will.

E. Questions: How often?

*Write **How often** in the questions.*

1. ___**How often**___ can people use the ATM? —Every day.

2. _____ does Raquel see Ming at the International Center? —Every Wednesday.

3. _____ does Sasha deposit his paycheck? —Once a week.*

4. _____ does Simon withdraw his money? —On Monday and Friday.

5. _____ do Jorge and Elena receive a bank statement? —Every month.

6. _____ does it snow in Russia? —Every winter.

7. _____ does it snow in the Dominican Republic? —Never.

8. _____ does it rain in your city? —A few days a month.

*once a week = one time a week; twice a week = two times a week

F. Adverbs of Frequency

100%	always	Elena *always* goes to the supermarket on Saturday.
80%	usually	Sasha *usually* paints apartments.
60%	often	Raquel *often* cooks dinner in the evening.
40%	sometimes	Jorge *sometimes* cooks dinner for Elena.
20%	rarely	Simon *rarely* cooks dinner for Raquel.
0%	never	Ming *never* works in the restaurant on Sunday.

1. People can ____**always**____ use the ATM. (every day)

2. The bank is ____**usually**____ open from 8:00 A.M. to 4:00 P.M. (Monday to Friday, Saturdays 9:00 to 3:00)

3. Sasha _____ deposits his paycheck into his account on Friday. (every Friday)

4. Banks _____ approve credit card applications. (4 out of 10 times)

5. It _____ snows in Russia in winter. (0° – 40° F.)

6. It _____ snows in the Dominican Republic. (70° – 90°F.)

7. Sasha _____ works on Sunday. (three times a year)

8. Simon _____ walks to the International Center. (four times a week)

9. Jorge and Elena _____ speak Spanish with each other. (not always)

10. They _____ speak English with Simon.

G. *Too* and *Enough*

A car is **too expensive.**   They don't have **enough money.**

*Write **too** or **enough** in the sentences.*

1. Can Jorge and Elena buy a car now?

—No, they can't. A car is ____**too**____ expensive.

2. Can Elena make lasagna?

—Yes, she can. She has ___enough___ tomato sauce.

3. Can Simon make chicken curry?

—No, he can't. It's _____ difficult.

4. Can Ming go to the supermarket today?

—Yes, she can. She has _____ time.

5. Can Ming lift a refrigerator?

—No, she can't. It's _____ heavy.

6. Can Sasha paint houses?

—Yes, he can. He has _____ experience.

7. Can Sasha wear Jorge's shoes?

—No, he can't. They're _____ small.

8. Can Jorge wear Sasha's shoes?

—No, he can't. They're _____ big.

9. Can Simon teach high school English?

—Yes, he can. He has _____ education.

10. Can Jorge and Elena rent an apartment?

—Yes, they can. They have _____ money.

H. Object Pronouns

<u>Simon</u> takes <u>Jorge and Elena</u> to the bank.
subject   object

<u>He</u> takes <u>them</u> to the bank.
subject   object

SUBJECT	OBJECT	SUBJECT	OBJECT
I	me	we	us
you	you	you	you
he	him		
she	her	they	them
it	it		

Write the sentence using an object pronoun.

1. Simon will meet <u>Raquel</u> at the center.
   Simon will meet her at the center.

2. Jorge and Elena will ask <u>Sasha</u> to paint their new apartment.
   _____

3. The bank teller will mail <u>a loan application</u> to Jorge and Elena.
   _____

4. Ming will serve <u>people</u> in the restaurant.
   _____

5. Raquel will take <u>the book</u> to the library.
   _____

6. Simon gives <u>his students</u> homework every day.
   _____

7. You can get <u>cash</u> from the ATM.
   _____

8. Jorge can teach <u>Simon</u> to cook.
   _____

9. Elena can show <u>Ming</u> her new apartment.
   _____

10. Sasha can take <u>a sandwich</u> to work.
    _____

I. If Clauses: Bank Advice

If it rains, you'll get wet. 　　If you take your umbrella,
　　　　　　　　　　　　　　　　　　you won't get wet.

Write the missing word.

1. If you go to the bank, you can get an ___application___ .
   (apple/application)

2. If you are married, you can open a _____ account.
   (joint/individual)

3. If you deposit money, your _____ will go up.
   (deposit/balance)

4. If you withdraw money, your _____ will
   go down.　(balance/paycheck)

5. If the bank is closed, you can use the _____ .
   (ATM/teller)

6. If you save money, your _____ will grow.
   (savings account/bills)

7. If you have an account, you can apply for a _____ card.
   (credit/loan)

8. If you're going on a trip, you can get traveler's _____ .
   (cards/checks)

9. If you're going to buy a car, you can ask for a _____ .
   (loan/ fee)

10. If you get a loan, you will have to pay _____ .
    (fees/interest)

J. A Bank Statement

Look at Jorge and Elena's bank statement and answer the questions.

Jorge and Elena Gonzalez 1735 Beals Boulevard Center City, USA				**Checking Account** Account Number: 407238	

Date	Check No.	Description	Deductions (-)	Additions (+)	Balance
11-01		Starting Balance			1,000.00
11-01	0001	Beals Blvd. Mgmt.	850.00		150.00
11-01		Deposit		1,500.00	1,650.00
11-05	0002	City Electric	36.64		1,613.36
11-07	0003	City Telephone	68.12		1,545.24
11-10	0004	Super Shop	29.67		1,515.57
11-12		Withdrawal ATM	50.00		1,465.57
11-15	0005	City Gas	12.74		1,452.83
11-20	0006	Best Dressed	29.99		1,422.84
11-25		Withdrawal ATM	50.00		1,372.84
11-31		**Ending Balance**			**1,372.84**

1. Check 0001 is for rent. How much is it? _____**$850**_____

2. When does Jorge deposit his paycheck of $1,500? _____

3. How much is the telephone bill? _____

4. How many ATM withdrawals are there? _____

5. What is the ending balance? _____

K. Conjunctions: *And* Versus *Or*

- Jorge and Elena are opening a checking and a savings account.

- You can pay by check or credit card.

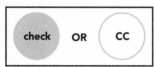 

- They do **not** allow dogs **or** cats in the apartment building.

*Write **and** or **or** in the sentences.*

1. Jorge and Elena pay for electricity, gas, ____**and**____ telephone.

2. They don't pay for water _____ parking.

3. Jorge can take a bus _____ a train to work.

4. Ming works at the restaurant on Monday, Wednesday, _____ Friday.

5. Simon likes Dominican _____ American food.

6. Will Simon make spaghetti _____ tacos?

L. Conjunctions: *And* Versus *But*

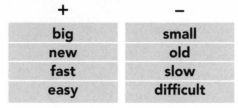

+	−
big	small
new	old
fast	slow
easy	difficult

BUT: (+/-)   or   (-/+)   AND: (+/+)   or   (-/-)

The apartment on Owens Avenue is new and big. (+/+)

The apartment on Beals Boulevard is big but old. (+/-)

The apartment on Stanford Street is old but nice. (-/+)

*Write **and** or **but** in the sentences.*

1. The apartment on Stanford Street is big ___**but**___ old.

2. Using the ATM is fast _____ easy.

3. Jorge and Elena are going to apply for a credit card, _____ not for a loan.

4. A wire transfer is fast _____ secure.

5. Today is cold _____ sunny.

6. Ming works on weekdays _____ not on weekends.

M. Real People...Real Language

1. Where is your bank account?

Circle the bank you hear.

a. (BankBoston)   Fleet Bank   U.S. Trust

b. BankBoston   Fleet Bank   U.S. Trust

c. BankBoston   Fleet Bank   U.S. Trust

2. Do you prefer big banks or small banks?

Check the one you hear.

a. ✔ big   _____ small

b. _____ big   _____ small

c. —— big   —— small

d. —— big   —— small

e. —— big   —— small

f. —— big   —— small

g. —— big   —— small

3. What services do you use at the bank?

Put a ✔ *under the ones you hear.*

	CHECKING	SAVINGS	ATM
a.	✔	✔	
b.			
c.			

4. How often do you use the ATM?

Draw a line to the correct phrase.

a.   not often

b.   3 or 4 times a week

c.   a lot

d.   twice a week

5. Which do you use more often: checks or credit cards?

Draw a box around the words you hear.

a.   checks   credit cards

b.   checks   credit cards

c.   checks   credit cards

d.   checks   credit cards

e.   checks   credit cards

f.   checks   credit cards

g.   checks   credit cards

Video Transcript

Watch and Listen

Ms. Lee: So, what can I do for you today?

Jorge: We'd like to open a bank account.

Ms. Lee: Individual accounts or a joint account?

Elena: A joint one is better.

Ms. Lee: Yes, and you can get both checking and savings.

Jorge: Do we have to pay a service fee?

Ms. Lee: If you have a minimum balance of $1,500, there are no fees.

Elena: I hope we can do that.

Jorge: Don't worry; we both work.

Ms. Lee: Okay. How much would you like to deposit now?

Jorge: $1,000 now and more next week.

Ms. Lee: Good. You'll get a statement with your balance every month.

Elena: And when do we get our checks and ATM cards?

Ms. Lee: You'll get temporary checks now and permanent checks and your ATM cards in about a week.

Jorge: So, we deposit our paychecks at the teller's window, right?

Elena: Or ATM.

Ms. Lee: Yes, and some companies offer direct deposit, so your paycheck can be deposited into your account automatically.

Jorge: So, no waiting in line!

Ms. Lee: That's right... Any other questions?

Elena: Can we have a credit card application, too?

Ms. Lee: Sure. You can fill it out at home and bring it in later.

Elena: How do we send money home to our families in Mexico?

Ms. Lee: You can do that by money order or wire transfer.

Jorge: We're also thinking about buying a car. Do you think we can get a loan?

Ms. Lee: It depends on how much you want to borrow and how much you earn. Would you like to fill out an application?

Jorge: Let's come back and talk about it in a few months.

Elena: Good idea.

Ms. Lee: Thank you for banking with us. See you again soon.

Jorge: Thank you. Good-bye.

Elena: Good-bye.

Simon: That wasn't too difficult, was it? Let's go over some phrases you'll need at the bank.

When someone at a bank or store sees you, they might say:

> **How may I help you?**   or
>
> **What can I do for you today?**

You can reply like this:

> **I'd like** some traveler's checks.   or
>
> **We'd like to** apply for a loan.

To show ownership, you say:

> **You have** a new credit card.   or
>
> **She has** a checking account here.

To show that something is necessary, you say:

> **You have to** mail your payment on time.   or
>
> **She has to** open a savings account.

Now let's listen to people talk about different bank services.

Unit 7
Using the Telephone

A. Vocabulary Practice

Write the words in the sentences.

1. When the telephone rings, you _p i c k_ it up.

2. When the telephone is busy, you _h_ _ _ _ up.

3. When you aren't home, the answering machine takes
   a _m_ _ _ _ _ _ _ .

4. When you dial a number, the phone _r_ _ _ _ _ .

5. When you call the _o_ _ _ _ _ _ _ _ , she gives you
   information.

6. You can buy a _p_ _ _ _ _ _c_ _ _ _ at a store.

7. You can dial a _t_ _ _ _ - _f_ _ _ _ number without
   paying.

8. You have to go to the airport to take a _f_ _ _ _ _ _ .

9. You have to call the airlines to check the plane
   _s_ _ _ _ _ _ _ _ .

10. You pay less for a round-trip ticket than two _o_ _ _ - _w_ _ _
    tickets.

B. Verbs: Simple Past—Regular

_____ + ed

I	worked	we	worked
you	worked	you	worked
he/she/it	worked	they	worked

yesterday   today   tomorrow

past:
yesterday
last week/month/year
a long time ago
in 1960

Write the verbs in the past tense.

1. want __**wanted**__

2. look _____

3. dial _____

4. ask _____

5. call _____

6. receive* _____

7. pick _____

8. press _____

9. listen _____

10. offer _____

*e + ed = ed

Now write the verbs in the sentences.

1. Ming __**wanted**__ to go to her sister's wedding.

2. Raquel _____ in the newspaper for cheap flights.

3. Ming _____ 1-800-555-TOUR.

4. She _____ about ticket prices to Hong Kong.

5. Sasha's friends _____ from Russia.

6. They _____ their visas to come to the U.S.

7. Sasha _____ up the phone to make a call.

8. He _____ the buttons for train schedules.

9. He _____ to the information.

10. Then he _____ to put up Ming's bookshelves.

C. Negatives

I	did not work	we	did not work
you	did not work	you	did not work
he/she/it	did not work	they	did not work

Contraction: did not = didn't

Write the subject pronoun and the negative form of the verbs in Exercise B.

1. **She didn't want** to go to her cousin's wedding.

2. _____ in the newspaper for expensive flights.

3. _____ 1-800-666-TOUR.

4. _____ about ticket prices to Russia.

5. _____ from Mexico.

6. _____ their visas to come to Canada.

7. _____ up the newspaper to make a call.

8. _____ the buttons for plane schedules.

9. _____ to the time and temperature.

10. _____ to put up Raquel's bookshelves.

D. Questions and Yes/No Answers

Ming **wanted** to go to Hong Kong.

Did Ming **want** to go to Hong Kong?

Circle the correct short answer for the questions.

1. Did Ming want to go to Hong Kong for the wedding?

Yes, she did.   No, she didn't.

2. Did Raquel find a cheap ticket to Hong Kong?

   Yes, she did.   No, she didn't.

3. Did Ming want to buy the ticket for $899?

   Yes, she did.   No, she didn't.

4. Did she call for a cheaper ticket?

   Yes, she did.   No, she didn't.

5. Did she find a cheaper ticket?

   Yes, she did.   No, she didn't

6. Did Sasha's friends call him from Russia?

   Yes, they did.   No, they didn't.

7. Did Sasha call for bus schedules to the airport?

   Yes, he did.   No, he didn't.

8. Did he find out the price of a plane ticket?

   Yes, he did.   No, he didn't.

9. Did Raquel call Simon at work?

   Yes, she did.   No, she didn't.

10. Did she talk to him?

    Yes, she did.   No, she didn't.

E. Verbs: Simple Past—Irregular

come	came	have	had
cost	cost	leave	left
feel	felt	meet	met
fly	flew	take	took
get	got	tell	told
go	went	think	thought

To be: am/is → was; are → were.

Write verbs in the past tense in the sentences.

1. Ming and Sasha _____**met**_____ at the International Center. (meet)

2. Sasha's friends _____ from Russia. (fly)

3. Raquel _____ to Ming's apartment. (come)

4. Simon _____ a good time at the party. (have)

5. Ms. Lee _____ Jorge and Elena about bank services. (tell)

6. A ticket to Hong Kong _____ a lot of money. (cost)

7. Ming and Sasha _____ on the city tour. (go)

8. Raquel _____ the center at 8:00 P.M. (leave)

9. Jorge and Elena _____ a nice apartment. (get)

10. Sasha _____ the train to the airport. (take)

11. Raquel _____ better after shopping. (feel)

12. Ming _____ about her sister's wedding. (think)

F. Question Words

How **did** Simon and Raquel **meet**?
—They **met** on vacation.

Circle the correct question word.

1. (Where)/ When did Simon go? —To the Dominican Republic.

2. Who / How did he get there? —He flew.

3. When / How long was he there? —For one week.

4. Where / When did he meet Raquel? —At the hotel.

5. How / Why was she at the hotel? —She was on vacation.

6. Where / How did he invite her? —To dinner.

7. When / Where was the restaurant? —By the sea.

8. Who / What did they do after dinner? —They danced.

9. What / How did Simon ask Raquel to do? —To write to him.

10. How / When did Raquel feel when Simon left? —She felt sad.

G. Verbs in Questions

Write verbs in the past tense in the questions.

1. Where ____did____ Simon ____fly____ ? (fly)

2. Why _____ he _____ there? (go)

3. How _____ he _____ Raquel? (meet)

4. Why _____ she at the hotel? (be)

5. What _____ she _____ of Simon? (think)

6. How _____ the dinner? (be)

7. Why _____ Simon _____ Raquel to write him? (want)

8. How _____ they _____ ? (feel)

9. Why _____ they sad when the vacation ended? (be)

10. When _____ they _____ married? (get)

H. *How much?/How long?*

Draw a line to the correct answer.

1. How much is a cheap ticket to Hong Kong?

2. How long is the trip to the airport?

3. How much is a one-way train ticket to the airport?

4. How long was Simon in the Dominican Republic?

5. How much is a round-trip ticket to the airport?

6. How long will Raquel work at the center?

7. How much is an 800 number phone call?

8. How long will Sasha wait at the airport?

a. $8.00.

b. Until 9:00 P.M.

c. $12.00.

d. Until late.

e. It's free.

f. Thirty minutes.

g. About $900.

h. One week.

I. Possessives: Nouns, Adjectives, and Pronouns

1. Raquel is __Simon's__ wife.

2. Elena is _____ wife.

3. Ming is _____ friend.

4. Simon is __Raquel's__ husband.

5. Jorge is _____ husband.

6. Sasha is _____ friend.

ADJECTIVE + NOUN	PRONOUN	ADJECTIVE + NOUN	PRONOUN
my ticket	mine	our house	ours
your phone	yours	your class	yours
his furniture	his		
her apartment	hers	their car	theirs
its food	—		

Cross out the possessive adjective + noun and write the possessive pronoun.

7. Where are the tickets?

   <del>My ticket</del> **Mine** is on the table, and <del>your ticket</del> **yours** is on the desk.

8. Where are the phones?

   His phone is in his hand, and *her phone* is in her bag.

9. Where is the dog's food?

   Its food is on the floor.

10. Where is your house?

    Our house is near *your house*—on the same street.

11. Where are the cars?

    Their car is in the parking lot, and *our car* is on the street.

J. Modals: *Should, Could, Might*

Read the dialogues and answer the questions.

SASHA: Ming, what time **should** I go to the airport? (*advice*)

MING: What time will the plane arrive?

SASHA: It **should** arrive at 9:00 P.M. (*probability*), but it **could** be late. (*possibility*)

MING: It **might** be early, too. (*possibility*) Take the 8:00 train to be safe.

SASHA: That's a good idea.

---

1. What time **should** the plane arrive? —At _____ **9:00 P.M.** _____

2. What time **could** it arrive? —Before/after _____

3. Which train **should** Sasha take to the airport?

    —The _____ train.

MING: It takes a long time to go through immigration.

SASHA: I know. It **might** take half an hour.

MING: You **could** watch TV in the waiting area.

SASHA: I **should** bring a book to read.

MING: Yes, you **might** not get home until eleven.

---

4. How long **might** it take to pass through immigration and

    customs? — _____ minutes.

5. What time **could** Sasha's friends be ready to go?

    —After _____ .

6. What time **might** he get home? —Around _____ .

K. Real People...Real Language

1. Making a local directory assistance call...

Write the answers on the lines.

a. City: _____ **Boston** _____

b. Listing: _____ **Boston Museum of Science** _____

c. Number: _____

2. Calling for the time and temperature...

Circle what you hear.

a. At the tone, the time will be ⟨3:35 PM⟩ 3:15 PM

b. The temperature is: 73° 93°

3. Calling for the hours of the Science Museum...

Write what you hear.

a. open Tuesday through __**Sunday**__

b. hours are _____ A.M. to _____ P.M.

c. Admission: _____ adults, _____ students,

_____ children

4. Calling for plane fares...

Circle what you hear.

a. Hong Kong ⟨New York⟩

b. round-trip one-way

c. $19 $90

VIDEO TRANSCRIPT

Watch and Listen

Raquel: So, your sister's getting married.

Ming: Yes, I wish I could go to Hong Kong for the wedding.

Raquel: Well, some airlines have cheap flights to Hong Kong. You know what, we can look in the paper. Here's something right here: a round-trip ticket for $899.

Ming: Not bad, but I can't afford it.

Raquel: Let's call and see if there's anything cheaper.

Ming: Okay, what's the number?

Raquel: 1-800-555-TOUR.

Ming: Tour?

Raquel: Yes, you have to press the buttons for the letters.

Ming: Oh, I see... T-O-U-R... The line is busy.

Raquel: Well, that's okay. Let's try again later.

(doorbell sounds)

Ming: Come in. It's open.

Raquel: Who is that?

Ming: Sasha said he might stop by.

Sasha: Ming! ... Oh, hello, Raquel.

Raquel: Hi, Sasha.

Ming: Come in. Sit down.

Sasha: Guess what!

Raquel: What?

Sasha: An old friend from Russia called me. He and his family are arriving today!

Ming: Really?

Sasha: Yes, they finally got a visa after two years.

Ming: That's so exciting!

Sasha: I'm going to the airport to pick them up. Do you want to come?

Ming: Okay.

Raquel: How are you going to get there?

Sasha: By train. But I have to call for the times. They're arriving on a 9:00 flight.

Ming: You can use this phone.

Raquel: I think the number for the train schedules is 555-9244.

Sasha: The airport train, right?

Raquel: Right. It takes about half an hour.

TRAINCHECK: Welcome to TrainCheck. For city trains, press 1. For commuter trains, press 2. For city train routes, press 1. For schedules and prices, press 2. The A train, which goes to the airport, leaves every fifteen minutes from Central Station. It takes approximately 30 minutes. The fare is $8 one-way, or $12 round-trip.

Sasha: It only costs $12 for a round-trip ticket to the airport. Not bad.

Raquel: No, not bad at all.... Ming, can I borrow your phone? I have to tell Simon I'm going to be working late tonight.

Ming: Of course.

Raquel: Hi, may I speak to Simon, please?...Oh, that's right, he's still in class. Can I leave a message for him?...Yes, it's Raquel. Could you please tell him that I'm going to be working late tonight?...Thank you...Okay. Bye...So, Ming, are you all unpacked?

Ming: Yes, mostly. But I still have to put up bookshelves in my room.

Sasha: I can help you with that, Ming.

Ming: Oh, thank you. Let me show you how I want it set up.

Raquel: That's all for now. Here are a few phrases you can use on the phone.

To ask to speak to someone, you can say:

> **May I speak to** Simon, please?   or
>
> **Is** Sasha **there?**

To introduce yourself on the phone, you say:

> **Hi, this is** Raquel.   or
>
> **It's** Raquel.

To leave a message for someone, you can say:

> **Please call me back.**   or
>
> **I'll call you back later.**
>
> **My number is** 555-3890.   or
>
> **You can reach me at** 555-3890.

Now let's listen to people using different services on the phone.

Answer Key: Everyday Life

Unit 1: **Unit 1:** At The International Center: Introductions

A. Introductions
1. Hello 2. are 3. Fine 4. you
5. This 6. meet 7. is 8. My

B. Countries
1. China 2. Russia 3. United States
4. Mexico

C. Professions
1. d. 2. a. 3. e. 4. c. 5. b.

D. Verbs: Present Tense—*To Be*
1. is 2. are 3. is 4. is 5. is 6. is
7. are 8. am 9. are 10. are

E. Contractions
1. you're 2. they're 3. it's 4. I'm
5. we're 6. he's

F. Negatives
1. am not 2. are not 3. is not 4. is not
5. is not 6. is not 7. are not
8. are not 9. are not 10. is not

G. Negative Contractions
1. he's not/he isn't 2. they're not/they aren't 3. we're not/we aren't 4. I'm not 5. you're not/you aren't 6. she's not/she isn't

H. Questions and Yes/No Answers
1. No, he is not. 2. Yes, he is. 3. Yes, she is. 4. No, I am not. 5. No, they are not. 6. Is Simon from the United States? 7. Are you from Hong Kong? 8. Are Sasha and Ming at the International Center? 9. Are Elena and Jorge hungry? 10. Is the food on the table?

I. Question Words
1. Who 2. Who 3. What 4. Who
5. Where 6. What 7. Where 8. What

J. Short answers
1. Ming is. 2. From Mexico. 3. Sasha is. 4. From the D.R. 5. Simon is.

K. Country/Nationality/Language
1. Portuguese 2. Dominican 3. China
4. —— 5. —— 6. —— 7. Mexican
8. Russian 9. American 10. ——

L. People/Countries
1. Dominican Republic 2. Chinese
3. Mexico 4. Russian 5. United States
6. Spanish 7. Russian 8. Chinese
9. English

M. Dialogue
1. Simon 2. you, is 3. meet 4. My
5. you 6. Nice 7. you 8. this 9. meet
10. pleasure 11. Are, I

N. Professions and Workplaces
1. teacher 2. cashier 3. waitress
4. engineer

O. Real People...Real Language
1. computer 2. student 3. Taiwan
4. consultant 5. Mexican 6. Ukraine
7. Taipei 8. Colombia 9. mother
10. Puerto Rico 11. Jamaica
12. technology

Unit 2: A City Tour: The Time and Date

A. Days, Months, and Seasons
1. Sunday, Monday, Tuesday,
Wednesday, Thursday, Friday,
Saturday 2. March, April, May 3.
June, July, August 4. September,
October, November 5. December,
January, February

B. Verbs: Present Continuous—To Be + _ing
1. is waiting 2. is coming 3. are
talking 4. is asking 5. is looking 6. is
telling 7. is walking 8. are going
9. are writing 10. am finishing

C. Negatives
1. is not going 2. is not waiting 3. are
not shopping 4. is not having 5. is not
talking 6. are not sitting 7. am not
getting up 8. are not eating 9. are not
watching 10. is not sleeping

D. Yes/No Answers
1. Yes, she is. 2. No, he isn't./No, he's
not. 3. Yes, it is. 4. Yes, they are.
5. Yes, it is. 6. No, they aren't./No,
they're not. 7. Yes, it is. 8. Yes, they
are. 9. No, he isn't./No, he's not.
10. Yes it is.

E. Question Words
1. When 2. Which 3. When
4. Which 5. When 6. When
7. When 8. Which 9. When

F. Prepositions of Time
1. at, in 2. in 3. on 4. at 5. on 6. at,
at 7. in 8. on 9. in 10. on

G. Dialogue
1. sorry 2. right 3. at 4. What
5. you 6. are 7. Let's 8. on
9. fall

H. Number Practice
(no answers)

I. Telling Time
1. 1:10/one-ten 2. 2:25/two-twenty-
five 3. 12:15/twelve-fifteen
4. 8:55/eight-fifty-five 5. 11:45/eleven-
forty-five 6. 9:05/nine-o-five
7. 3:35/three-thirty-five 8. 4:30/ four-
thirty 9. 5:00/five o'clock
10. 7:20/seven-twenty 11. 6:50/six-
fifty 12. 10:40/ten-forty

J. What's the date?
1. Thursday 2. Tuesday
3. Wednesday 4. Friday 5. Monday

K. Real People...Real Language
1. a. 8:30 b. 7:00 c. 8:00 d. 11:00
e. 7:00 f. 6:00 g. 9:00
2. a. dinner in a restaurant b. stopped
having parties c. party with family and
friends d. no party e. dinner and
phone calls
3. a. summer b. winter c. summer
d. fall e. spring f. summer g. summer

Unit 3: Asking for Directions

A. What is it?
1. stop 2. box 3. post 4. movie

B. Odd One Out
1. letter 2. stamp 3. movie 4. theater

C. Opposites
1. right 2. off 3. far 4. there

D. Verbs: Simple Present
1. sits 2. answers 3. asks 4. wants
5. needs 6. takes 7. live 8. eat
9. speak 10. study

E. Negatives
1. doesn't speak 2. doesn't drive
3. doesn't work 4. don't go 5. doesn't
paint 6. don't know 7. don't drink
8. don't buy 9. don't watch
10. doesn't eat

F. Yes/No Answers
1. Yes, he does. 2. No, they don't.
3. Yes, I do. 4. No, she doesn't.
5. No, you don't. 6. Yes, it does.
7. Yes, he does. 8. Yes, I do. 9. No,
they don't. 10. Yes, you do.

G. Short Answers
1. Elena does. 2. Near the
supermarket. 3. Jorge does. 4. Two
blocks. 5. Raquel does. 6. I do. 7. It
costs $1.50. 8. Four stops. 9. Near
the pharmacy. 10. Ming does.

H. Questions
1. Where 2. Where 3. Who 4. How
much 5. Who 6. How many 7. How
much 8. Who 9. How many
10. Where

I. Plurals
1. banks 2. blocks 3. letters 4. maps
5. stops 6. trains

J. *There is.../There are...*
1. There are 2. There is 3. There is
4. There are 5. There are 6. There is

K. Prepositions of Place: *In/On/At*
1. in 2. at 3. on 4. at 5. at or in 6. in
7. on 8. on 9. at 10. on

L. Dialogue
1. post 2. bus 3. Where 4. Center
5. I'm 6. supermarket 7. you 8. are
9. am 10. go

M. Real People...Real Language
1. a. 10, 5 b. —— c. 8 d. 10
2. a. 5 or 3 b. 2 c. 1 d. —— e. 1
3. a. walk b. drive c. drive d. drive
e. walk f. drive g. drive h. walk

Unit 4: Shopping for Food

A. Odd One Out
1. bananas 2. carrots 3. soup 4. juice
5. sauce

B. What is it?
1. apples, oranges, bananas,
strawberries 2. potatoes, onions,
carrots, tomatoes 3. milk, eggs, butter
4. soup, sauce

C. Verbs: Future with *Going To*
1. are going to go 2. is going to buy
3. is going to get 4. is going to look
for 5. are going to have 6. am going
to see 7. are going to drive 8. is going
to snow 9. are going to take 10. is
going to rent

D. Negatives
1. They aren't going to/They're not going to 2. She isn't going to/She's not going to 3. She isn't going to/She's not going to 4. She isn't going to/She's not going to 5. They aren't going to/They're not going to 6. He isn't going to/He's not going to 7. You aren't going to/You're not going to 8. I'm not going to 9. It isn't going to/It's not going to 10. We aren't going to/We're not going to

E. Yes/No Answers
1. No, she isn't. 2. Yes, she is. 3. No, she isn't. 4. Yes, they are. 5. No, he isn't. 6. No, they aren't.

F. Short Answers
1. d. 2. h. 3. i. 4. e. 5. a. 6. j. 7. b. 8. c. 9. g. 10. f.

G. Questions
1. How much 2. How many 3. How much 4. How many 5. How many 6. How much 7. How many 8. How many 9. How much 10. How much

H. Singular/Plural Nouns
1. apples 2. bananas 3. carrots 4. eggs 5. onions 6. potatoes 7. tomatoes 8. strawberries 9. raspberries 10. cherries

I. Money
Raquel: Total = $8.54 Change = $1.46
Ming: Total = $6.36 Change = $3.64
Elena: Total = $9.21 Change = $.79

J. Count and Noncount Nouns
1. apples, potatoes, eggs, bananas, onions, oranges, tomatoes 2. bread, soup, juice, rice, milk, spaghetti, tomato sauce

K. Recipe: Jorge's Tacos
BEEF, LETTUCE TOMATO, SALT, TACO, CHEESE, SALSA, CREAM

L. Dialogue
1. you 2. cook 3. What 4. tacos 5. need 6. cheese 7. do 8. some 9. tonight 10. need 11. dinner 12. her

M. Containers
Other answers are also correct!
1. apples, grapefruit 2. beer, champagne 3. pasta, rice 4. plantains, collard greens 5. peaches, tuna 6. soy milk, eggs 7. cauliflower 8. mayonnaise, kimchee 9. cookie dough 10. ointment, hand cream

N. Real People...Real Language
1. a. once a month b. once or twice a week c. hardly ever d. once every two weeks 2. a. cheese b. eggs c. rice 3. a. onions b. bananas c. rice d. sauce 4. a. 2 b. 2 c. 2 5. a. $80 to $100 b. $50 c. $150 d. $200

Unit 5: Finding an Apartment

A. Odd One Out
1. bed 2. shower 3. oven 4. microwave

B. Verbs: Present Tense—Can/Can't
1. can 2. can't 3. can 4. can't 5. can't 6. can 7. Can/No, he can't. 8. Can/Yes, he can. 9. Can/Yes, she can. 10. Can/No, she can't.

C. Verbs: Past Tense—Could/Couldn't
1. could 2. couldn't 3. could 4. couldn't 5. could 6. could 7. Could/No, they couldn't. 8. Could/Yes, they could. 9. Could/Yes, he could. 10. Could/No, she couldn't.

D. *Can/Can't or Could/Couldn't*
1. can't 2. could 3. could 4. can't
5. couldn't 6. can 7. couldn't
8. could

E. Short Answers
1. Yes, I can. 2. No, he couldn't.
3. Yes, they can. 4. Yes, she could.
5. Yes, I can. 6. No, he couldn't.
7. Yes, we can. 8. No, I couldn't.
9. No, they can't. 10. Yes, she could.

F. Adjectives: Opposites
1. new, large, expensive 2. old, small,
pretty 3. large, old, interesting

G. Adjectives: Comparative and Superlative
1. large, larger, largest 2. small,
smaller, smallest 3. new, newer,
newest 4. old, older, oldest 5. heavy,
heavier, heaviest 6. pretty, prettier,
prettiest 7. easy, easier, easiest
8. expensive, more expensive, most
expensive 9. interesting, more
interesting, most interesting
10. difficult, less difficult, least difficult
11. Serious, less serious, least serious

H. More Comparatives and Superlatives
1. older 2. newer 3. larger 4. more
expensive 5. more interesting 6. more
modern 7. newest 8. cheapest 9. most
expensive 10. most interesting

I. Questions: *Which/Which one*
1. Which 2. Which one 3. Which
4. Which one 5. Which 6. Which one
7. Which one 8. Which 9. Which one
10. Which one

J. Dialogue
1. nice 2. Where 3. near 4. much
5. expensive 6. many 7. large 8. can
9. you 10. tomorrow 11. like
12. can't

K. Newspapers: Classified Ads
Apt. 1: 1, 1, yes, yes, yes, $800 Apt. 2:
3, 1¹/₂, no, no, yes, $1,500 Apt. 3: 2,
2, yes, yes, yes, $1,200 Apt. 4: 4, 2,
yes, yes, yes, $2,000

L. Real People...Real Language
1. a. Mission Hill b. Hyde Park
c. West Roxbury d. North Cambridge
2. a. realtor b. friend c. doctor
d. driving e. real estate agent 3. a. 2 b.
3 c. 3 d. 3 e. 2 4. a. $575 b. $300
each/$600 total c. $2,500 before/
$1,500 now d. high e. $800 5. a. yes
b. no c. yes d. no e. no

Unit 6: Opening a Bank Account

A. Vocabulary Practice
1. savings account, to save money
2. ATM card, credit card 3. checking
account, paycheck, traveler's checks
4. deposit 5. withdraw 6. teller
7. cash

B. Verbs: Future with *Will/Won't*
1. will 2. won't 3. will 4. will 5. will
6. won't 7. will 8. will 9. won't
10. will

C. Yes/No Answers
1. No, they won't. 2. Yes, they will.
3. Yes, they will. 4. Yes, they will.
5. No, they won't. 6. Yes, I will.
7. No, it won't. 8. Yes, we will.
9. Yes, it will. 10. No, I won't.

D. Questions
1. h. 2. a. 3. b. 4. c. 5. f. 6. g. 7. d.
8. i. 9. j. 10. e.

E. Questions: How often?
1. How often 2. How often 3. How
often 4. How often 5. How often
6. How often 7. How often 8. How
often

F. Adverbs of Frequency
1. always 2. usually 3. always
4. sometimes 5. always 6. never
7. rarely 8. often 9. usually 10.
always

G. *Too* and *Enough*
1. too 2. enough 3. too 4. enough
5. too 6. enough 7. too 8. too
9. enough 10. enough

H. Object Pronouns
1. Simon will meet her at the center.
2. Jorge and Elena will ask him to
paint their new apartment. 3. The
bank teller will mail it. 4. Ming will
serve them in the restaurant. 5. Raquel
will take it to the library. 6. Simon
gives them homework. 7. You can get
it from the ATM. 8. Jorge can teach
him to cook. 9. Elena can show her
her new apartment. 10. Sasha can take
it to work.

I. If Clauses: Bank Advice
1. application 2. joint 3. balance
4. balance 5. ATM 6. savings account
7. credit 8. checks 9. loan 10. interest

J. A Bank Statement
1. $850 2. 11-01 3. $68.12 4. 2
5. $1,372.84

K. Conjunctions: *And* Versus *Or*
1. and 2. or/and 3. or 4. and 5. and
6. and/or

L. Conjunctions: *And* Versus *But*
1. but 2. and 3. but 4. and
5. but 6. but

M. Real People...Real Language
1. a. BankBoston b. BankBoston
c. Fleet Bank 2. a. big b. big
c. small d. big e. small f. big g. big
3. a. checking/savings b. checking/
savings/ATM c. checking/savings/
ATM 4. a. twice a week b. not often
c. three or four times a week
d. a lot 5. a. credit cards b. checks
c. checks d. credit cards e. credit cards
f. checks g. credit cards

Unit 7: Using the Telephone

A. Vocabulary Practice
1. pick 2. hang 3. message 4. rings
5. operator 6. phone card 7. toll-free
8. flight 9. schedule 10. one-way

B. Verbs: Simple Past—Regular
1. wanted 2. looked 3. dialed
4. asked 5. called 6. received
7. picked 8. pressed 9. listened
10. offered 1. wanted 2. looked 3.
dialed 4. asked 5. called
6. received 7. picked 8. pressed 9.
listened 10. offered

C. Negatives
1. She didn't want 2. She didn't look
3. She didn't dial 4. She didn't ask
5. They didn't call 6. They didn't
receive 7. He didn't pick 8. He didn't
press 9. He didn't listen 10. He didn't
offer

D. Questions and Yes/No Answers
1. Yes, she did. 2. Yes, she did. 3. No, she didn't. 4. Yes, she did. 5. No, she didn't 6. Yes, they did. 7. Yes, he did. 8. No, he didn't. 9. Yes, she did. 10. No, she didn't.

E. Verbs: Simple Past—Irregular
1. met 2. flew 3. came 4. had 5. told 6. cost 7. went 8. left 9. got 10. took 11. felt 12. thought

F. Question Words
1. Where 2. How 3. How long 4. Where 5. Why 6. Where 7. Where 8. What 9. What 10. How

G. Verbs in Questions
1. did, fly 2. did, go 3. did, meet 4. was 5. did, think 6. was 7. did, want 8. did, feel 9. were 10. did, get

H. *How much?/How long?*
1. g. 2. f 3. a. 4. h. 5. c. 6. d. 7. e. 8. b.

I. Possessives: Nouns, Adjectives, and Pronouns
1. Simon's 2. Jorge's 3. Sasha's 4. Raquel's 5. Elena's 6. Ming's 7. Mine, yours 8. His, hers 9. —— 10. Ours, yours 11. Theirs, ours

J. Modals: *Should, Could, Might*
1. 9:00 2. 9:00 3. 8:00 4. 30 5. 10:00 6. 11:00

K. Real People...Real Language
1. a. Boston b. Boston Museum of Science c. 555-1700 2. a. 3:35 b. 73° 3. a. Sunday b. 10, 6 c. $10, $8, $6 4. a. New York b. round-trip c. $90

Word List: Everyday Life

a few
a little
a lot
account
afternoon
again
agent
aisle
always
American
and
answering
    machine
any
apartment
apples
are
area code
ATM
bag
balance
bananas
bank
basket
bathroom
bedroom
birthday
block
bottle
box
Brazil
Brazilian
bread
building

bunch
bus
bus stop
busy signal
butter
bye
call
can
cardinal numbers
cards
carrots
cart
carton
cash
cashier
center
chair
cheap
check
child
children
China
Chinese
classified ads
clothing store
collector
college
Colombia
Colombian
Colorado
community
company
computer
consultant

container
convenience
corner
could
cross the street
dark
date
daughter
day
deposit
dial
dining room
directory
    assistance
do
does
doesn't
Dominican
Dominican
    Republic
don't
electricity
Elena
engineer
evening
expensive
father
fee
fine
floor
French
gas
Georgia
get off

get on
go straight
good morning
good-bye
great
had
Haiti
Haitian
half-past
hang up
has
has to
have
have to
he
hello
her
hers
hi
high
his
home
Hong Kong
house
how
how long
how many
how much
how often
hungry
husband
I
identification
information

interest	movie theater	Sasha	today
international	my	sauce	token
is	nationalities	school	tomatoes
it	negative	secretary	tomorrow
its	neighborhood	see	train
Jamaica	never	seldom	traveler's checks
Jamaican	new	service	turn left
Japan	New York	she	turn right
Japanese	newspaper	should	Ukraine
jar	nice	signature	United States
Jorge	night	Simon	Uruguay
juice	o'clock	small	usually
know	office	social worker	utilities
Korea	often	some	vacation
Korean	old-fashioned	sometimes	verb
large	onions	son	very well
later	operator	soon	Vietnam
laundry	oranges	soup	Vietnamese
lease	ordinal numbers	Spain	waitress
leave	our	Spanish	we
letter	ours	stamp	where
light	painter	statement	wife
living room	parking	stick	will
loaf	people	store	window
loan	pharmacy	strawberries	withdraw
local	phrases	student	word
long-distance	pick up	subway	would
low	Port-au-Prince	supermarket	wrong number
machine	Portugal	table	years
mailbox	Portuguese	tai chi	yogurt
math	post office	Taipei	you
mechanic	potatoes	Taiwan	your
meet	pound	teacher	yours
message	Puerto Rican	technology	
Mexican	Puerto Rico	telephone	
Mexico	quarter	teller	
milk	Raquel	Thailand	
mine	rarely	that	
Ming	real estate	their	
minimum	restaurant	theirs	
modern	rice	they	
months	ring	this	
Moscow	Russia	time	
mother	Russian	to	

Audio Script: Everyday Life

Unit 1: Introductions

Greetings

Listen and repeat.

1. Hi.
2. Hello.
3. How are you?
4. Fine, thanks.
5. And you?
6. Very well.
7. Good morning.
8. Good afternoon.
9. Good evening.
10. Good night.

Professions and Countries

Listen and repeat.

1. engineer
2. cashier
3. teacher

4. social worker

5. painter

6. waitress

7. United States

8. Mexico

9. China

10. Russia

Introductions

Listen and repeat.

1. Hi, I'm Raquel.

2. My name is Jorge.

3. Nice to meet you.

4. I'd like you to meet Ming.

5. How do you do?

6. Nice to meet you.

7. This is Sasha.

8. Hi, Sasha. How are you?

9. Nice to meet you.

10. My pleasure.

Verbs: *To Be*

Listen and repeat.

1. I am

2. you are

3. he is

4. she is

5. it is

6. we are

7. you are

8. they are

Sentences

Make a sentence from these words.

First, listen to the example:

    Ming/Chinese   Ming is Chinese.

Now it's your turn.

1. Simon/American   Simon is American.

2. Raquel/Simon's wife   Raquel is Simon's wife.

3. Jorge/Mexican   Jorge is Mexican.

4. Elena/housewife   Elena is a housewife.

5. Sasha/tall   Sasha is tall.

Negatives: *To Be*

Listen and repeat.

1. I'm not   I'm not

2. you're not   you aren't

3. he's not   he isn't

4. she's not   she isn't

5. it's not   it isn't

6. we're not   we aren't

7. you're not   you aren't

8. they're not   they aren't

Negatives: Sentences

Make a sentence from these words.

First, listen to the example:

   Simon/painter   Simon isn't a painter.

Now it's your turn.

1. They/engineers   They aren't engineers.

2. Raquel/waitress   Raquel isn't a waitress.

3. Jorge/painter   Jorge isn't a painter.

4. Elena/teacher   Elena isn't a teacher.

5. Sasha/social worker   Sasha isn't a social worker.

Who?

Answer these questions.

First, listen to the example:

   Who is a painter?   Sasha is.

Now it's your turn.

1. Who is a painter?   Sasha is.

2. Who is a social worker?   Raquel is.

3. Who is a cashier?   Elena is.

4. Who is a waitress?   Ming is.

5. Who is an engineer?   Jorge is.

Where?

Answer these questions.

First, listen to the example:

> Where is the teacher? (school)

> He's at school.

Now it's your turn.

1. Where are Jorge and Elena? (theater)

   They're at the theater.

2. Where is the waitress? (restaurant)

   She's at the restaurant.

3. Where is the engineer? (office)

   He's at the office.

4. Where is the cashier? (store)   She's at the store.

5. Where is the painter? (house)   He's at the house.

What?

Answer the questions.

First, listen to the example:

> What is on the table? (glasses)

> The glasses are on the table.

Now it's your turn.

1. What is on the desk? (book)   The book is on the desk.

2. What is in the refrigerator? (food)

   The food is in the refrigerator.

3. What is in the closet? (clothes)

   The clothes are in the closet.

4. What is on the bed? (pillows)

   The pillows are on the bed.

5. What is in the living room?   The furniture is in the living
    (furniture)   room.

Unit 2: A City Tour: The Time and Date

Numbers

Listen and repeat.

one	twelve	twenty-three	seventy
two	thirteen	twenty-four	eighty
three	fourteen	twenty-five	ninety
four	fifteen	twenty-six	one hundred
five	sixteen	twenty-seven	one hundred one
six	seventeen	twenty-eight	
seven	eighteen	twenty-nine	two hundred
eight	nineteen	thirty	one thousand
nine	twenty	forty	
ten	twenty-one	fifty	
eleven	twenty-two	sixty	

Telling Time

Listen and repeat.

What time is it?

1. It's one-ten.

2. It's two-twenty-five.

3. It's twelve-fifteen.

4. It's five-fifty-five.

5. It's five-o'clock.

Days of the Week

Listen and repeat.

What day is it?

1. Today is Sunday.

2. Today is Monday.

3. Today is Tuesday.

4. Today is Wednesday.

5. Today is Thursday.

6. Today is Friday.

7. Today is Saturday.

Months of the Year

Listen and repeat.

1. January

2. February

3. March

4. April

5. May

6. June

7. July

8. August

9. September

10. October

11. November

12. December

Ordinal Numbers

Listen and repeat.

first	twelfth	twenty-third	seventieth
second	thirteenth	twenty-fourth	eightieth
third	fourteenth	twenty-fifth	ninetieth
fourth	fifteenth	twenty-sixth	one hundredth
fifth	sixteenth	twenty-seventh	one hundred first
sixth	seventeenth	twenty-eighth	
seventh	eighteenth	twenty-ninth	two hundredth
eighth	nineteenth	thirtieth	one thousandth
ninth	twentieth	fortieth	
tenth	twenty-first	fiftieth	
eleventh	twenty-second	sixtieth	

Seasons

Listen and repeat.

1. spring
2. summer
3. fall
4. winter

Sentences in the Present Progressive

Make a sentence from these words.

First, listen to the example:

Ming/talk　　　　　　Ming is talking.

Now it's your turn.

1. Ming/talk	Ming is talking.
2. You/speak	You are speaking.
3. They/run	They are running.
4. I/eat	I am eating.
5. It/rain	It is raining.

Negative Sentences

Make sentences from these words.

Listen to the example:

Ming/shop	Ming isn't shopping.

Now it's your turn.

1. Ming/shop	Ming isn't shopping.
2. We/drink	We aren't drinking.
3. You/write	You aren't writing.
4. It/snow	It isn't snowing.
5. I/call	I'm not calling.

Unit 3: Asking for Directions

Vocabulary

Listen and repeat.

1. bus
2. bus stop
3. subway
4. machine
5. token

6. train

7. bank

8. ATM

9. mailbox

10. letter

11. stamp

12. post office

13. movie theater

14. ticket counter

Directions

Listen and repeat.

1. turn left

2. turn right

3. go straight

4. cross the street

5. one block

6. on the corner

7. get on the bus

8. get off the train

Singular and Plural

Listen to the singular and say the plural.

First, listen to the example:

bank   banks

Now it's your turn:

1. bank   banks
2. block   blocks
3. car   cars
4. corner   corners
5. letter   letters

Sentences in the Present Simple

Make a sentence from these words.

First, listen to the example:

Simon/teach/English   Simon teaches English.

Now it's your turn.

1. Simon/teach/English   Simon teaches English.
2. He/work/International   He works at the International
   Center   Center.
3. I/study/English   I study English.
4. You/watch/video   You watch the video.
5. We/answer/questions   We answer the questions.

Negative Sentences

Make a sentence from these words.

First, listen to the example:

Simon/teach/French   Simon doesn't teach French.

Now it's your turn.

1. He/work/supermarket   He doesn't work at the
                               supermarket.

2. They/go out/weekdays · They don't go out on weekdays.

3. We/speak/Russian · We don't speak Russian.

4. Jorge/take/train · Jorge doesn't take the train.

5. The train/go/pharmacy · The train doesn't go to the pharmacy.

Short Answers

Answer these questions.

First, listen to the example:

Does Elena work at the International Center? · No, she doesn't.

Now it's your turn.

1. Does Elena work at the International Center? · No, she doesn't.

2. Does Simon teach English? · Yes, he does.

3. Does Elena go to the post office? · No, she doesn't.

4. Do they study Spanish? (No) · No, they don't.

5. Do we use the ATM? (Yes) · Yes, we do.

How Much and How Many?

Answer these questions.

First, listen to the example:

How much is a subway token? ($2.00) · It's $2.00.

Now it's your turn.

1.	How much is a subway token? ($2.00)	It's $2.00.
2.	How much is a bus ticket? ($1.50)	It's $1.50.
3.	How much is an airmail stamp? ($1.00)	It's $1.00.
4.	How many blocks does Elena walk? (two)	Two blocks.
5.	How many stops does Jorge go? (four)	Four stops.

Prepositions of Place

Answer these questions with "in," "on," or "at."

First, listen to the example:

Where is the International Center? (Boston)	It's in Boston.

Now it's your turn.

1.	Where is the International Center? (Boston)	It's in Boston.
2.	Where is Simon? (information desk)	He's at the information desk.
3.	Where is the map? (wall)	It's on the wall.
4.	Where is Elena? (supermarket)	She's at the supermarket.
5.	Where is the supermarket? (corner)	It's on the corner.

Unit 4: Shopping for Food

Fruits and Vegetables

Listen and repeat.

1. apple
2. banana
3. carrot
4. cherry
5. grape
6. lettuce
7. onion
8. orange
9. potato
10. raspberry
11. tomato
12. strawberry

Other Foods

Listen and repeat.

1. beef
2. bread
3. butter
4. cream
5. egg
6. juice
7. milk
8. pepper

9. rice

10. salt

11. sauce

12. soup

13. spice

14. chicken

Singular and Plural

Listen to the singular and then say the plural.

First, listen to the example:

 apple   apples

Now it's your turn.

1. apple	apples
2. banana	bananas
3. carrot	carrots
4. cherry	cherries
5. cookie	cookies
6. egg	eggs
7. grape	grapes
8. onion	onions
9. orange	oranges
10. pepper	peppers
11. potato	potatoes
12. raspberry	raspberries

| 13. strawberry | strawberries |
| 14. tomato | tomatoes |

Affirmative Sentences

Make a sentence from these words.

First, listen to the example:

| Raquel/go/shopping | Raquel is going to go shopping. |

Now it's your turn.

1. Raquel/go shopping	Raquel is going to go shopping.
2. They/eat lunch later	They are going to eat lunch later.
3. I/visit my friends	I am going to visit my friends.
4. You/make spaghetti tomorrow	You are going to make spaghetti tomorrow.
5. We/have a party next week	We are going to have a party next week.

Negative Sentences

Make a sentence from these words.

First, listen to the example:

| Jorge/make tacos | Jorge isn't going to make tacos. |

Now it's your turn.

1. Jorge/make tacos	Jorge isn't going to make tacos.
2. Ming/buy bread and potatoes	Ming isn't going to buy bread and potatoes.
3. Elena/get soup and rice	Elena isn't going to get soup and rice.

4. You/eat a lot of lasagna

You aren't going to eat a lot of lasagna.

5. We/drink beer

We're not going to drink beer.

How Much or How Many?

Ask a question with these words.

First, listen to the examples:

__eggs is Raquel going to buy?

How many eggs is Raquel going to buy?

__rice is Ming going to get?

How much rice is Ming going to get?

Now it's your turn.

1. __eggs is Raquel going to buy?

How many eggs is Raquel going to buy?

2. __lasagna is Elena going to make?

How much lasagna is Elena going to make?

3. __potatoes Simon going to eat?

How many potatoes is Simon going to eat?

4. __salad is Jorge going to have?

How much salad is Jorge going to have?

A Lot, a Little, a Few

Answer these questions.

First, listen to the example:

How many potatoes is Raquel going to buy? (a lot)

A lot of potatoes.

Now it's your turn.

1. How many potatoes is Raquel going to buy? (a lot)	A lot of potatoes.
2. How much juice is Ming going to get? (a little)	Only a little.
3. How many tomatoes is Elena going to use? (a few)	Only a few.
4. How much salad is Jorge going to have? (a lot)	A lot of salad.
5. How much cheese is Simon going to need? (a little)	Only a little.

Containers

Say the containers for these products.

First, listen to the examples:

onions, apples (bag)	A bag of onions, a bag of apples
wine, juice (bottle)	A bottle of wine, a bottle of juice

Now it's your turn.

1. onions, apples (bag)	A bag of onions, a bag of apples
2. rice, cereal (box)	A box of rice, a box of cereal
3. carrots, grapes (bunch)	A bunch of carrots, a bunch of grapes
4. peas, beans (can)	A can of peas, a can of beans
5. milk, eggs (carton)	A carton of milk, a carton of eggs
6. cabbage, lettuce (head)	A head of cabbage, a head of lettuce

7. jam, olives (jar)	A jar of jam, a jar of olives
8. toilet paper, film (roll)	A roll of toilet paper, a roll of film
9. toothpaste, hand cream (tube)	A tube of toothpaste, a tube of hand cream

Unit 5: Finding an Apartment

Apartment Vocabulary

Listen and repeat.

1. apartment
2. balcony
3. bathroom
4. bedroom
5. building
6. classified ads
7. dining room
8. entrance
9. for rent
10. garage
11. house
12. kitchen
13. laundry
14. living room
15. newspaper
16. parking lot
17. real estate office
18. three floors

Sentences with *Can*

Make sentences from these words.

First, listen to the example:

Elena/see the apartment/next week	Elena can see the apartment next week.

Now it's your turn.

1. Elena/see the apartment/next week	Elena can see the apartment next week.
2. Sasha/paint/the apartment/soon	Sasha can paint the apartment soon.
3. They/move/next month	They can move next month.
4. I/speak a little/English	I can speak a little English.
5. You/cook/Mexican food	You can cook Mexican food.

Sentences with *Can't*

Make sentences from these words.

First, listen to the example:

Jorge/pay much rent	Jorge can't pay much rent.

Now it's your turn.

1. Jorge/pay much rent	Jorge can't pay much rent.
2. Elena/lift heavy furniture	Elena can't lift heavy furniture.
3. They/have pets in the apartment	They can't have pets in the apartment.
4. I/help you next week	I can't help you next week.
5. You/eat spicy food	You can't eat spicy food.

Answers with *Could*

Give short answers to the questions.

First, listen to the example:

> Could Jorge find an apartment?
>
> Yes, he could.

Now it's your turn.

1. Could Jorge find an apartment?

   Yes, he could.

2. Could Simon help Jorge?

   Yes, he could.

3. Could the agent answer his questions?

   Yes, she could.

4. Could you understand the video?

   Yes, I could.

5. Could we do the exercises in the workbook?

   Yes, we could.

Answers with *Couldn't*

Give short answers to the questions.

First, listen to the example:

> Could Jorge pay a lot of rent?
>
> No, he couldn't.

Now it's your turn.

1. Could Jorge pay a lot of rent?

   No, he couldn't.

2. Could Ming help them move?

   No, she couldn't.

3. Could Simon paint the apartment?

   No, he couldn't.

4. Could Elena get a cat? No, she couldn't.

5. Could you remember all the No, I couldn't.
   words?

Adjectives

Repeat these words.

1. boring
2. cheap
3. different
4. difficult
5. easy
6. expensive
7. fast
8. funny
9. heavy
10. interesting
11. large
12. light
13. new
14. old
15. pretty
16. same
17. serious
18. short
19. slow
20. small

21. tall

22. ugly

Comparative and Superlative

Say the comparative and superlative forms of these adjectives.

First, listen to the example:

| fast | faster | fastest |

Now it's your turn.

1. fast	faster	fastest
2. cheap	cheaper	cheapest
3. tall	taller	tallest
4. easy	easier	easiest
5. funny	funnier	funniest

Now listen to the example again.

| boring | more boring | most boring |

6. boring	more boring	most boring
7. modern	more modern	most modern
8. beautiful	more beautiful	most beautiful
9. delicious	more delicious	most delicious
10. intelligent	more intelligent	most intelligent

Which?

Make questions with these words.

First, listen to the example:

| __ apartment is cheaper? | Which apartment is cheaper? |

Now it's your turn.

1. __ apartment is cheaper?   Which apartment is cheaper?

2. __ bedroom is larger?   Which bedroom is larger?

3. __ kitchen is more modern?   Which kitchen is more modern?

4. __ living room is more   Which living room is more
   spacious?   spacious?

5. __ lamp is the prettiest?   Which lamp is the prettiest?

6. __ sofa is the heaviest?   Which sofa is the heaviest?

Unit 6: Opening a Bank Account

Vocabulary

Listen and repeat.

1. ATM

2. balance

3. bank card

4. cash

5. checking

6. deposit

7. fees

8. individual account

9. interest

10. joint account

11. loan

12. paycheck

13. savings

14. statement

15. teller

16. traveler's checks

17. window

18. withdraw

Subject Pronouns

Substitute the subject pronoun for the noun.

First, listen to the example:

| Ms. Sato talks to Jorge and Elena. | She talks to Jorge and Elena. |

Now it's your turn.

1. Ms. Sato talks to Jorge and Elena.   She talks to Jorge and Elena.

2. Jorge and Elena listen to Ms. Sato.   They listen to Ms. Sato.

3. Jorge asks about service fees.   He asks about service fees.

4. Elena asks about checks.   She asks about checks.

5. The bank will send a monthly statement.   It will send a monthly statement.

6. Jorge and I have ATM cards.   We have ATM cards.

Short Answers

Answer these questions.

First, listen to the example:

Will Jorge and Elena open a joint account?   Yes, they will.

Now it's your turn.

1. Will Jorge and Elena open a joint account?   Yes, they will.

2. Will they have both checking and savings?   Yes, they will.

3. Will Ms. Sato send them checks?   Yes, she will.

4. Will they get bank cards?   Yes, they will.

5. Will you use the ATM this week?   Yes, I will.

6. Will we send money to our families?   Yes, we will.

Negative Short Answers

Answer these questions.

First, listen to the example:

Will Ms. Sato give them a loan today?   No, she won't.

Now it's your turn.

1. Will Ms. Sato give them a loan now?   No, she won't.

2. Will they get traveler's checks tomorrow?   No, they won't.

3. Will Jorge deposit money every day?   No, he won't.

4. Will Elena buy a car next week?   No, she won't.

5. Will you spend a lot of money today?   No, I won't.

6. Will it snow this summer?   No, it won't.

Object Pronouns

Substitute the object pronoun for the noun.

First, listen to the example:

Ms. Sato talks to Jorge and Elena.   Ms. Sato talks to them.

Now it's your turn.

1. Ms. Sato talks to Jorge and Elena.   Ms. Sato talks to them.

2. Jorge asks Ms. Sato a question.   Jorge asks her a question.

3. Ms. Sato answers Jorge.   Ms. Sato answers him.

4. The teller talks to my friend and me.   The teller talks to us.

5. Simon teaches high school students.   Simon teaches them.

6. Raquel helps Elena and Jorge.   Raquel helps them.

Questions with *Enough*

Answer these questions.

First, listen to the example:

Why can't Jorge and Elena buy a car now? (enough money)   Because they don't have enough money.

Now it's your turn.

1. Why can't Jorge and Elena buy a car now? (enough money) — Because they don't have enough money.

2. Why can't Raquel take tennis lessons? (enough time) — She doesn't have enough time.

3. Why can't Sasha stop smoking? (enough willpower) — Because he doesn't have enough willpower.

4. Why can't Mr. Smith be president? (enough votes) — Because he doesn't have enough votes.

Here's another example:

Why can't Ming lift the sofa? (strong enough) — Because she's not strong enough.

Now it's your turn.

5. Why can't Ming lift the sofa? (strong enough) — Because she's not strong enough.

6. Why can't Jorge cook lasagna? (patient enough) — Because he's not patient enough.

7. Why can't children go to a disco? (old enough) — Because they're not old enough.

8. Why can't Barbara win the race? (fast enough) — Because she's not fast enough.

Short Conversations: At the Bank

Listen and repeat.

- How may I help you?

- We'd like to apply for a loan.

- Just fill out this application.

- Thank you.

- What can I do for you today?

- I'd like some traveler's checks.

- How many would you like?

- I'd like ten of $100 each.

- I'll be right back.

- I lost my credit card.

- What is the number?

- I don't remember it.

- Okay, I have to look it up.

- Can you cancel it?

- Yes, I'll do it right away.

Unit 7: Using the Telephone

Vocabulary

Listen and repeat.

1. airport
2. answering machine
3. busy
4. dial
5. dial tone
6. directory assistance
7. flights
8. hang up
9. information
10. luggage

11. message

12. number

13. one way

14. operator

15. phone card

16. pick up

17. press

18. ring

19. round-trip

20. schedule

21. telephone

22. toll-free

Past Tense: Regular Verbs

Listen to the present tense and say the past tense.

The past tense of these verbs ends in /t/.

First, listen to the example:

    ask   asked

Now it's your turn.

1. ask   asked

2. check   checked

3. look   looked

4. pick   picked

5. press   pressed

The past tense of these verbs ends in /d/.

First, listen to the example:

    call   called

Now it's your turn.

  6. call   called

  7. charge   charged

  8. dial   dialed

  9. listen   listened

10. offer   offered

The past tense of these verbs ends in /ed/.

First, listen to the example:

    end   ended

Now it's your turn.

11. end   ended

12. land   landed

13. need   needed

14. start   started

15. wait   waited

Questions and Answers

Answer these questions in the past tense.

First, listen to the example:

    Did Ming call her sister or   She called the airlines.
    the airlines?

Now it's your turn.

1. Did Ming call her sister or the airlines?	She called the airlines.
2. Did Raquel look in the paper or the phone book?	She looked in the paper.
3. Did Ming want a cheap ticket or an expensive one?	She wanted a cheap ticket.
4. Did Sasha's friends arrive from Germany or Russia?	They arrived from Russia.
5. Did Sasha pick them up at the train station or the airport?	He picked them up at the airport.

Past Tense: Irregular Verbs

Listen to the present tense and say the past tense.

First, listen to the example:

buy	bought

Now it's your turn.

1. buy	bought
2. come	came
3. cost	cost
4. drink	drank
5. drive	drove
6. eat	ate
7. feel	felt
8. find	found
9. fly	flew

10. get	got
11. go	went
12. have	had
13. leave	left
14. meet	met
15. pay	paid
16. put	put
17. say	said
18. take	took
19. tell	told
20. think	thought

Questions and Short Answers

Give short answers to these questions.

First, listen to the example:

Did Ming find a cheap ticket to Hong Kong?	No, she didn't.

Now it's your turn.

1. Did Ming find a cheap ticket to Hong Kong? — No, she didn't.

2. Did Raquel give her the number from the paper? — Yes, she did.

3. Did Sasha come to Ming's house to visit? — Yes, he did.

4. Did his friends get their visas to visit the U.S.? — Yes, they did.

5. Did Sasha hear the plane   No, he didn't.
   information?

Question Words and Short Answers

Listen to the question and give a short answer.

First, listen to the example:

Who helped Ming find a   Raquel did.
cheap ticket?

Now it's your turn.

1. Who helped Ming find a   Raquel did.
   cheap ticket?

2. Where did Ming want to go? To Hong Kong.

3. What did she want to do in   Go to her sister's wedding.
   Hong Kong?

4. How much was a round-trip $12.00.
   ticket to the airport?

5. When did Sasha's friends   At 9:00 in the evening.
   arrive at the airport?

Work and School

PART

2

Unit 1
Finding a Job

A. Greetings and Introductions

Hi! = Hello!

I'm Raquel. = My name is Raquel.

How are you? = How do you do?

This is Sasha. = I'd like you to meet Sasha.

Nice to meet you. = My pleasure.

Write the word.

1. Hi! = __Hello__ !

2. _____ Simon. = My name is Simon.

3. How are you? = _____ do you do?

4. This is Elena. = I'd like _____ to meet Elena.

5. Nice to _____ you. = My pleasure.

B. Where do they work?

Draw a line to the picture.

1. teacher / child care / driver

2. social worker / clerical worker

3. engineer / painter

4. cashier / salesperson

5. waitress / cook

C. Verbs: Present Tense—*To Be*

Subject Pronouns

SINGULAR   PLURAL

 I   we

 you   you

 he

 she   they

 it

SINGULAR		PLURAL	
I	am	we	are
you	are	you	are
he	is	they	are
she	is	they	are
it	is	they	are

yesterday	today	tomorrow

present

Write the verbs in the sentences.

1. Simon _____ **is** _____ at the International Center.

2. The newspapers _____ **are** _____ on the table.

3. Raquel _____ Simon's wife.

4. Jorge _____ Elena's husband.

5. Ming _____ from China.

6. Sasha _____ a painter.

7. Raquel and Simon _____ volunteers.

8. I _____ at home.

9. We _____ in class.

10. You _____ a teacher.

D. Contractions

I am = I'm	we are = we're
you are = you're	you are = you're
he is = he's	they are = they're
she is = she's	they are = they're
it is = it's	they are = they're

Write the contractions.

1. you are = __you're__

2. they are = _____

3. it is = _____

4. I am = _____

5. we are = _____

6. he is = _____

E. Negatives

Simon is a teacher.   He **is not** a driver.

Raquel is a social worker.   She **is not** a salesperson.

Ming is a waitress.   She **is not** a cook.

I am not		**we are not**
you are not		**you are not**
he is not		**they are not**
she is not		**they are not**
it is not		**they are not**

Write the negative form of the verb.

1. I __am not__ at the International Center.

2. Simon and Raquel __are not__ at home.

3. Ming _____ an engineer.

4. Elena _____ a painter.

5. Sasha _____ from Mexico.

6. Jorge _____ a teacher.

7. You _____ a social worker.

8. Elena and Jorge _____ from Russia.

9. We _____ at an interview.

10. The newspapers _____ on the floor.

F. Negative Contractions

I'm not	we're not / we aren't
you're not / you aren't	you're not / you aren't
he's not / he isn't	they're not / they aren't
she's not / she isn't	they're not / they aren't
it's not / it isn't	they're not / they aren't

Write the contractions:

1. he is not = **he isn't/he's not**

2. they are not = _____

3. we are not = _____

4. I am not = _____

5. you are not = _____

6. she is not = _____

G. Questions and Yes/No Answers

Jorge is an engineer.   Is Jorge an engineer?   **Yes, he is.**

Elena is a cashier.   Is Elena a waitress?   **No, she is not.**

Write a "yes" or "no" short answer after the question.

1. Is Sasha from the Dominican Republic? __No, he is not.__

2. Is Sasha from Russia? _____

3. Are Elena and Jorge from Mexico? _____

4. Are you from China? _____

5. Is Simon from the United States? _____

Change the sentence to a question.

6. Simon is with Jorge and Elena.

_____ **Is Simon with Jorge and Elena?** _____

7. You are child-care workers.

_____

8. Raquel is with Sasha and Ming.

_____

9. They are at the table.

_____

10. The ads are in the newspaper.

_____

H. Questions and Short Answers

Who?

What?

Where?

Circle the correct short answer to the question.

1. **Who** is a waitress?
   Elena is.   (Ming is.)

2. **Where** are Jorge and Elena from?
   From Mexico.   From Colombia.

3. **What** is on the table?
   The newspapers are.   The drinks are.

4. **Where** is Simon from?
   From the D.R.   From the U.S.

5. **Who** is an engineer?
   Jorge is.   Sasha is.

6. **Where** is Sasha's interview?
   At the hardware store.   At the restaurant.

7. **What** is in the newspapers?
   The classified ads.   The applications.

8. **Who** is with Ming and Sasha?
   Raquel is.   Simon is.

9. **Where** are the Help Wanted ads?
   In the classified ads.   On the front page.

10. **Who** is a painter?
    Elena is.   Sasha is.

I. Question Words

*Write **Who**, **What**, or **Where** in the question.*

1. _____Who_____ is at the International Center?
   —Simon and Raquel are.

2. _____ is with Simon and Raquel?
   —Jorge, Elena, Sasha, and Ming.

3. _____What_____ is on the table? —The newspapers are.

4. _____ is with you? —My friends are.

5. ___**Where**___ are the children? —In school.

6. _____ does Sasha do? —He's a painter.

7. _____ are you? —At home.

8. _____ do you do? —I'm a student.

J. Plurals

a pen

pens

a letter

letters

Give the plurals.

	Singular (=1)	Plural (>1)
1.	cashier	cashiers
2.	cook	
3.	teacher	
4.	driver	
5.	engineer	
6.	painter	

K. *There is/There are*

	an application on the table. a pen in Sasha's hand. a letter of reference at Sasha's house.		applications at the International Center. pens on the desk. letters of reference at Raquel's office.
There is		**There are**	

Write There is or There are.

1. __**There are**__ cooks in the restaurant.

2. __**There is**__ a clerical worker in the office.

3. _____ a driver on the bus.

4. _____ cashiers in the store.

5. _____ an engineer in the building.

6. _____ teachers in the school.

L. More Question Words

Write the question words in the questions.

How much   money?   time?   experience?

1. _____ money does Ming make? —$300 a week.

2. _____ time does she spend at work? —Thirty hours a week.

3. _____ experience does she have? —Ten months.

How many   dollars?   hours?   years?

4. _____ dollars per hour will Elena make?
   —$8 per hour.

5. _____ hours will she work? —40 hours per week.

6. _____ years will she work? —2 years.

M. Classified Ads: Help Wanted

Look at these classified ads and fill in the chart.

1. Cashiers: P/T in sm. store, $7/hr., evenings & weekends, no exp. nec., 2 ref., 10% disc. incl., call 555-4872 bet. 9–5.

2. Salesperson: hardware store, P/T weekends, 10% disc., duties incl. stock & sales, no exp. nec., $8/hr., call 555-1234 bet. 10–4.

3. Cashiers: P/T or F/T in lg. supermarket, days, exp. nec., 15% disc., $8.50/hr., ref., call 555-0712 bet. 8–8 for appt.

4. Paint Dept.: large bldg. supply store, F/T days, paint exp. nec., $10/hr., 15% disc., 3 ref., call 555-9583 for appt. bet. 10–6.

	Job 1	Job 2	Job 3	Job 4
Full-time	No			
Part-time	Yes			
Pay	$7/hr.			
Discount	10%			
Hours	evenings/ weekends			
Experience	No			
References	Yes			
Hours to call	9–5			

5. Which job is for Elena?

6. Which job is for Sasha?

_____

_____

N. Real People...Real Language

1. What kind of work do you do?

Circle the words you hear.

a. Boston public high school   Boston University

b. interpersonal   entrepreneur

c. contractor   computer

d. waitress   wellness

e. technical   television

f. realtor   repairs

g. manager   magician

h. marriage counselor   martial arts

i. horse stable   horoscope

160

2. Do you work part-time or full-time?

Cross out the wrong word.

a. full-time   ~~part-time~~

b. full-time   part-time

c. full-time   part-time

d. full-time   part-time

e. full-time   part-time

f. full-time   part-time

3. Do you earn a good salary?

Circle the words you hear.

a. (good)   average   not good

b. good   average   not good

c. good   average   not good

d. good   average   not good

e. good   average   not good

f. good   average   not good

4. How did you find your job?

Cross out the wrong word.

a. ~~family~~   friend

b. busy street   office

c. friends   teachers

d. word-of-mouth   classified ads

e. newspaper   jobs on campus

f. headhunter   hairdresser

g. bartender   board member

5. If you could do anything, what kind of work would you do?

Circle the words you hear.

a. (artist)   art dealer   art supplier

b. moviegoer   movie ticket   movie producer

c. deal with kids   deal with people   deal with students

d. shop for food   shop for clothes   shop for people

e. go to school   go to work   go home

f. job I hated   job I loved   job that paid well

g. philatelist   Philippines   philanthropist

h. what I do now   what I did before   what I'll do later

VIDEO TRANSCRIPT

Watch and Listen

Simon: I'd like you to meet Jorge and his wife, Elena.

Jorge: How do you do?

Elena: Nice to meet you.

Simon: Today we're looking at classified ads to help Elena find a job.

Raquel: And I'd like you to meet Ming and Sasha.

Ming: Pleased to meet you.

Sasha: My pleasure.

Raquel: Today we're helping Sasha fill out a job application. Why don't you join us?

Simon: What kind of work are you looking for, Elena?

Elena: As a cashier... or maybe child care.

Simon: Here is the Help Wanted section... Let's see... "Cashiers"

Elena: Are there any jobs?

Simon:　Yes, some are part-time and some are full-time.

Jorge:　How many hours is full-time?

Simon:　Usually forty hours per week.

Elena:　What's the salary?

Simon:　It depends... between six and ten dollars an hour.

Elena:　Can I see?

Jorge:　This one at the supermarket pays eight dollars an hour.

Elena:　What is the number?

Jorge:　555-7500. This one, too, but it's part-time.

Elena:　No, I don't want that. I want to work full-time.

Simon:　Why don't we call the first number and make an appointment for an interview.

Jorge:　Good idea.

Simon:　How are you guys doing over there?

Raquel:　Fine. Sasha is filling out an application to work in a hardware store.

Ming:　Okay, here it says "Experience."

Sasha:　What does that mean?

Raquel:　It means your other jobs.

Sasha:　Well, they were in Russia. I painted for a remodeling company.

Raquel:　That's fine. "Duties" means what you did there.

Sasha:　I painted!

Raquel:　Then write that down. What else?

Ming:　"References."

Raquel:　Who can tell them that you were a good painter?

Ming:　Me! His apartment is nice!

Sasha:　My bosses are in Russia.

Raquel:　Then you can write down my name and number as a reference.

Sasha:　Okay. I think I'm finished.

Raquel:　Good. Now take it to the hardware store.

Sasha: All right. Do you want to come?

Ming: Sure, I'm not working today.

Raquel: Good luck.

Sasha: Thanks a lot, Raquel.

Raquel: You're welcome. While they're looking for jobs, let's review some useful phrases.

To introduce yourself, you say:

> **Hi, I'm Raquel.**   or
>
> **My name is Raquel.**

To introduce someone else, you say:

> **I'd like you to meet Ming.**   or
>
> **This is Sasha.**

To answer, you say:

> **Nice to meet you.**   or
>
> **How do you do?**

Now let's listen to some people talk about work.

Unit 2
Enrolling a Child in
School

A. Odd One Out

Cross out the word that does not belong.

1. teacher   school   office   ~~doctor~~   registration form
2. doctor's exam   ESL   medical form   shots   child
3. math   science   art   enroll   music   social studies
4. students   classroom   tutor   testing   medicine

B. What is it?

Write the missing word.

1. REGISTRATION <u>F</u> <u>O</u> <u>R</u> <u>M</u>

2. DOCTOR'S __ __ __ __

3. __ __ __ __ __ __ STUDIES

4. PHYSICAL __ __ __ __ __ __ __ __

5. __ __ __ __ __ ROOM

C. Spelling

Write the missing letters (A – E – I – O – U).

1. **A** R T   4. M __ T H
2. C __ M P __ T __ R S   5. M __ S __ C
3. __ N G L __ S H   6. S C __ __ N C __

D. Verbs: Present Simple

SINGULAR		PLURAL	
I	sit	we	sit
you	sit	you	sit
he	sits	they	sit
she	sits	they	sit
it	sits	they	sit

yesterday   today   tomorrow

present:
always
usually
sometimes
never

Use the present simple tense with these words:

day	Mondays	March
every week	**on** weekends	**in** winter
year	my birthday	the morning

Write the verbs in the sentences.

1. Ms. Roberts ___sits___ at the table with Ming and Raquel. (sit)

2. Ming _____ questions. (ask)

3. The teacher _____ her questions. (answer)

4. She _____ her nephew to go to school. (want)

5. Her nephew _____ some shots. (need)

6. The children _____ to school every day. (go)

7. They _____ math, science, and English. (study)

8. They _____ lunch at school. (eat)

9. You _____ slowly. (speak)

10. I _____ English every day. (study)

E. Negatives

	SINGULAR		PLURAL
I	do not speak	we	do not speak
you	do not speak	you	do not speak
he	does not speak	they	do not speak
she	does not speak	they	do not speak
it	does not speak	they	do not speak

Remember the contractions: I do not = I don't; he does not = he doesn't; etc.

Write the contraction of the negative form of the verb.

1. Ming's nephew **doesn't speak** English. (speak)

2. He _____ to an American school. (go)

3. Ming's brother _____ the teacher. (know)

4. He _____ his son to feel bad in school. (want)

5. Ms. Roberts _____ sixth grade. (teach)

6. Ming _____ at the school. (work)

7. Raquel _____ any children. (have)

8. The doctor _____ many shots to children. (give)

9. The children _____ German or French. (study)

10. They _____ TV in school. (watch)

F. Questions and Yes/No Answers

Ms. Roberts works at the school.

Does Ms. Roberts **work** at the school?   Yes, she does.

Ming and her brother speak Chinese.

Do Ming and her brother **speak** Spanish?   No, they don't.

Write a "yes" or "no" short answer after the question.

1. Does Ms. Roberts work at the school?   **Yes, she does.**

2. Do Ming and her brother speak Spanish? **No, they don't.**

3. Does Raquel teach children?   **No,** _____

4. Does Ming work in a school?   **No,** _____

5. Do the children study many subjects?   **Yes,** _____

6. Does Ming's nephew speak English?   **No,** _____

7. Does the tutor help children in ESL class?   **Yes,** _____

8. Do the children need a doctor's exam
   to enroll in school?   **Yes,** _____

9. Do they take tests every day?   **No,** _____

10. Do you write the answers to the
    questions?   **Yes,** _____

G. Short Answers

Circle the correct answer.

1. Who asks Ms. Roberts questions?   ⬭Ming does.⬭
                                      Elena does.

2. Where is the office?   In the school.
                          In the store.

3. Who goes with Ming?   Simon does.
                                        Raquel does.

4. How old is Ming's nephew?   Eight years old.
                                        Twelve years old.

5. Who teaches third grade?   Raquel does.
                                        Ms. Roberts does.

6. When will Ming's nephew start   Next week.
   school?   Next year.

7. How big are the ESL classes?   About 30 students.
                                        About 15 students.

8. Where are the computers?   In the classroom.
                                        In the music room.

9. When will Ming's nephew visit   In a few days.
   a class?   In a few years.

10. How long is the school day?   Ten hours.
                                        Six hours.

H. Questions

*Write **Who, Where, How much,** or **How many** in the question.*

1. _____**Where**_____ is Ming's nephew? —At home.

2. _____ are Ming and Raquel? —At school.

3. _____ answers questions? —Ms. Roberts does.

4. _____ does a doctor's exam cost? —About $50.

5. _____ wants his son in school? —Ming's brother
   does.

6. _____ subjects do children study? —About six.

7. _____ does a school lunch cost? —It's about $2.00.

8. _____ teaches third grade? —Ms. Roberts does.

9. _____ students are in each class? —About 25.

10. _____ do you get the forms? —In the office.

I. Possessives: Nouns, Adjectives, and Pronouns

Write the missing word.

1. Raquel is __Simon's__ wife.   4. Simon is _____ husband.

2. Elena is _____ wife.   5. Jorge is _____ husband.

3. Ming is _____ friend.   6. Sasha is _____ friend.

Adjective+Noun	Pronoun	Adjective+Noun	Pronoun
my nephew	mine	our house	ours
your class	yours	your job	yours
his teacher	his	their salary	theirs
her computer	hers	their class	theirs
its food	—	their toys	theirs

*Cross out the **possessive noun** and write the **possessive adjective**.*

Her
7. ~~Ming's~~ nephew is at home.

8. *Ms. Robert's* class is small.

9. *Simon's* car is at work.

10. *The students'* books are on the desk.

Cross out the possessive adjective + noun and write the possessive pronoun.

Mine   **yours**

11. Where are the tests?   ~~My test~~ is on the table, and ~~your test~~ is on the desk.

12. Where are the classes?   *His class* is in the music room, and *her class* is in the computer room.

13. Where is the cat's food?   *Its food* is on the floor. (no change)

14. Where is your tutor?   *Our tutor* is with *your tutor* in the office.

15. Where are the children?   *Their child* is at the playground, and *our child* is in the gym.

J. Dialogue

Read the dialogue and write the missing words.

NURSE: Please _____**come**_____ in and take off your clothes.
                1. (come/eat)

FATHER: May I _____ in, too?
               2. (come/stand)

NURSE: Yes, you can sit down and wait for the _____.
                                       3. (teacher/doctor)

FATHER: Thank you. I'll help my _____.
                      4. (son/wife)

SON: Daddy, what will the _____ do?
                       5. (doctor/nurse)

FATHER: He'll examine _____.
                  6. (me/you)

SON: Will he give me a _____?
                      7. (shot/class)

FATHER: He may, but _____ won't hurt much.
8. (I/it)

SON: I _____ want a shot.
9. (don't/do)

FATHER: I know, but _____ should have one.
10. (I/you)

SON: Could we _____ to the park later?
11. (go/study)

FATHER: Of course. I have some food. We can go to the

_____ and eat lunch and play all afternoon.
12. (office/park)

SON: Yippee! Then it's okay for the doctor to _____
13. (give/enroll)

me a shot.

K. School Subjects

Write the name of the subject in front of the words.

1. ___**math**___ problem numbers multiply divide

2. _____ melody piano sing guitar

3. _____ paint crayons draw picture

4. _____ plants animals nature experiment

5. _____ exercise basketball running sports

6. _____ typing games printing Internet

7. _____ speaking listening   reading   writing

8. _____ history   geography   culture   government

9. _____ stories   compositions novels   poems

L. Countries, Nationalities, and Languages

Country: Ming is from <u>Hong Kong.</u>

Nationality: She is <u>Chinese.</u>

Language: She speaks <u>Chinese.</u>

Fill in the chart with a country, nationality, or language.

Country	Nationality	Language
Brazil	**Brazilian**	Portuguese
Dominican Republic	1.	Spanish
2.	Chinese	Chinese
Haiti	Haitian	French
Japan	Japanese	Japanese
Korea	Korean	Korean
Mexico	3.	Spanish
4.	Russian	Russian
United States	5.	English
Vietnam	Vietnamese	Vietnamese

M. People and Countries

Write a country, nationality, or language in the sentence.

1. Raquel is from the **Dominican Republic**. She's Dominican.

2. Elena and Jorge are from _____. They're Mexican.

3. Raquel, Elena, and Jorge speak _____ and English.

4. Ming is from China. She's _____.

5. She speaks _____ and English.

6. Sasha is from Russia. He's _____.

7. He speaks _____ and English.

8. Simon is from the _____. He's American.

9. He speaks only _____!

10. Ms. Roberts speaks only _____, too.

◉ ◉

N. Real People...Real Language

1. Are you from this country?/Where are you from?

Write the person's age or the country of origin.

a. Jamaica _____ **14** _____

b. _____ **U.S.** _____ born here

c. Puerto Rico _____

d. born here _____

e. 12 years ago _____

f. Mexican _____

g. 12 years old _____

h. Another country _____

i. Puerto Rico _____

2. What do you study in school?

Circle the word you hear.

a.   (fine arts)   science

b.   acting   accounting

c.   psychology   philosophy

d.   television   computer technology

e.   computer graphics   container grabbing

f.   math   music

3. Do you like your teachers?

Cross out the wrong word.

a.   good   ~~bad~~

b.   fine   mean

c.   great   awful

d.   wonderful   terrible

4. What is your favorite subject?

Circle the correct word.

a.   (printmaking)   dressmaking   toolmaking

b.   cuisine   culture   cabinetry

c.   fudge   forests   film

d.   physics   philosophy   philanthropy

e.   numbers   nautical   nutrition

5. Do you like the other students in your school?

Write the missing word.

a. Still go out with _____ from school...

b. Don't know too _____ other students...

c. _____ I could have done without...

d. I got along pretty _____ with colleagues...

VIDEO TRANSCRIPT

Watch and Listen

Raquel:	Today I'm going with Ming to ask about enrolling her nephew in school. Why don't you come along?
Teacher:	Good morning. I'm Ms. Roberts. I teach third grade.
Raquel:	Good morning. I'm Raquel Bradford, and this is Ming Lui. We'd like to enroll Ming's nephew in school.
Teacher:	How old is the child?
Ming:	He's eight years old—third grade, I think.
Teacher:	Have a seat. Here's a registration form.
Ming:	"Name, address, date of birth, country." This looks easy.
Raquel:	You can help your brother fill it out.
Teacher:	He'll need a doctor's exam as well. Here's the form. Do you have any questions?
Raquel:	The child is from Hong Kong. He doesn't speak English.
Teacher:	We have ESL classes for children from other countries.
Ming:	How big are the classes?
Teacher:	There are about fifteen students per class.
Raquel:	What other subjects will he study?
Teacher:	Math, science, social studies, computers, music, art, physical education...

Ming: How will he learn if he doesn't know English?

Teacher: Children learn quickly....Bring him in for a visit. He can sit in class for an hour or two. There is another Chinese boy who can help him, as well.

Raquel: That's a good idea.

Teacher: The ESL teacher will test him. He'll be in class with children at his level. He may also need a tutor.

Ming: I'm a little worried about him. He doesn't have any friends here.

Teacher: We'll play games to make him feel welcome. It may be difficult at first, but he'll feel better later.

Raquel: You seem to have a lot of experience in these situations.

Teacher: Yes, we have many international students at our school.

Ming: That's good to know.

Raquel: Thank you for your time.

Teacher: You're welcome. See you next week.

Ming: Thank you. Good-bye.

Raquel: That's all for now. Here are some useful phrases to remember.

To make a request, you can say:

May I ask a question?   or

Can I have a registration form?   or

Could I speak with his teacher?

You might hear these responses:

Yes, of course.   or

Here you are.   or

Certainly.

Now let's listen to some other people talk about education.

Unit 3
A Job Interview

A. What is it?

Write the word.

1. ___interview___

2. _____

3. _____

4. _____

5. _____

6. _____

B. What day is it?

1. *Write the days on the calendar.*

JULY						
Sunday						
			1	2	3	4
5	6	7	8	9	10	11
12	13	14	15	16	17	18
19	20	21	22	23	24	25
26	27	28	29	30	31	

C. Verbs: Future with *Will/Won't*

I	will / won't	we	will / won't
you	will / won't	you	will / won't
he/she/it	will / won't	they	will / won't

Contractions: will not = won't; will='ll

yesterday	today	tomorrow

future:
tomorrow
next week/month/year
in a week/month/year

*Write **will** or **won't** in the sentences.*

1. Tomorrow, Jorge and Elena __will__ go to the supermarket at 10:15.

2. They __won't__ go to the supermarket at 10:45.

3. Mr. Hart _____ talk to Elena about the job.

4. He _____ talk to Jorge about the job.

5. He _____ look at Elena's application.

6. He _____ ask Elena questions.

7. Elena _____ start to work after the interview.

8. She _____ start to work the next day.

9. Mr. Hart _____ pay her $7.00 per hour.

10. He _____ pay her $8.00 per hour.

D. Questions and Yes/No Answers

Write a "yes" or "no" short answer after the question.

1. Will Jorge and Elena be early for
   the interview?   **Yes, they will.**

2. Will Mr. Hart interview Jorge?   **No, he won't.**

3. Will Elena ask Mr. Hart questions?   **Yes,** _____

4. Will he tell her about benefits?   **Yes,** _____

5. Will she get health insurance?   **Yes,** _____

6. Will she get dental insurance?   **No,** _____

7. Will she have two weeks of training?   **No,** _____

8. Will she work alone after training?   **Yes,** _____

9. Will her coworkers be helpful?   **Yes,** _____

10. Will her boss be unfriendly?   **No,** _____

E. Questions

Draw a line to the correct affirmative or negative short answer.

1. Who will Jorge and Elena speak with today? $8 per hour.

2. What kind of job will Elena interview for?   A cashier's job.

3. How much will she earn per hour?   The manager.

4. When will she start to work?   A coworker.

5. Will they tell Simon about the interview?   In six months.

6. Who will teach Elena about her job?   Tomorrow.

7. Will Jorge work with Elena?   Yes, they will.

8. When will Elena get a raise?   No, he won't.

F. Number Practice

Practice saying these numbers.

1 one	11 eleven	21 twenty-one	40 forty
2 two	12 twelve	22 twenty-two	50 fifty
3 three	13 thirteen	23 twenty-three	60 sixty
4 four	14 fourteen	24 twenty-four	70 seventy
5 five	15 fifteen	25 twenty-five	80 eighty
6 six	16 sixteen	26 twenty-six	90 ninety
7 seven	17 seventeen	27 twenty-seven	100 one hundred
8 eight	18 eighteen	28 twenty-eight	101 one hundred-one
9 nine	19 nineteen	29 twenty-nine	200 two hundred
10 ten	20 twenty	30 thirty	1000 one thousand

G. Telling Time

Write the time in numbers.

What time is it?

1. __9:30__   2. _____   3. _____   4. _____

What's the time?

5. _____   6. _____   7. _____   8. _____

Do you have the time?

9. ————— 10. ————— 11. ————— 12. —————

A.M.: 12:00 midnight to 12:00 noon (00:00–11:59)

P.M.: 12:00 noon to 12:00 midnight(12:00–23:59)

Write the time in letters.

1. **It's nine-thirty.**   7. ——————————

2. **It's eleven-fifteen.**   8. ——————————

3. ——————————   9. ——————————

4. ——————————   10. ——————————

5. ——————————   11. ——————————

6. ——————————   12. ——————————

H. Prepositions of Time

in	July the summer the morning / the afternoon / the evening
on	Monday / Tuesday afternoon June second
at	9:00 / noon night

Write in, on, or *at in the sentences.*

1. Elena will go to work _____ **at** _____ 7:30 _____ **in** _____ the morning.

2. Jorge will meet her ——————— the afternoon at 2:30.

3. Elena will work ——————— Monday, Tuesday, Wednesday, Thursday, and Friday.

4. The children will go to the cafeteria _____ noon.

5. Ming's nephew will have a birthday party _____ July 16 (sixteenth).

6. Sasha will go to his job interview _____ Saturday.

7. You will go on vacation _____ August.

8. Jorge and Elena will go to Ming's restaurant _____ Sunday.

9. Simon will call Raquel _____ night from the center.

10. Jorge's birthday is _____ January 6 (sixth).

I. Singular and Plural Nouns

Write the plural next to the singular.

	Singular (=1)	Plural (>1)
1.	apple	apples
2.	banana	
3.	carrot	
4.	egg	
5.	onion	
6.	potato	potatoes *
7.	tomato	
8.	strawberry	strawberries †
9.	raspberry	
10.	cherry	

*Remember: after *o* or *u*, add *es*. †Remember: *y* → *ie* before *s*.

J. Money

| dollar | quarter | dime | nickel | penny |

How much money did Elena's customers spend?

1. SuperShop		2. SuperShop		3. SuperShop	
• apples	$1.69	• bananas	$2.11	• peaches	$2.58
• tomatoes	$2.09	• onions	$1.09	• raspberries	$1.99
• eggs	$1.59	• juice	$1.99	• potatoes	$1.39
• bread	$2.49	• rice	$1.49	• milk	$1.59
• pasta	$1.09	• cereal	$2.99	• soup	$ .99
Total	**$8.95**	Total	_____	Total	_____
Cash	$10.00	Cash	$10.00	Cash	$10.00

How much change did Elena give them?

4. **$1.05** _____   5. _____   6. _____

K. Count and Noncount Nouns

Here are some words to use with count and noncount nouns.

   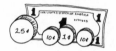

COUNT		NONCOUNT	
a	banana	—	milk
some	bananas	some	milk
a few	bananas	a little	milk
a lot of	bananas	a lot of	milk
many	bananas	much	milk
no	bananas	no	milk
not many	bananas	not much	milk

Write the food from the receipts.

1. some / a few / a lot of / many	2. some / a little / a lot of / much
apples	bread
tomatoes	pasta
eggs	

L. Dialogue

Write the words in the dialogue.

MR. HART: Hello, Elena. Nice to see you again.

ELENA: I'm happy to be here.

MR. HART: _____**Come**_____ and say hello to your coworkers.
              1. (Come/Eat)

ELENA: Oh, good. I want to meet them.

MR. HART: Good morning, everyone. This is Elena.

ELENA: Hi! How are you?

COWORKERS: Nice to meet you.

MARIA: I'm Maria. You'll work with me today.

MR. HART: Now _____ on this blue jacket and
              2. (learn/put)
              _____ at this cash register with Maria.
              3. (stand/sleep)

ELENA: All right. What do I do now?

MR. HART: Just _____ Maria. She'll teach you how
              4. (think/watch)
              to run the register. Don't _____ afraid to
              5. (be/sit)
              ask questions.

ELENA: I hope I can do a good job.

MARIA: Don't _____, Elena. It's not hard.
                         6. (go/worry)

MR. HART: I'll check in from time to time. _____ a
                                              7. (Have/Move)

             nice day!

ELENA: Thank you, Mr. Hart. See you later!

M. Real People...Real Language

1. How do you prepare for a job interview?

Check the phrases you hear.

a. _____ Bring your car.   ✔ _____ Bring personal references.

    ✔ _____ Dress neatly.   _____ Eat your lunch there.

    ✔ _____ Show up on time.

b. _____ Get background   _____ Bring your dog.
           information.

    _____ Wear shorts.   _____ Wear business clothing.

    _____ Be prompt.

c. _____ Talked to several   _____ Redid my résumé.
           teachers.

d. _____ Learned about the   _____ Talked to a friend.
           company.

e. _____ Got another job.   _____ Got online brochures.

2. Tell me about your job.

Circle the words you hear.

a. (job)   waking   training   educating   animals

   families   school   children

b. wait tables serve food on feet dealing with children

   customers busy relaxing stressful slow

   fast not so bad

c. difficult job greatest job watching TV teaching

   boring learning

3. Do you have benefits at work?

Underline the benefits you hear.

a. no benefits   <u>health insurance</u>   dental care
   eye care   life/personal insurance
   stock options   retirement   vacation
   sick days

b. no benefits   health insurance   dental care
   eye care   life/personal insurance
   stock options   retirement   vacation
   sick days

c. no benefits   health insurance   dental care
   eye care   life/personal insurance
   stock options   retirement   vacation
   sick days

d. no benefits   health insurance   dental care
   eye care   life/personal insurance
   stock options   retirement   vacation
   sick days

e. no benefits   health insurance   dental care
   eye care   life/personal insurance
   stock options   retirement   vacation
   sick days

f. no benefits   health insurance   dental care
    eye care   life/personal insurance
    stock options   retirement   vacation
    sick days

4. What hours do you work?

Fill in the numbers.

a. From __**9:30**__ to __**5:00**__ with a lunch break.

b. From _____ to _____, Monday to Friday,

    _____ hours a week.

c. From _____ to _____, Thursday to Saturday.

d. From _____ to _____ at night.

5. Do you like your schedule?

Write Yes or No in the blank.

a. __**Yes**__ flexibility   part-time bookkeeping jobs

b. _____ fits around classes   fits around my needs

c. _____ It's so flexible.   I'm in charge.

d. _____ time for my son   do stuff in the evening

VIDEO TRANSCRIPT

Watch and Listen

Jorge: Hey, Simon, guess what! Elena just had an interview at the supermarket.

Simon: Really? How did it go?

Elena: Oh, I was really nervous, but it went great!

Simon: What did they ask you?

Elena: About my experience, just like you told me.

Jorge: What time is it?

Elena: It's 10:20.

Jorge: Relax. It's early. How do you feel, Elena?

Elena: I'm a little nervous.

Jorge: Don't worry... you'll do fine.

Mr. Hart: Hello, I'm Mr. Hart, the store manager. Are you Elena Gonzales?

Elena: Yes, I am. This is my husband, Jorge.

Mr. Hart: Nice to meet you. Right this way, please. I can take that from you. Have a seat. I see that you have a diploma from Mexico City.

Elena: I took courses there for two years after high school.

Mr. Hart: Do you have any experience as a cashier?

Elena: Yes, I worked in a department store.

Mr. Hart: For how long?

Elena: For three years.

Mr. Hart: Good. We pay $8 an hour to start. You get a raise in six months. Do you have any questions?

Elena: How many days do cashiers work?

Mr. Hart: Full-time cashiers work five days a week, six hours a day.

Elena: What are the hours?

Mr. Hart: Eight to two or two to eight. Part-timers work eight to midnight.

Elena: I prefer eight to two.

Mr. Hart: Good. Which days can you work?

Elena: I can work weekdays and maybe some weekends.

Mr. Hart: Okay. We'll work out your schedule. First, there is a week of training. You'll be at a register next to a coworker.

Elena: Then I'll work alone?

Mr. Hart: That's right. Employees get a half-hour break for lunch or dinner.

Elena: What are the benefits?

Mr. Hart: Health insurance, one sick day per month, and ten days' vacation.

Elena: Do employees get a discount on food?

Mr. Hart: Yes, there is a 10% discount.

Elena: That's really good.

Mr. Hart: Your coworkers are friendly and helpful. And your boss is, too.

Elena: Who is my boss?

Mr. Hart: I am. So when can you start?

Elena: You mean I have the job?

Mr. Hart: Yes, I think you'll do fine.

Elena: Thank you, Mr. Hart. I can start tomorrow.

Mr. Hart: Great! I need your Social Security number for your paycheck.

Elena: It's on the application.

Mr. Hart: Oh, yes. Then I'll see you tomorrow at eight. Don't be late!

Elena: Don't worry. I won't. See you tomorrow!

Simon: So you got the job, Elena. Congratulations! I know you're gonna be great. I hope you do well on your job interview. Here are a few expressions to practice.

To tell someone to do something, say:

> **Come** tomorrow at 8:00.   or

> **Write** down your Social Security number.   or

> **Tell** me about your work experience.

To tell someone not to do something, say:

> **Don't come** at 8:00. Come at 9:00.   or

> **Don't worry.** Everything will be fine.   or

> **Don't be** nervous. I'm sure you'll get the job.

Simon: Now let's listen to other people talk about their jobs.

Unit 4
Adult Education

A. Time of Day

Write the words in the sentences.

1. We get up in the ___morning___ and go to work.

2. We come home in the _____ .

3. We watch TV in the _____ .

4. We go to bed at _____ .

B. Time of Year

Write the seasons next to the months of the year.

1. ___SPRING___ March
April
May

3. _ _ _ _ September
October
November

2. _ _ _ _ _ _ June
July
August

4. _ _ _ _ _ _ December
January
February

C. Taking a Class

Write the missing word in the sentence.

1. It is easy to take a **course** _____ .

2. First, look at the **c** _____ .

3. Then **s** _____ **u** _____ .

4. Fill out the **r** _____ **f** _____ .

5. Check the **s** _____ for the time.

6. Meet your **i** _____ in class.

7. Do all your **h** _____ .

8. Study for the **t** _____ .

9. You will get good **g** _____ .

10. Your class may be **e** _____ or **h** _____ .

11. Or it may be **b** _____ or **i** _____ .

Just do your best!

D. Verbs: Future with *Going To*

I	am going to __	we	are going to __
you	are going to __	you	are going to __
he/she/it	is going to __	they	are going to __

yesterday	today	tomorrow

← →

future:
tomorrow
next week
next month
next year

Write the verbs in the sentences.

1. Raquel, Ming, and Jorge **are going to sign up** for courses. (sign up)

2. They _____ between December second and ninth. (register)

3. Raquel _____ aerobics with Elena. (take)

4. Ming _____ bookkeeping. (study)

5. Jorge _____ his equivalency degree in engineering. (get)

6. Ming and her brother _____ a Chinese restaurant. (open)

7. Her brother _____ . (cook)

8. Ming _____ the manager. (be)

9. They _____ a good restaurant. (have)

10. They _____ delicious food. (make)

E. Negatives

I	am not going to __	we	are not going to __
you	are not going to __	you	are not going to __
he/she/it	is not going to __	they	are not going to __

Remember the contractions: I am = I'm; you are = you're; he is = he's
or: are not = aren't; is not = isn't

Write the subject pronoun and the contracted negative form of the verb.

1. **They're not going to** go to the movie theater.
   (Raquel, Ming, and Jorge)

2. _____ take ballroom dancing. (you)

3. _____ study engineering. (Ming)

4. _____ get a teaching degree. (Jorge)

5. _____ sign up for a class. (Sasha)

6. _____ take a test next week. (I)

7. _____ sleep all day. (the dog)

8. _____ pay much for the course. (we)

F. Questions and Yes/No Answers

Raquel is going to take a class with Elena.

Is Raquel going to take a class with Elena? —Yes, she is.

Is Raquel going to take a class with Ming? —No, she isn't.

Write the correct answer.

1. Is Raquel going to take a class with Ming? **No, she isn't.**
2. Is Ming going to study bookkeeping? **Yes,** _____
3. Is Jorge going to go to aerobics with Raquel? **No,** _____
4. Are they going to sign up soon? **Yes,** _____
5. Is Simon going to learn about engineering? **No,** _____
6. Are Sasha and Simon going to be instructors? **No,** _____

Write the questions.

7. The instructor is going to give a test.

   Is the instructor going to give a test?

8. The students are going to get good grades.

   _____

9. The homework is going to be easy.

   _____

10. The new catalogs are going to be out soon.

    _____

11. Ming is going to take classes at night.

    _____

12. Elena and Raquel are going to take afternoon classes.

    _____

G. Questions and Short Answers

Write the number of the question next to the answer.

1. How many courses is Raquel going to take?

2. How much is the tuition?

3. What kind of class is Jorge going to take?

4. How much homework does Ming have?

5. How hard is Jorge's class?

6. When is Jorge going to take a class next semester?

7. What kind of class is Elena going to take?

8. How many more courses is Jorge going to take?

9. What kind of restaurant is Ming going to open?

10. How much are Jorge and Elena going to pay for tuition?

____ a. An exercise class.

____ b. Another math class.

____ c. In the evening.

____ d. Only four more.

____ e. A Chinese restaurant.

____ f. $300.

__1__ g. Only one.

____ h. $150 per course.

____ i. It's easy.

____ j. A lot.

H. Conjunctions: *And* Versus *Or*

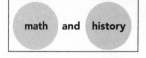 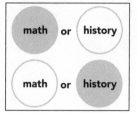 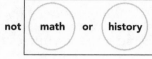

Ming's Schedule

	MONDAY	TUESDAY	WEDNESDAY	THURSDAY	FRIDAY
1 (9:50–11:10)	Computers		Computers		
2 (11:30–12:50)	ESL		ESL		
3 (1:10–2:30)		History			
4 (2:50–4:10)	work	History	work	work	
5 (4:30–5:50)	work		work	work	
6 (6:10–7:30)	work		work	work	

*Write **and** or **or** in the sentences.*

1. Ming has a computer class on Monday **and** Wednesday.

2. She does not have class on Thursday _____ Friday.

3. Ming works on Monday, Wednesday, _____ Thursday.

4. She does not go to classes _____ to work on Friday.

5. Ming has history during periods 3 _____ 4 on Tuesday.

6. For next semester, Ming can register from 9:00 to 11:00 in the morning _____ from 2:00 to 5:00 in the afternoon.

I. Conjunctions: *And* Versus *But*

+	
interesting	
easy	
small	
like	

–	
boring	
hard	
big	
don't / doesn't like	

BUT: (+/-) or (-/+)   AND: (+/+) or (-/-)

The ESL class is easy *and* small. (+/+)

The computer class is interesting *but* hard. (+/-)

The history class is boring *but* easy. (-/+)

*Write **and** or **but** in the sentences.*

1. Computer science is interesting ____**but**____ hard for Ming.

2. Calculus is boring _____ easy for Jorge.

3. They can sign up for classes in the beginning of December _____ not the end of December.

4. Raquel _____ Elena want to take aerobics.

5. Jorge wants to take a history course, _____ it's only offered in the afternoon. He needs an evening class.

6. Simon likes Dominican _____ American food.

7. Elena wants to work weekdays _____ not weekends.

J. Course Catalog

Cooking: Learn the basics of food preparation. Prepare and eat simple meals with your class based on chicken, beef, and fish recipes. Bring your apron and your appetite. *Sat. 2:00–4:00* P.M., *6 wks., $240.*

Swimming: Learn the basic strokes in indoor pool. Instructors trained by Red Cross. Must have doctor's permission if over 40. Bring bathing suit, swim cap, and towel. *Mon./Wed./Fri. 8:00–8:30* A.M., *4 wks., $60.*

Intro to Computers: Learn about hardware and software. Practice word-processing applications. Create documents, tables, graphs, and spreadsheets. No prior experience necessary. *Mon./Wed. 6:00–7:00* P.M., *8 wks.,* $160.

Personal Finance: Learn how to balance your checkbook, read your bank statement, and monitor your savings. Plan for the future and save for a rainy day. Simple math skills required. *Tues./Thur. 7:30–9:00* P.M., *6 wks., $180.*

Answer the questions about the courses.

1. Should a gourmet chef take the cooking class? _____**No.**_____

2. If I'm 55, can I take the swimming class? _____

3. Should a new secretary take the computer class? _____

4. Can a child take the personal finance class? _____

5. What must you bring to the cooking class? _____

6. What must you bring to the swimming class? _____

7. Should you know word processing for the computer class? _____

8. Should you know accounting to take the personal finance class? _____

9. Which class is the shortest? _____

10. Which class lasts the longest number of weeks? _____

K. Sign up!

Choose a class and fill in the registration form.

Name _____	Course _____
Address _____	Days _____
City/State/Zip _____	Times _____
Telephone _____	Tuition _____
E-mail _____	Reg. Fee $20 _____
Please circle as many as apply:	Total $ _____
New student Continuing student	Check Cash
18–29 30–45 46–59 60 +	Credit card # __
(Senior-citizen discount: 50% of tuition)	Exp. date __

L. Real People...Real Language

1. Are you taking any classes?

Write the name of the courses you hear.

a. H&R Block ___**tax**___ course

b. Complex Variables, Intro. to _____ Science, Statistical Physics, Asian Art

c. children's _____ illustration

d. _____ workshop

e. _____ classes

f. personal _____

g. _____ class

2. How do you like your class?

Underline the word you hear.

a. <u>yes</u> / no   but I don't play the <u>flute</u> / piano very well.

b. yes / no   but they're interesting / challenging.

c. yes / no   but not Spanish / French.

d. yes / no   but very intense / expensive.

3. When is your class?

Write the times and days you hear.

Time	A.M. / P.M.	Days
a. **8:30–9:45**	**A.M.**	**M, T, W, Th**
b.		
c.		
d.		
e.		
f.		

4. What are the people in your class like?

Circle the words you hear.

a. teenagers / early 30s to 40s / single / married /
    fresh out of school / older

b. working people / rich / nice / busy / intelligent / hard-working

c. senior citizens / very different / young / older / poor /
    working full-time

VIDEO TRANSCRIPT

Watch and Listen

Raquel:	Hi, guys! How are you?
Ming:	Hi, Raquel. Have a seat.
Raquel:	How are your classes going?
Ming:	My computer class is interesting, but it's hard. I have a lot of homework, but I don't have time to do it.
Jorge:	Well, at least you're learning something.
Raquel:	You don't like your class, Jorge?
Jorge:	No. It's boring, and the tests are too easy!
Raquel:	What are you taking?
Jorge:	Calculus. I need it to get an equivalency degree in engineering.
Raquel:	Is that the new catalog?
Jorge:	Yes, we have to register for next semester.
Raquel:	Which classes are you going to be taking next semester?
Jorge:	There's a U.S. history class I want to take, but it's in the afternoon, and I need an evening class.
Ming:	And I'm going to take bookkeeping.
Raquel:	Bookkeeping?
Ming:	Yes, I'll need it when I start my own business.
Raquel:	You're going to start your own business, Ming?
Ming:	Yes, someday I'll own a restaurant.
Raquel:	That's great! What about a cooking class, then?
Ming:	No, my brother can cook, and I'll be the manager.
Raquel:	That's really wonderful! Can I see that catalog a second? Maybe I'll take a class, too.
Jorge:	What will you take?
Raquel:	I'm thinking about an exercise class, but there are so many, it's hard to decide.

Jorge: Oh, Elena wants to take aerobics.

Raquel: Really? Maybe we can take it together. How much is the tuition?

Jorge: It's $150.

Raquel: I think I'll be able to pay that much. And when is registration?

Jorge: From December second to the ninth.

Raquel: That's great! Maybe I can call Elena, and we can register together.

Ming: I've got to run, or I'll be late for my class.

Jorge: And I've got to go to work this afternoon. See you later.

Raquel: See you later, guys!

That's all for now. Here are a few phrases to remember from this lesson.

If you're talking about the future, you say:

I'm going to take a class.   or

We're going to exercise together.   or

Ming is going to open a restaurant.

You can also say:

I'll study hard.   or

We'll go to the 10:00 class.   or

Ming's brother **will cook.**

Now let's listen to some people talk about their classes.

Unit 5
First Day on the Job

A. What is it?

Make a word from the letters.

1. morning food: **BREAKFAST**
   AKRSTABEF

2. afternoon food: _____
   HUCLN

3. evening food: _____
   NEDRIN

4. they (1–3) are: _____
   ALMES

5. keeps food cold: _____
   RAIGORETREFR

6. keeps food hot: _____
   EVOST

7. cook food in them: _____
   STOP and SNAP

B. Odd One Out

Cross out the word that does not belong.

1. insurance   accident   dental   disability   ~~weekly~~
2. boiling   chopping   frying   serving   washing
3. paycheck   medical   time clock   overtime   time card

C. Verbs: Present Continuous Tense—*To Be* + ___*ing*

cook + ing = cooking   serve + ing = serving

fry + ing = frying   write + ing = writing

I	am ___ ing	we	are ___ing
you	are ___ing	you	are ___ing
he/she/it	is ___ing	they	are ___ing

Remember the contractions: I am = I'm; you are = you're, etc.

| yesterday | today | tomorrow |

present continuous:
now
at the moment

Write the verbs in the sentences.

1. Simon __is waiting__ for Ming at the center. (wait)

2. Ming __is coming__ from the Jade Palace Restaurant. (come)

3. They _____ about Ming's first day on the job. (talk)

4. Simon _____ Ming about her duties. (ask)

5. Ming _____ him about Ms. Chan. (tell)

6. Ms. Chan _____ the job to Ming. (explain)

7. She _____ Ming the kitchen. (show)

8. She _____ out where things are in the kitchen. (point)

9. We _____ the verbs. (write)

10. I _____ this exercise. (finish)

D. Negatives

I	am not ____ ing	we	are not ____ing
you	are not ____ing	you	are not ____ing
he	is not ____ing	they	are not ____ing
she	is not ____ing	they	are not ____ing
it	is not ____ing	they	are not ____ing

Remember the contractions: I am not = I'm not;
you are not = you're not; he is not = he's not;
we are not = we're not; they are not = they're not

Remember to drop the –e before you add –ing:
come + ing = coming; have + ing = having

Write the contracted negative form of the verb.

1. Ming _____**isn't going**_____ back to work. (go)

2. Raquel _____ at the International Center. (wait)

3. Simon and Raquel _____ dinner at the restaurant tonight. (have)

4. You _____ dinner now. (eat)

5. We _____ TV. (watch)

E. Questions

Make the sentences from part D into questions.

1. __Is Ming going back to work?__

2. _____

3. _____

4. _____

5. _____

F. Questions and Yes/No Answers

Write a "yes" or "no" short answer after the question.

1. Is Ming talking to Simon? **Yes, she is.**

2. Is Simon waiting for Ms. Chan? **No, he isn't.**

3. Is Ming working this week? **Yes,**

4. Are Sasha and Jorge going to the restaurant? **No,**

5. Is Ming working forty hours every week? **Yes,**

6. Are Jorge and Elena at the center? **No,**

7. Is Ming going to cook at the restaurant? **No,**

8. Is she going to assist the chef? **Yes,**

9. Is Raquel going to work there, too? **No,**

10. Are you going to eat at the Jade Palace? **Yes,**

G. Object Pronouns

Simon sees Ming. → He sees her.
subject   object   subject   object

SUBJECT	OBJECT	SUBJECT	OBJECT
I	me	we	us
you	you	you	you
he	him	they	them
she	her		
it	it		

Cross out the object and write the pronoun.

1. Simon sees ~~Raquel.~~ **her**

2. Ming talks to *Ms. Chan.*

3. Sasha likes *Russian food.*

4. Elena loves *Jorge.*

5. Elena and Jorge invite *Simon and Raquel* to dinner.

6. The teacher smiles at *you and me.*

7. The girl loves *the dog.*

8. Ming washes *the pots and pans.*

9. Ming and Raquel help *Sasha* with the application.

10. Jorge looks at *cars* with *Raquel.*

H. Questions: *Which/Which one*

Jade Palace is a Chinese restaurant.

Los Charros is a Mexican restaurant.

St. Petersburg is a Russian restaurant.

Fisherman's Catch is an American seafood restaurant.

Which restaurant serves fried rice and wonton soup?
>>—Jade Palace.

Which one serves tacos and burritos?
>>—Los Charros.

*Write **Which** or **Which one** in the question. Answer the question.*

1. _____**Which**_____ restaurant serves borsch (beet soup)?
    _____**St. Petersburg**_____

2. _**Which one**_ serves trout and salmon (fish)?
    _____**Fisherman's Catch**_____

3. _____ restaurant has Chinese chefs?
    _____

4. _____ has a Russian chef?
    _____

5. _____ has guitar players on weekends?
    _____

6. _____ restaurant serves fresh shellfish?
    _____

7. _____ has dim sum on weekends?
    _____

8. _____ has enchiladas and guacamole?
    _____

9. _____ restaurant does Ming work at?
    _____

10. _____ does Sasha eat at on Saturday night?
    _____

I. Recipe: Jade Palace Fried Rice

Unscramble the words in Chef Lee's recipe.

1. a cup of ___RICE___
   ERIC

2. two cups of _____
   TRAWE

3. some _____
   BAGBACE

4. a little _____
   YOS ACSUE

5. one _____
   ROTRAC

6. a few _____
   NEGRE SNONOI

7. some _____
   ANEB TROSPUS

8. one _____
   GEG

- *Put the rice in a pot with 2 cups of water. Boil until the water is gone.*
- *Wash and chop the cabbage, carrot, green onions, and bean sprouts .*
- *Fry the chopped vegetables in the wok or a big frying pan.*
- *Add the rice and stir. Fry together a few minutes.*
- *Add the egg and mix well.*
- *Pour in a little soy sauce and stir again.*
- *Enjoy your fried rice!*

J. Prepositions of Place: *In/On/At*

in   on   at

in	the kitchen / the frying pan / New York
on	the table / Center Street / the bus
at	the stove / the restaurant / the bus stop / 34 Stanton St.

Underline the correct preposition.

1. The vegetables are <u>on</u> / in the table.

2. The chef is at / on the stove.

3. The pot is on / at the stove.

4. Ming is standing on / at the table.

5. The eggs are at / in the refrigerator.

6. The meal is in / on the table.

7. The customers are sitting at / on the chairs.

8. Ming's paycheck is on / in Ms. Chan's desk.

9. The time cards are in / at the time clock.

10. The Jade Palace is at / on Main Street.

K. Adverbs

Chef Lee chops vegetables **fast.**   Ming chops them **slowly.**

Chef Lee cooks **well.**   Ming cooks **badly.**

Chef Lee works **hard.**   Ming works **hard,** too.

Answer the questions.

1. How does Chef Lee chop vegetables? <u>He chops them fast.</u>

2. How does Ming chop them? _____

3. How does Chef Lee cook? _____

4. How does Ming cook? _____

5. How do Chef Lee and
   Ming work? _____

L. Real People...Real Language

1. How often do you go out to eat in a restaurant?

Circle the words you hear.

a. one time (two times) a week (a month)

b. once   twice   every other week   every other month

c. once   twice   a week   a month

d. once   twice   a week   a month

e. not very often very often   for lunch   for dinner

f. one–two   three–four   nights a week   nights a month

2. What kind of food do you like?

Cross out the words you don't hear.

a. sushi   ~~rice~~   fried chicken   Chinese   Japanese

b. Indian   South American   Malaysian

c. Spanish   Mexican   Italian   Pakistani   American

d. Japanese   Israeli   Thai   German   French

e. few kinds of food   some kinds of food   all kinds of food

f. Dominican   Japanese   Chinese   Italian   Spanish

g. Russian   Puerto Rican   Japanese   Indian

h. appetizers   main courses   desserts   drinks

3. Have you ever worked in a restaurant?

Write "yes" or "no."

a. **yes** in a fast-food restaurant when I was a teenager.

b. _____ as a teenager.

c. _____ never.

d. _____ one day.

4. What kinds of restaurants are popular nowadays?

Underline the correct words.

a.	pastry shops	<u>coffee shops</u>
b.	ethnic restaurants	expensive restaurants
c.	slow food	fast food
d.	diet food	health food
e.	natural food	Asian food

VIDEO TRANSCRIPT

Watch and Listen

Ming: Hi!

Simon: Hi, Ming! So how was your first day on the job?

Ming: It was great! I like my new boss, Ms. Chan, a lot.

In the kitchen at the Jade Palace.

Ms. Chan: Hello, I'm Ms. Chan, the kitchen supervisor. Welcome to the Jade Palace.

Ming: Nice to meet you. Wow! This kitchen is really modern.

Ms. Chan: It's only two years old. So let me tell you how things work around here.

Ming: Thank you.

Ms. Chan: First, here's your time card. When you come in and when you leave, put your card in the time clock. You're going to work forty hours a week.

Ming: So that means if I work more than forty hours, I'll get overtime?

Ms. Chan: Right, you'll get time-and-a-half. Your paycheck is going to come every week on Friday.

Ming: What are the hours?

Ms. Chan: The lunch shift is from ten to four. The dinner shift is from four to midnight.

Ming: Okay. Oh, do I have insurance?

Ms. Chan: You have medical, dental, accident, and disability. You can read this later.

Ming: Am I going to work in the kitchen?

Ms. Chan: Yes. The pots and pans are over there, and the plates are here. And that's the refrigerator.

Ming: Can you tell me a little about my duties?

Ms Chan: Yes, you're going to assist Mr. Lee. He's a famous chef from Hong Kong.

Ming: Oh, I'm from Hong Kong, too!

Ms. Chan: You're going to help him prepare meals. He's probably going to ask you to wash vegetables and chop them. As his assistant, you're going to follow his directions.

Ming: Does that mean I won't be cooking?

Ms. Chan: He may ask you to boil or fry something, but he's the chef. You're going to learn a lot from helping him.

Ming: That sounds exciting. I can't wait to start.

Ms. Chan: We're happy to have you, Ming.

Simon: That's great, Ming. Congratulations!

Ming: Thanks, Simon! You have to come to the restaurant sometime.

Simon: Maybe Raquel and I can come Saturday night.

Ming: Oh, that would be great. Oh, bye!

Simon: That's all for now. Here are a few phrases to practice from this lesson.

To ask for information, say:

> **Can you tell me** about my duties?　or
>
> **I'd like to know** how things work.

To ask for more information, say:

> **Does that mean** I won't be cooking?　or
>
> **So that means** I'll get overtime?

Now let's listen to people talk about food.

Unit 6
Getting a Driver's License and Buying a Car

A. What is it?

Write the first word in the group.

1. R E G I S T R Y OF M _ _ _ R V _ _ _ _ _ _ _ S:
   written test, road test, photo, license

2. D _ _ _ _ _ _ 'S E _ _ _ _ _ _ _ _ _ N:
   driver's manual, safety, seat belts

3. C _ R D _ _ _ _ _ R:
   new cars, used cars, test drive, warranty

B. Opposites

Write the contrasting words.

1. **new** cars	used cars
2. written test	test
3.	expensive
4. easy	
5.	high
6. less	
7.	there

C. Verbs: Present Tense—*Can/Can't*

I	can / can't	we	can / can't
you	can / can't	you	can / can't
he/she/it	can / can't	they	can / can't

Remember the contraction: cannot = can't

yesterday   today   tomorrow

present

She **can drive** the car.   He **can't drive** the car.

*Write **can** or **can't** in the sentences.*

1. Jorge _____ **can** _____ drive a car.

2. He _____ **can't** _____ drive a truck.

3. Sasha _____ work as a painter.

4. He _____ work as an engineer.

5. Ming _____ cook Chinese food.

6. She _____ cook Mexican food.

7. She _____ help Chef Lee in the kitchen.

8. Elena _____ work at the supermarket.

9. She _____ work at the Jade Palace.

10. Raquel and Simon _____ help their friends.

D. Questions and Yes/No Answers

Jorge **can buy** a used car.

Can Jorge **buy** a used car? —Yes, he **can.**

Can he **buy** a new car? —No, he **can't.**

*Write **Can** in the questions and **can** or **can't** in the answers.*

1. __Can__ Raquel cook Russian food?   **No, she can't.**
2. __Can__ she cook Dominican food?   **Yes, she can.**
3. _____ Elena work as a cashier?   **Yes,** _____
4. _____ she work as a teacher?   **No,** _____
5. _____ Simon teach English?   **Yes,** _____
6. _____ he teach Chinese?   **No,** _____
7. _____ he teach Spanish?   **No,** _____
8. _____ Simon and Raquel speak Russian?   **No,** _____
9. _____ they speak English?   **Yes,** _____
10. _____ dogs speak?   **No,** _____

E. Verbs: Past Tense—*Could/Couldn't*

I	could / couldn't	we	could / couldn't
you	could / couldn't	you	could / couldn't
he/she/it	could / couldn't	they	could / couldn't

yesterday   today   tomorrow

past

Last week, Jorge **could pass** the driving test.

Simon **couldn't go** with him.

Write could or couldn't in the sentences.

1. Simon _____couldn't_____ look at cars with Jorge.

2. But Raquel _____ look at cars with him.

3. Jorge _____ buy a new car.

4. He _____ buy a used car.

5. He _____ bargain with the salesman.

F. More Questions and Yes/No Answers

Last Friday, Jorge **could go** for a test drive.

Could Jorge **go** for a test drive? —Yes, he **could.**

Could Elena **go** for a test drive?—No, she **couldn't.**

Write Could in the questions and could or couldn't in the answers.

1. _____Could_____ Jorge and Elena buy a $7,000 car?
   _____No, they couldn't._____

2. _____ Jorge bargain for the price?
   Yes, _____

3. _____ the salesman lower the price to $5,000?
   No, _____

4. _____ they agree on a price?
   Yes, _____

5. _____ Jorge take the car for a test drive?
   Yes, _____

6. _____ Jorge and Elena buy a car without a down payment?
   No, _____

7. _____ the salesman offer them financing?
   Yes, _____

8. _____ they get a warranty?

Yes, _____

9. _____ they buy the car?

Yes, _____

G. Can/Can't or Could/Couldn't?

Circle the correct verb in the sentence.

1. I   can / (can't)   speak English well now.

2. Simon   could / couldn't   go with Jorge last Friday.

3. Jorge and Elena   could / couldn't   spend more than $6,000 on a car.

4. The salesman   could / couldn't   sell the car for less than $5,500.

5. Raquel   can / can't   speak Chinese.

6. Ming   could / couldn't   get a job in the Jade Palace.

7. Elena   can / can't   work at the checkout counter.

8. She   could / couldn't   go to the car dealer last Friday.

9. Raquel   could / couldn't   take an aerobics class with Elena.

10. Sasha   can / can't   work in a hardware store.

H. Short Answers

Write a short answer after the question.

1. Can Sasha speak Russian?   Yes, he can.

2. Could Jorge speak English ten years ago?   No, he couldn't.

3. Can dogs run fast?   Yes, _____

4. Could Ming take a bookkeeping class? **Yes,** _____

5. Can you understand the video? **Yes,** _____

6. Could Jorge and Elena buy an expensive car? **No,** _____

7. Can people use coupons at the checkout counter? **Yes,** _____

8. Could you write in English last year? **No,** _____

9. Could Sasha find a job in the classified ads? **Yes,** _____

10. Can Ming help Chef Lee prepare food? **Yes,** _____

I. Adjectives: Opposites

cheap	expensive
comfortable	uncomfortable
fast	slow
high	low
large	small
light	heavy
new	old
pretty	ugly
simple	luxurious
short	long

1997 coupe	**1998 sedan**	**2000 van**
good condition, 2 doors, standard shift, black, low down payment. $5,999 + tax	bright red, CD / stereo, automatic shift, 4 doors, convertible. $9,999 + tax	room for 10, removable seats, 4 doors, green, CD / radio / cassette deck. $12,999 + tax

Jorge looked at three cars:

The coupe is **small** and **cheap.**

The sedan is **fast** and **pretty.**

The van is **large** and **expensive.**

1. Which car is large? _____ The van.

2. Which one is cheap? _____

3. Which one is pretty? _____

4. Which one is small? _____

5. Which one is fast? _____

6. Which one is expensive? _____

J. Adjectives: Comparative and Superlative

Superlative	Comparative	Adjective	Comparative	Superlative
-est	-er		-er	-est
least	less		more	most

Use the **comparative** when comparing **two** things or people.
Use the **superlative** when comparing **three or more** things or people.

Jorge is taller than Ming. Sasha is taller than Jorge.

Sasha is tallest of the three.

Fill in the chart with the comparative and superlative forms.

	ADJECTIVE	COMPARATIVE (+/-)	SUPERLATIVE (+++/- - -)
1.	cheap ($)	**cheaper** (¢¢)	**cheapest** (¢)
2.	small		
3.	new		
4.	old		
5.	heavy*	**heavier**	**heaviest**
6.	pretty*		
7.	ugly*		
8.	expensive ($$$)	**more expensive**($$$$) **less expensive** ($$)	**most expensive** ($$$$$$) **least expensive** ($)
9.	comfortable		
10.	luxurious	**more luxurious** **less luxurious**	**most luxurious** **least luxurious**

*y + er = ier; y + est = iest

The coupe is **smaller** and **cheaper than** the sedan.

The sedan is **faster** and **prettier than** the coupe.

The van is **larger** and **more expensive than** the sedan.

Write the comparative in the sentences.

11. The coupe is ____**older**____ than the sedan. (old)

12. The van is _____ than the coupe. (new)

13. The van is _____ than the sedan. (large)

14. The sedan is **more expensive** than the coupe. (expensive)

15. The van is _____ than the coupe. (luxurious)

16. The coupe is _____ than the sedan. (comfortable)

The coupe is **the oldest** of the three cars.

The sedan is **the prettiest** of the three cars.

The van is **the most luxurious** of the three cars.

Write the superlative in the sentences.

17. The van is the ____**newest**____ of the three. (new)

18. The coupe is the _____ of the three. (cheap)

19. The sedan is the _____ of the three. (pretty)

20. The van is the _____ of the three. (heavy)

21. The van is the _____ of the three. (expensive)

22. The coupe is the _____ of the three. (luxurious)

K. Dialogue

Choose the correct word.

JORGE: Do we have to fill out the **papers** now?
1. (papers/cars)

SALESMAN: Yes, _____ sit down at my desk.
2. (let's/it's)

ELENA: Do we have to pay the full _____ ?
3. (bargain/price)

SALESMAN: No. You _____ put 25% down. That's about $1,500.
4. (can/can't)

ELENA: Then _____ do we pay every month?
5. (how many/how much)

SALESMAN: If you pay $175 a month, the _____ will be
6. (car/van)
yours in about two years.

JORGE: Now that Elena is working, we _____ afford
7. (can/can't)
that.

SALESMAN: Here are the papers. This is the bill of sale, the

monthly _____ plan, and the title to the
8. (safety/payment)
car.

JORGE: Okay, I'm going to look them over with my

_____ for a few minutes.
9. (wife/friend)

SALESMAN: Take your time. Call me when you're _____.
10. (leaving/ready)

L. Real People...Real Language

1. When did you get your driver's license?

Write the age you hear.

a. __16 1/2__

b. _____

c. _____

d. _____

e. _____

2. What kind of car do you drive?

Write the name of the car.

a. __Mazda__ 323 1988 standard

b. _____ sedan

c. _____ 4x4

d. 1993 _____ Civic

3. Are you happy with your car?

Fill in the missing words.

a. Yes, because it's brand ____**new**____ and doesn't give me any trouble.

b. Yes, it's twelve years old and still going _____ .

c. Yes, because it's new and plush and _____ .

d. Yes, because it's sporty and low to the ground and has a great _____ system, and the _____ attracts many girls.

4. Did you buy a new or used car?

Underline the word you hear.

a. Used   ten/twelve years old

b. Used   couldn't afford a nice/new one

5. Did you get good financing?

Fill in the missing words.

a. Bought for ____**cash**____; didn't have to finance.

b. A good price; bought it from my _____ .

c. _____ cash.

d. _____ financing.

e. Lease; good _____; $178 a month plus 3% interest.

VIDEO TRANSCRIPT

Watch and Listen

Raquel: Jorge should be finished with his driver's test by now. I hope he passed it!

Jorge: Raquel! Guess what?

Raquel: You passed?

Jorge: Yes, I passed! The written test was easy. I really studied the driver's manual. But the road test was harder than I thought.

Raquel: Did you do everything right?

Jorge: Yes, except I didn't buckle my seat belt, and I almost failed.

Raquel: Oh, no! Let me see your license. Oh, you look much younger in this picture, but you look a lot better in person.

Jorge: Do you have time to go to a car dealer?

Raquel: I have about an hour before my aerobics class with Elena.

Jorge: Let's go to the dealer in Cambridge. I think the cars are cheaper there.

At the car dealer's.

Raquel: Well, it looks like the new cars are right here, and the used cars are over there.

Jorge: Well, we can only afford a used car for now.

Raquel: Right, yeah.

Jack: Howdy, folks! What can I do for you today?

Raquel: We'd like to look at some used cars.

Jack: We have a lot of used cars you can look at. What do you have in mind?

Jorge: I'd like one that's a few years old and not too expensive.

Jack: What's your price range?

Jorge: Under $6,000.

Jack: There are a few over there you can look at. They're all around that price. Low down payment, low monthly installments.

Jorge: How much is your down payment?

Jack: We ask for 25% of the sale price.

Jorge: And what about the monthly installments?

Jack: You can spread them out over a year or two.

Raquel: Jorge, you know you don't have to pay that price. You can bargain.

Jorge: I was counting on it. (*to Jack*) I'd like to offer $5,000 for this one.

Jack: Oh, I couldn't let you have it for less than $5,800.

Jorge: Well, I'm going to have to talk to my wife...

Jack: How about $5,700?

Jorge: She doesn't want me to spend more than $5,200.

Jack: Okay, let's make it an even $5,500.

Jorge: I think we can afford that. Does it have a warranty?

Jack: Six months. Would you like to take it for a test drive?

Jorge: Sure!

Jack: I have the keys right here.

Raquel: While they're going for a ride, let's review some phrases from this lesson.

To say you want something, say:

> **I'd like** a used car.   or
>
> **We'd like** something less expensive.

To say you want to do something, say:

> **I'd like to buy** a car.   or
>
> **We'd like to see** some cars.

To say you want to do something with someone else, say:

> **Let's go** to the dealer in Cambridge.   or
>
> **Let's take** the car for a test drive.

Now let's listen to some people talk about their cars.

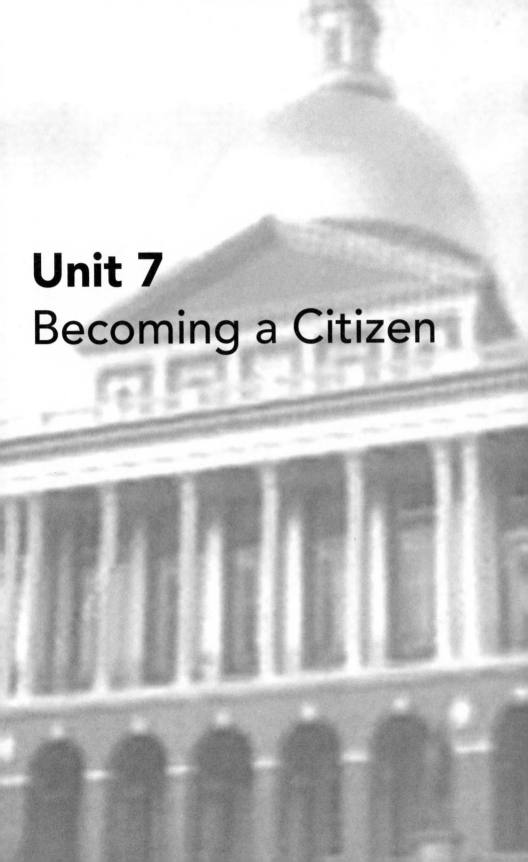

Unit 7
Becoming a Citizen

A. Odd One Out

Cross out the word that does not belong.

1. birth certificate   marriage certificate   ~~presidents~~
   Social Security number   alien registration card

2. government   federal   fingerprints
   state   Constitution

3. fingerprints   oral exam   written exam
   federal   swearing-in ceremony

4. history   Revolutionary War   Constitution
   presidents   birth certificate

B. What is it?

Write the word of the category.

1. <u>**E X A M**</u>:
   oral   written   school   medical

2. _ _ _ _ _ _ _ _ _ _ _ :
   Washington   Jefferson   Lincoln   Kennedy

3. _ _ _ _ _ _ _ _ _ _ _ _ :
   birth   school   marriage   death

4. _ _ _ _ _ _ _ _ _ _ _ :

town   city   state   federal

C. Verbs: Simple Past—Regular

_____ + ed

I	worked	we	worked
you	worked	you	worked
he/she/it	worked	they	worked

yesterday   today   tomorrow

past:
yesterday
last week/month/year
a long time ago
in 1960

Write the verbs in the past tense.

1. ask __asked__

2. call _____

3. visit _____

4. want _____

5. announce* _____

6. prepare* _____

7. use* _____

8. submit __submitted__

9. apply† __applied__

10. study† _____

*e + ed = ed   †y + ed = ied

237

D. More Verb Practice

Write the verbs in the sentences.

1. Raquel ____**wanted**____ to become a U.S. citizen. (want)

2. She _____ for citizenship. (apply)

3. She _____ about the United States. (study)

4. Elena _____ her fingerprints. (submit)

5. She _____ her Employment Authorization Card. (receive)

6. Jorge _____ his green card. (use)

7. He _____ his country. (visit)

8. Raquel _____ for the exam. (prepare)

9. Simon _____ her questions. (ask)

10. Then he _____ the citizenship classes. (announce)

E. Negatives

I	did not work	we	did not work
you	did not work	you	did not work
he/she/it	did not work	they	did not work

Remember the contraction: did not = didn't

Write the contracted negative form of the verbs.

1. Raquel ___**didn't want**___ to become a Canadian citizen. (want)

2. Elena _____ for citizenship. (apply)

3. She _____ about the United States. (study)

4. She _____ her citizenship application. (submit)

5. She _____ her green card. (receive)

6. Sasha _____ a ticket to Russia. (buy)

7. He _____ his country yet. (visit)

8. He _____ for his trip. (prepare)

9. Simon _____ ESL classes. (announce)

10. He _____ the citizenship classes yet. (start)

F. Questions and Yes/No Answers

Sasha **wanted** to go to Russia.

Did Sasha **want** to go to Russia?　　—Yes, he **did.**

Did he **want** to go to China?　　—No, he **didn't.**

Circle the correct short answer for the questions.

1. Did Simon help Raquel prepare for the citizenship exam?

　(Yes, he did.)　　　　No, he didn't.

2. Did Raquel know the answers to his questions?

Yes, she did.   No, she didn't.

3. Did she study hard?

Yes, she did.   No, she didn't.

4. Did Sasha get his green card?

Yes, he did.   No, he didn't.

5. Did Elena get her green card?

Yes, she did.   No, she didn't

6. Did she get her Employment Authorization Card?

Yes, she did.   No, she didn't.

7. Did she submit all of her papers?

Yes, she did.   No, she didn't.

8. Did Simon announce the new citizenship classes?

Yes, he did.   No, he didn't.

9. Did Jorge take them already?

Yes, he did.   No, he didn't.

10. Did Elena want to tell him about them?

Yes, she did.   No, she didn't.

G. Verbs: Simple Past—Irregular

begin	began	know	knew
come	came	read	read
feel	felt	say	said
get	got	see	saw
go	went	take	took
have	had	think	thought

To be: am/is → was; are → were.

Write verbs in the past tense in the sentences.

1. Simon and Raquel __were__ at the International Center. (be)

2. Sasha and Elena _____ there, too. (be)

3. Raquel _____ the answers to Simon's questions. (know)

4. She _____ a book about American history. (read)

5. She also _____ educational programs on TV. (see)

6. She __didn't feel__ nervous about the test. (feel + not)

7. Jorge _____ his interview at the I.N.S. (have)

8. He _____ his green card. (get)

9. Elena _____ for an interview yet. (go + not)

10. Jorge _____ citizenship classes. (take + not)

11. The new course _____ yet. (begin + not)

12. Sasha _____ that Simon was a good teacher. (say)

H. Questions in the Past Tense

How **did** Raquel **get** her citizenship?

She **completed** all the steps.

Underline the correct question word.

1. <u>When</u> / Why did Raquel marry Simon? —Seven years ago.

2. What / Where did Raquel need to apply for an Alien

Registration Card? —Several certificates and forms.

3. Where / What did she get her fingerprints taken?
   —At the police station.

4. When / What did she do with her papers? —She sent them to I.N.S.

5. Where / When will she get a Social Security number?
   —Right away.

6. How / What kind of job did she get? —As a social worker.

7. Where / How did she get her equivalency degree?
   —At a city college.

8. When / Where did she graduate? —A few years ago.

9. Who / When did she get her green card? —Five years ago.

10. How much / How long has she lived in the U.S.?
    —For five years.

I. Verbs in Questions

*Write **verbs in the past tense** in the questions.*

1. Why ___did___ Raquel ___marry___ Simon? (marry)

2. Where _____ she _____ her application? (take)

3. What _____ she _____ at the police station? (do)

4. When _____ she _____ her papers to I.N.S.? (send)

5. Where _____ she _____ her Social Security number?
   (get)

6. How _____ she _____ for a job? (apply)

7. How _____ she _____ her courses? (finish)

8. Where _____ she _____ from? (graduate)

9. Who _____ with her when she got her green card? (be)

10. How much _____ she _____ I.N.S.? (pay)

J. How much?/How many?/How long?

Draw a line to the correct answer.

1. How much is a ticket to Russia?   Only $30.

2. How much is the tuition for citizenship classes? $200,000.

3. How much does the president earn?   About $1,000.

4. How many years must you live in the U.S.
   as a resident?   Fifty.

5. How many stripes are on the U.S. flag?   Five.

6. How many states are there in the union?   Thirteen.

7. How long has Raquel lived in the U.S.?   About an hour.

8. How long is the U.S. president's term?   Seven years.

9. How long is the swearing-in ceremony?   Four years.

K. How often?

How often?

*Write **How often** in the questions.*

1. **How often** is there a presidential election?
   —Every four years.

2. _____ does Simon teach the citizenship course?
   —Every three months.

3. _____ does Sasha work at the hardware store?
   —Every weekend.

4. _____ does Raquel work at the center?
   —On Monday and Friday.

5. _____ does Jorge take classes?
   —Every semester.

6. _____ does Elena visit her family?
   —Every other year.

7. _____ do you have to submit fingerprints?
   —Only once.

8. _____ does Ming call her family?
   —Once a week.

L. Adverbs of Frequency

100%	always	Elena *always* goes to the center on Monday.
80%	usually	Sasha *usually* paints houses, not offices.
60%	often	Raquel *often* stops by the International Center after work.
40%	sometimes	Jorge *sometimes* drives Elena to work.
20%	rarely	Simon *rarely* goes out to lunch.
0%	never	Ming *never* works at the Jade Palace on Sunday.

Write the correct adverb.

1. There are ____**always**____ classes offered at the International Center. (every day)

2. The center is ____**usually**____ open from 10:00 A.M. to 8:00 P.M. (Monday to Friday)

3. Elena _____ gets her paycheck on Friday. (every Friday)

4. Ming _____ gets a good tip from a customer. (4 out of 10 times)

5. People who take the citizenship class _____ pass the citizenship exam. (8 out of 10)

6. It _____ snows in Mexico. (70°–90° F)

7. Sasha _____ works on Sunday. (three times a year)

8. Simon _____ walks to the International Center. (four times a week)

9. Jorge and Elena _____ speak Spanish with each other. (not always)

10. They _____ speak English with Simon. (every day)

M. *Too* and *Enough*

A ticket to Russia is
too expensive.

Sasha doesn't have
enough money.

*Write **too** or **enough** in the sentences.*

1. Can Sasha buy a ticket now?

   No, he can't. A ticket is _____**too**_____ expensive.

2. Can Raquel pass the exam?

   Yes, she can. She has _____**enough**_____ information.

3. Does Ming like her computer class?

   No, she doesn't. It's _____ difficult.

4. Can Elena work at a cash register?

   Yes, she can. She has _____ training.

5. Can Jorge buy a new car?

   No, he can't. It's _____ expensive.

6. Can Ming help Chef Lee?

   Yes, she can. She has _____ experience.

7. Can she be a chef?

   No, she can't. She's _____ young.

8. Does Jorge like his calculus class?

   No, he doesn't. It's _____ easy.

9. Can Ming lift a refrigerator?

   No, she can't. It's _____ heavy.

10. Can Sasha paint houses?

Yes, he can. He has _____ experience.

N. Real People...Real Language

1. Were you born in this country?

Circle the word you hear.

a. (Kiev, Ukraine)   Rockport, Maine

b. Taichi, Szechuan   Taipei, Taiwan

c. Puerto Rico   Costa Rica

d. Jakarta   Jamaica

2. What do you like about being an American citizen?

Underline the right answer.

a. I enjoy two worlds   I enjoy two walks

b. freedom to choose   free socks and shoes

c. lights and rivers   rights and liberties

d. right to vote   right to smoke

e. espresso with onion   express my opinion

f. anything is possible   nothing is impossible

3. Was it difficult to pass the citizenship exam?

Circle the word you hear.

a. (easy)   difficult

b. easy   difficult

c. easy   difficult

d. easy   difficult

4. Do you go back to your country often?

Write the word you hear.

a. at least ___ **twice** ___ a year

b. _____ since we left

c. I _____ go back

d. _____ times for educational reasons

e. _____ a year

VIDEO TRANSCRIPT

Watch and Listen

Simon:	Today I'm helping Raquel study for her citizenship exam. So, how many states are there in the United States?
Raquel:	Fifty.
Simon:	And how many stripes are there on the flag?
Raquel:	Thirteen.
Simon:	And what do they stand for?
Raquel:	The first thirteen colonies.
Simon:	Very good! I see you've been studying.
Raquel:	I have.
Simon:	Hi, Elena!
Elena:	Hi, Simon and Raquel! What are you doing?
Simon:	I was giving Raquel a little quiz.
Raquel:	For my citizenship exam. Hey, Sasha!
Sasha:	Hey, everybody! What's up?
Simon:	I'm quizzing Raquel for her exam tomorrow. And we're announcing citizenship classes here at the International Center.

Elena:	What do you have to study?
Sasha:	American history and government.
Raquel:	Very good.
Elena:	Oh, then you can become a citizen?
Raquel:	It takes a few years.
Simon:	You both have your green cards, right?
Sasha:	Yes, I got mine a few months ago. Now I can go back to Russia to visit.
Raquel:	Wonderful.
Elena:	Jorge has his, but I don't have mine yet, just the Employment Authorization Card. At least I can work.
Sasha:	Well, when the I.N.S. gets all your papers, you'll have an interview.
Elena:	I had to submit my fingerprints, medical forms, and birth and marriage certificates. Now I'm just waiting for the interview... and my green card.
Simon:	And after several years of permanent residence, you can apply for citizenship.
Elena:	And then you have to take a test?
Simon:	Yes, but it's not hard. You just have to know a little about the United States.
Elena:	Like what?
Simon:	Oh, the Revolutionary War, the Constitution, the presidents, and the structure of the state and federal governments.
Elena:	That sounds hard! When are the next classes offered?
Raquel:	A new course is offered here every few months.
Elena:	Maybe I should take it next time.
Simon:	You've got a lot of time to prepare, but it's good to start early.
Elena:	I'll speak with Jorge. I'm sure he'll be interested.
Sasha:	I should take it, too.
Raquel:	As a matter of fact, this is the schedule for this year's class. See, it's not expensive.

Sasha: Oh, and the teacher is great!

Elena: Who is it?

Sasha: Simon—the best teacher in the world!

Simon: Come on, you guys...

Sasha: Okay... one of the best.

Simon: That's all for now. Here are some phrases for you to practice.

To give advice to someone, you can say:

Sasha **could** take a citizenship course this year.   or

Jorge **should** study before his interview.   or

Why don't you practice the dictation more?

A person might respond like this:

I think he will.   or

I know he should.   or

That's a good idea.

Now let's listen to some people talk about their experiences.

Answer Key: Work and School

Unit 1

A. Greetings and Introductions
1. Hello 2. I'm 3. How 4. you
5. meet

B. Where do they work?
1. school 2. office 3. construction site
4. store 5. restaurant

C. Verbs: Present Tense—*To Be*
1. is 2. are 3. is 4. is 5. is 6. is
7. are 8. am 9. are 10. are

D. Contractions
1. you're 2. they're 3. it's 4. I'm
5. we're 6. he's

E. Negatives
1. am not 2. are not 3. is not 4. is not
5. is not 6. is not 7. are not 8. are not
9. are not 10. are not

F. Negative Contractions
1. he isn't/he's not 2. they're not/they
aren't 3. we're not/we aren't 4. I'm
not 5. You aren't/you're not 6. She
isn't/she's not

G. Questions and Yes/No Answers
1. No, he is not. 2. Yes, he is. 3. Yes,
they are. 4. No, I am not./Yes, I am.
5. Yes, he is. 6. Is Simon with Jorge
and Elena? 7. Are you child-care
workers? 8. Is Raquel with Sasha and
Ming? 9. Are they at the table?
10. Are the ads in the newspaper?

H. Questions and Short Answers
1. Ming is. 2. From Mexico. 3. The
newspapers are. 4. From the U.S.
5. Jorge is. 6. At the hardware store.
7. The classified ads. 8. Raquel is.
9. In the classified ads. 10. Sasha is.

I. Question Words
1. Who 2. Who 3. What 4. Who
5. Where 6. What 7. Where 8. What

J. Plurals
1. cashiers 2. cooks 3. teachers
4. drivers 5. engineers 6. painters

K. *There is/There are*
1. There are 2. There is 3. There is
4. There are 5. There is 6. There are

L. More Question Words
1. How much 2. How much 3. How
much 4. How many 5. How many
6. How many

M. Classified Ads: Help Wanted
1. no, yes, $7/hr., 10%,
evenings/weekends, no, yes, 9–5
2. no, yes, $8/hr., 10%, weekends, no,
no, 10–4
3. yes, yes, $8.50/hr., 15%, days, yes,
yes, 8–8
4. yes, no, $10/hr., 15%, days, yes, yes,
10–6 5. Job #3 6. Job #2

N. Real People...Real Language
1. What kind of work do you do?
a. Boston public high school
b. entrepreneur c. computer
d. waitress e. technical f. repairs
g. manager h. martial arts
i. horse stable

2. Do you work full-time or part-time?
(crossed out)
a. part-time b. full-time c. full-time
d. part-time e. part-time f. full-time

3. Do you earn a good salary?
a. good b. good c. not good
d. average e. average f. average

4. How did you find your job?
(crossed out)
a. family b. busy street c. teachers
d. classified ads e. newspaper
f. hairdresser g. bartender

5. If you could do anything, what kind of work would you do?
a. artist b. movie producer c. deal with people d. shop for people e. go to school f. job I loved
g. philanthropist h. what I do now

Unit 2
A. Odd One Out
1. doctor 2. ESL 3. enroll 4. medicine

B. What is it?
1. form 2. exam 3. social
4. education 5. class

C. Spelling
1. A 2. O, U, E 3. E, I 4. A 5. U, I
6. I, E, E

D. Verbs: Present Simple
1. sits 2. asks 3. answers 4. wants
5. needs 6. go 7. study 8. eat
9. speak 10. study

E. Negatives
1. doesn't speak 2. doesn't go
3. doesn't know 4. doesn't want
5. doesn't teach 6. doesn't work
7. doesn't have 8. doesn't give
9. don't study 10. don't watch

F. Questions and Yes/No Answers
1. Yes, she does. 2. No, they don't.
3. No, she doesn't. 4. No, she doesn't.
5. Yes, they do. 6. No, he doesn't.
7. Yes, she does. 8. Yes, they do.
9. No, they don't. 10. Yes, I do.

G. Short Answers
1. Ming does. 2. In the school.
3. Raquel does. 4. Eight years old.
5. Ms. Roberts does. 6. Next week.
7. About 15 students. 8. In the classroom. 9. In a few days. 10. Six hours.

H. Questions
1. Where 2. Where 3. Who 4. How much 5. Who 6. How many 7. How much 8. Who 9. How many
10. Where

I. Possessives: Nouns, Adjectives, and Pronouns
1. Simon's 2. Jorge's 3. Sasha's
4. Raquel's 5. Elena's 6. Ming's
7. Her 8. Her 9. His 10. Their
11. Mine, yours 12. His, hers 13. Its
14. Ours, yours 15. Theirs, ours

J. Dialogue
1. come 2. come 3. doctor 4. son
5. doctor 6. you 7. shot 8. it
9. don't 10. you 11. go 12. park
13. give

K. School Subjects
1. math 2. music 3. art 4. science
5. physical education 6. computers
7. ESL 8. social studies 9. English

L. Countries, Nationalities, and Languages
1. Dominican 2. China 3. Mexican
4. Russia 5. American

M. People and Countries
1. Dominican Republic 2. Mexico
3. Spanish 4. Chinese 5. Chinese
6. Russian 7. Russian 8. United States
9. English 10. English

N. Real People...Real Language
1. Are you from this country? Where are you from?
a. 14 b. U.S. c. 10 d. U.S.
e. Colombia f. Born here. g. Ukraine
h. 14 i. 7

2. What do you study in school?
a. fine arts b. accounting
c. psychology d. computer technology
e. computer graphics f. math

3. Do you like your teachers?
(crossed out)
a. bad b. fine c. awful d. terrible

4. What is your favorite subject?
a. printmaking b. culture c. film
d. physics e. nutrition

5. Do you like the other students in your school?
a. friends b. many c. People d. well

Unit 3
A. What is it?
1. interview 2. diploma 3. boss
4. coworkers 5. department store
6. cash register

B. What day is it?
1. Sunday, Monday, Tuesday, Wednesday, Thursday, Friday, Saturday

C. Verbs: Future with *Will/Won't*
1. will 2. won't 3. will 4. won't
5. will 6. will 7. won't 8. will
9. won't 10. will

D. Questions and Yes/No Answers
1. Yes, they will. 2. No, he won't.
3. Yes, she will. 4. Yes, he will.
5. Yes, she will. 6. No, she won't.
7. No, she won't. 8. Yes, she will.
9. Yes, they will. 10. No, he won't.

E. Questions
1. The manager. 2. A cashier's job.
3. $8 per hour. 4. Tomorrow. 5. Yes, they will. 6. A coworker. 7. No, he won't. 8. In six months.

F. Number Practice
(no answers)

G. Telling Time
1. 9:30, It's nine-thirty. 2. 11:15, It's eleven-fifteen. 3. 2:20, It's two-twenty.
4. 7:05, It's seven-o-five.
5. 4:35, It's four thirty-five. 6. 5:45, It's five forty-five. 7. 1:15, It's one-fifteen. 8. 6:50, It's six-fifty. 9. 3:10, It's three-ten. 10. 11:00, It's eleven o'clock. 11. 10:40, It's ten-forty.
12. 8:55, It's eight-fifty-five.

H. Prepositions of Time
1. at, in 2. in 3. on 4. at 5. on 6. on
7. in 8. on 9. at 10. on

I. Singular and Plural Nouns
1. apples 2. bananas 3. carrots
4. eggs 5. onions 6. potatoes
7. tomatoes 8. strawberries
9. raspberries 10. cherries

J. Money
1. Total: $8.95 2. Total: $9.67
3. Total: $8.54 4. Change: $1.05
5. Change: $.33 6. Change: $1.46

K. Count and Noncount nouns
1. apples, tomatoes, eggs, bananas, onions, peaches, raspberries, potatoes
2. bread, pasta, juice, rice, cereal, milk, soup

L. Dialogue
1. Come 2. put 3. stand 4. watch
5. be 6. worry 7. Have

M. Real People...Real Language
1. How do you prepare for a job interview?
a. Bring personal references, Dress neatly, Show up on time b. Get background information, Wear business clothing, Be prompt c. Redid my résumé d. Learned about the company e. Got online brochures

2. Tell me about your job.
a. job/training/educating/families/children b. wait tables/on feet/customers/busy/stressful/slow/not so bad c. greatest job/teaching/learning

3. Do you have benefits at work?
a. health insurance b. health insurance/dental care/eye care
c. health/dental d. health/dental/personal insurance/stock options
e. no benefits f. health/retirement/vacation/sick days

4. What hours do you work?
a. 9:30–5:00 b. 9–5, 40 c. 11–6
d. 8:30–7

5. Do you like your schedule?
a. Yes b. Yes c. Yes d. Yes

Unit 4
A. Time of Day
1. morning 2. afternoon 3. evening
4. night

B. Time of Year
1. spring 2. summer 3. fall 4. winter

C. Taking a Class
1. course 2. catalog 3. sign up
4. registration form 5. schedule
6. instructor 7. homework 8. tests
9. grades 10. easy, hard 11. boring, interesting

D. Verbs: Future with *Going To*
1. are going to sign up 2. are going to register 3. is going to take 4. is going to study 5. is going to get 6. are going to open 7. is going to cook
8. is going to be 9. are going to have
10. are going to make

E. Negatives
1. They're not going to 2. You're not going to 3. She's not going to 4. He's not going to 5. He's not going to
6. I'm not going to 7. It's not going to
8. We're not going to

F. Questions and Yes/No Answers
1. No, she isn't. 2. Yes, she is. 3. No, he isn't. 4. Yes, they are. 5. No, he isn't. 6. No, they aren't. 7. Is the instructor going to give a test? 8. Are the students going to get good grades?
9. Is the homework going to be easy?
10. Are the new catalogs going to be out soon? 11. Is Ming going to take classes at night? 12. Are Elena and Raquel going to take afternoon classes?

G. Questions and Short Answers
1. g 2. h 3. b 4. j 5. i 6. c 7. a 8. d
9. e 10. f

H. Conjunctions: *And* Versus *Or*
1. and 2. or 3. and 4. or 5. and
6. and (or)

I. Conjunctions: *And* Versus *But*
1. but (and) 2. but (and)
3. but 4. and 5. but 6. and 7. but

J. Course Catalog
1. No 2. Yes 3. Yes 4. No 5. Apron and appetite 6. Bathing suit, swim cap, towel 7. No 8. No 9. Swimming 10. Intro to Computers

K. Sign up!
(Answers will be different for each student)

L. Real People...Real Language
1. Are you taking any classes?
a. tax b. Computer c. book d. painting e. biology f. finance g. flute

2. How do you like your class?
a. Yes, flute b. Yes, challenging c. Yes, French d. Yes, intense

3. When is your class?
a. 8:30–9:45, A.M., M, T, W, Th
b. M 11:30, T 9:30, A.M., M–F
c. 11:00 A.M.–7:00 P.M. d. M–Th, M+W 12:30–3:00, T+Th 2:30–5:30
e. 4:30–7:00, P.M. f. 3 times a week, 6–9, 6–8 weeks

4. What are the people in your class like?
a. early 30s to 40s, married, fresh out of school b. working people, nice, busy, hard-working c. very different, young, older, working full-time

Unit 5
A. What is it?
1. breakfast 2. lunch 3. dinner 4. meals 5. refrigerator 6. stove 7. pots and pans

B. Odd One Out
1. weekly 2. washing 3. medical

C. Verbs: Present Tense— To Be + _ing
1. is waiting 2. is coming 3. are talking 4. is asking 5. is telling 6. is explaining 7. is showing 8. is pointing 9. are writing 10. am finishing

D. Negatives
1. isn't going 2. isn't waiting 3. aren't having 4. aren't eating 5. aren't watching

E. Questions
1. Is Ming going back to work? 2. Is Raquel waiting at the International Center? 3. Are Simon and Raquel having dinner at the restaurant tonight? 4. Are you eating dinner now? 5. Are we watching TV?

F. Questions and Yes/No Answers
1. Yes, she is. 2. No, he isn't. 3. Yes, she is. 4. No, they aren't. 5. Yes, she is. 6. No, they aren't. 7. No, she isn't. 8. Yes, she is. 9. No, she isn't. 10. Yes, I am.

G. Object Pronouns
1. her 2. her 3. it 4. him 5. them 6. us 7. it 8. them 9. him 10. them, her

H. Questions: *Which/Which one*
1. Which, St. Petersburg 2. Which one, Fisherman's Catch 3. Which, Jade Palace 4. Which one, St. Petersburg 5. Which one, Los Charros 6. Which, Fisherman's Catch 7. Which one, Jade Palace 8. Which one, Los Charros 9. Which, Jade Palace 10. Which one, St. Petersburg

I. Recipe: Jade Palace Fried Rice
1. rice 2. water 3. cabbage 4. soy
sauce 5. carrot 6. green onions
7. bean sprouts 8. egg

J. Prepositions of Place: *In/On/At*
1. on 2. at 3. on 4. at 5. in 6. on
7. on 8. on 9. at 10. on

K. Adverbs
1. He chops them fast. 2. She chops
them slowly. 3. He cooks well. 4. She
cooks badly. 5. They work hard.

L. Real People...Real Language
1. How often do you go out to eat in a
restaurant?
a. two times a month b. once every
other week c. twice a week d. twice a
week e. very often for lunch f. three-
four nights a week

2. What kind of food do you like?
(crossed out)
a. rice b. South American, Malaysian
c. Spanish, Pakistani d. Israeli,
German e. few kinds of food, some
kinds of food f. Dominican
g. Russian h. appetizers, main courses,
drinks

3. Have you ever worked in a
restaurant?
a. Yes b. Yes c. No d. Yes

4. What kinds of restaurants are
popular nowadays?
a. coffee shops b. ethnic restaurants
c. fast food d. health food e. natural
food

Unit 6
A. What is it?
1. Registry of Motor Vehicles
2. driver's education 3. car dealer

B. Opposites
1. new 2. road 3. cheap 4. hard
5. low 6. more 7. here

C. Verbs: Present Tense—*Can/Can't*
1. can 2. can't 3. can 4. can't 5. can
6. can't 7. can 8. can 9. can't 10. can

D. Questions and Yes/No Answers
1. Can/No, she can't. 2. Can/Yes, she
can. 3. Can/Yes, she can. 4. Can/No,
she can't. 5. Can/Yes, he can.
6. Can/No, he can't. 7. Can/No, he
can't. 8. Can/No, they can't.
9. Can/Yes, they can. 10. Can/No,
they can't.

E. Verbs: Past Tense—
Could/Couldn't
1. couldn't 2. could 3. couldn't
4. could 5. couldn't

**F. More Questions and Yes/No
Answers**
1. Could/No, they couldn't. 2. Could/
Yes, he could. 3.Could/No, he
couldn't. 4.Could/Yes, they could.
5. Could/Yes, he could. 6. Could/No,
they couldn't. 7. Could/Yes, he could.
8. Could/Yes, they could. 9. Could/
Yes, they could.

G. *Can/Can't* or *Could/Couldn't*.
1. can't 2. couldn't 3. couldn't
4. couldn't 5. can't 6. could 7. can
8. couldn't 9. could 10. can

H. Short Answers
1. Yes, he can. 2. No, he couldn't.
3. Yes, they can. 4. Yes, she could.
5. Yes, I can. 6. No, they couldn't.
7. Yes, they can. 8. No, I couldn't.
9. Yes, he could. 10. Yes, she can.

I. Adjectives: Opposites
1. The van. 2. The coupe. 3. The sedan. 4. The coupe. 5. The sedan. 6. The van.

J. Adjectives: Comparative and Superlative
1. cheap, cheaper, cheapest 2. small, smaller, smallest 3. new, newer, newest 4. old, older, oldest 5. heavy, heavier, heaviest 6. pretty, prettier, prettiest 7. ugly, uglier, ugliest 8. expensive, more/less expensive, most/least expensive 9. comfortable, more/less comfortable, least/most comfortable 10. luxurious, more/less luxurious, most/least luxurious 11. older 12. newer 13. larger 14. more expensive 15. more luxurious 16. less comfortable 17. newest 18. cheapest 19. prettiest 20. heaviest 21. most expensive 22. least luxurious

K. Dialogue
1. papers 2. let's 3. price 4. can 5. how much 6. car 7. can 8. payment 9. wife 10. ready

L. Real People...Real Language
1. When did you get your driver's license?
a. 16 1/2 b. 15 c. 28 d. 18 e. 17

2. What kind of car do you drive?
a. Mazda b. Volvo c. Toyota d. Honda

3. Are you happy with your car?
a. new b. strong c. comfortable d. stereo, color

4. Did you buy a new or used car?
a. used/ten b. used/new

5. Did you get good financing?
a. cash b. mom c. Paid d. Good e. deal

Unit 7
A. Odd One Out
1. presidents 2. fingerprints 3. federal 4. birth certificate

B. What is it?
1. exam 2. presidents 3. certificate 4. government

C. Verbs: Simple Past—Regular
1. asked 2. called 3. visited 4. wanted 5. announced 6. prepared 7. used 8. submitted 9. applied 10. studied

D. More Verb Practice
1. wanted 2. applied 3. studied 4. submitted 5. received 6. used 7. visited 8. prepared 9. asked 10. announced

E. Negatives
1. didn't want 2. didn't apply 3. didn't study 4. didn't submit 5. didn't receive 6. didn't buy 7. didn't visit 8. didn't prepare 9. didn't announce 10. didn't start

F. Questions and Yes/No Answers
1. Yes, he did. 2. Yes, she did. 3. Yes, she did. 4. Yes, he did. 5. No, she didn't. 6. Yes, she did. 7. Yes, she did. 8. Yes, he did. 9. No, he didn't. 10. Yes, she did.

G. Verbs: Simple Past—Irregular
1. were 2. were 3. knew 4. read 5. saw 6. didn't feel 7. had 8. got 9. didn't go 10. didn't take 11. didn't begin 12. said

H. Questions in the Past Tense
1. When 2. What 3. Where 4. What
5. When 6. What 7. Where 8. When
9. When 10. How long

I. Verbs in Questions
1. did/marry 2. did/take 3. did/do
4. did/send 5. did/get 6. did/apply
7. did/finish 8. did/graduate 9. was
10. did/pay

J. *How much?/How many?/How long?*
1. About $1,000. 2. Only $30.
3. $200,000. 4. Five. 5. Thirteen.
6. Fifty. 7. Seven years. 8. Four years.
9. About an hour.

K. How often?
1. How often 2. How often 3. How
often 4. How often 5. How often 6.
How often 7. How often 8. How
often

L. Adverbs of Frequency
1. always 2. usually 3. always
4. sometimes 5. usually 6. never
7. rarely 8. often 9. often 10. always

M. *Too* and *Enough*
1. too 2. enough 3. too 4. enough
5. too 6. enough 7. too 8. too 9. too
10. enough

N. Real People...Real Language
1. Were you born in this country?
a. Kiev, Ukraine b. Taipei, Taiwan
c. Puerto Rico d. Jamaica

2. What do you like about being an
American citizen?
a. I enjoy two worlds. b. freedom to
choose c. rights and liberties d. right
to vote e. express my opinion
f. nothing is impossible

3. Was it difficult to pass the
citizenship exam?
a. easy b. easy c. easy d. easy

4. Do you go back to your country
often?
b. once c. never d. three e. twice.

Word List: Work and School

a few
a little
a lot
account
afternoon
again
agent
aisle
always
American
and
answering
  machine
any
apartment
apples
are
area code
ATM
bag
balance
bananas
bank
basket
bathroom
bedroom
birthday
block
bottle
box
Brazil
Brazilian
bread
building

bunch
bus
bus stop
busy signal
butter
bye
call
can
cardinal numbers
cards
carrots
cart
carton
cash
cashier
center
chair
cheap
check
child
children
China
Chinese
classified ads
clothing store
collector
college
Colombia
Colorado
community
company
computer
consultant
container

convenience
corner
could
cross the street
dark
date
daughter
day
deposit
dial
dining room
directory
  assistance
do
does
doesn't
Dominican
  Republic
don't
electricity
Elena
engineer
evening
expensive
father
fee
fine
floor
France
French
gas
Georgia
get off
get on

go straight
good morning
good-bye
great
had
Haiti
Haitian
half-past
hang up
has
has to
have
have to
he
hello
her
hers
hi
high
his
home
Hong Kong
house
how
how many
how much
how often
hungry
husband
I
identification
information
interest
international

is
it
its
Jamaica
Jamaican
Japan
Japanese
jar
Jorge
juice
know
Korea
Korean
large
later
laundry
lease
leave
letter
light
living room
loaf
local
long distance
low
machine
mailbox
math
mechanic
meet
message
Mexican
Mexico
milk
mine
Ming
minimum
modern
months
Moscow
mother
movie theater
my
nationalities

negative
neighborhood
never
new
New York
newspaper
nice
night
o'clock
office
often
old-fashioned
onions
operator
oranges
ordinal numbers
our
ours
painter
parking
people
pharmacy
phrases
pick up
Port-au-Prince
Portugal
Portuguese
post office
potatoes
pound
Puerto Rican
Puerto Rico
quarter
Raquel
rarely
real estate
restaurant
rice
ring
Russia
Russian
Sasha
sauce
school

secretary
see
seldom
service
she
should
signature
Simon
small
social worker
some
sometimes
son
soon
soup
Spain
Spanish
stamp
statement
stick
store
strawberry
student
subway
supermarket
table
tai chi
Taipei
Taiwan
teacher
technology
telephone
teller
Thailand
that
their
theirs
they
this
time
to
today
token
tomatoes

tomorrow
train
traveler's checks
turn left
turn right
Ukraine
United States
Uruguay
usually
utilities
vacation
verb
very well
Vietnam
Vietnamese
waitress
we
where
wife
will
window
withdraw
word
would
wrong number
years
yogurt
you
your
yours

Audio Script: Work and School

Unit 1: Finding a Job

Vocabulary

Listen and repeat.

1. advertisement
2. application
3. appointment
4. cashier
5. child care
6. classified ads
7. clerical worker
8. company
9. cook
10. driver
11. duties
12. engineer
13. experience
14. full-time
15. hardware
16. help wanted

17. interview
18. job
19. newspaper
20. painter
21. part-time
22. references
23. remodeling
24. salary
25. salesperson
26. social worker
27. teacher
28. waitress
29. work

Affirmative Verbs

Listen and repeat.

1. I am
2. you are
3. he is
4. she is
5. it is
6. we are
7. you are
8. they are

Affirmative Sentences

Make a sentence from these words.

First, listen to the example:

    Simon/teacher   Simon is a teacher.

Now it's your turn.

1. Simon/teacher   Simon is a teacher.
2. Raquel/social worker   Raquel is a social worker.
3. Jorge/engineer   Jorge is an engineer.
4. Elena/cashier   Elena is a cashier.
5. Sasha/painter   Sasha is a painter.
6. Ming/waitress   Ming is a waitress.
7. You/salespersons   You are salespersons.
8. We/cooks   We are cooks.

Negative Verbs

Listen and repeat.

1. I'm not
2. you're not
3. he's not
4. she's not
5. it's not
6. we're not
7. you're not
8. they're not

Negative Sentences

Make a sentence from these words.

First, listen to the example:

    Simon/painter   Simon isn't a painter.

Now it's your turn.

1. Simon/painter   Simon isn't a painter.

2. Raquel/waitress   Raquel isn't a waitress.

3. Jorge/child care worker   Jorge isn't a child care worker.

4. I/clerical worker   I'm not a clerical worker.

5. They/drivers   They're not drivers.

Questions

Answer these questions.

First, listen to the example:

    Is Simon a teacher or a   He's a teacher.
    painter?

Now it's your turn.

1. Is Simon a teacher or a   He's a teacher.
   painter?

2. Is Raquel a cashier or a   She's a social worker.
   social worker?

3. Is Ming a waitress or a   She's a waitress.
   cook?

4. Are they bus drivers or taxi   They're taxi drivers.
   drivers?

5. Are you a student or a   I'm a student.
   teacher?

Questions and Short Answers

Answer these questions.

1.	Who is an engineer?	Jorge is.
2.	Who is at the table with Simon?	Jorge and Elena are.
3.	What is on the table?	The newspapers are.
4.	Who is looking for a job?	Elena is.
5.	Who is at the table with Raquel?	Sasha and Ming are.

There Is or *There Are*

Make sentences from these words.

First, listen to the example:

newspaper/table	There is a newspaper on the table.

Now it's your turn.

1.	newspaper/table	There is a newspaper on the table.
2.	people/at the table	There are three people at the table.
3.	application/on the table	There is an application on the table.
4.	pen/in Elena's hand	There is a pen in Elena's hand.
5.	cooks/restaurant	There are cooks in the restaurant.
6.	driver/bus	There is a driver on the bus.
7.	teachers/at the school	There are teachers at the school.

8. engineer/in the office   There is an engineer in the office.

Unit 2: Enrolling a Child in School

Vocabulary

Listen and repeat.

1. art
2. aunt
3. boy
4. brother
5. children
6. classroom
7. computers
8. desk
9. doctor's exam
10. English
11. enroll
12. ESL
13. father
14. girl
15. math
16. medical form
17. mother
18. music
19. nephew
20. niece

21. office

22. physical education

23. register

24. registration form

25. science

26. shots

27. sister

28. social studies

29. students

30. subjects

31. teacher

32. testing

33. tutor

34. uncle

Simple Present Tense—Affirmative Short Answers

Answer these questions.

First, listen to the example:

> Does Ming speak to Ms. Roberts?   Yes, she does.

Now it's your turn.

1. Does Ming speak to Ms. Roberts?   Yes, she does.

2. Does Raquel go to the school with her?   Yes, she does.

3. Do Ming and Raquel ask questions?   Yes, they do.

4. Does Ms. Roberts answer their questions? Yes, she does.

5. Does Ming's nephew speak Chinese? Yes, he does.

Simple Present Tense–Negative Short Answers

Answer these questions.

First, listen to the example:

Does Ming's nephew speak English? No, he doesn't.

Now it's your turn.

1. Does Ming's nephew speak English? No, he doesn't.

2. Does he have friends at school? No, he doesn't.

3. Does Ms. Roberts teach first grade? No, she doesn't.

4. Do Ming and Raquel teach ESL? No, they don't.

5. Does Ming fill out the forms? No, she doesn't.

Questions and Answers

Answer these questions.

First, listen to the example:

Who goes to school with Ming? Raquel does.

Now it's your turn.

1.	Who goes to school with Ming?	Raquel does.
2.	Who talks to them about enrollment?	Ms. Roberts does.
3.	Who studies in this school?	Children do.
4.	Who teaches third grade?	Ms. Roberts does.
5.	When do the children go to school?	In the morning.

Negative Sentences

Make negative sentences with these words.

First, listen to the example:

Ming's nephew/speak English	Ming's nephew doesn't speak English.

Now it's your turn.

1.	Ming's nephew/speak English	Ming's nephew doesn't speak English.
2.	Ms. Roberts/meet him	Ms. Roberts doesn't meet him.
3.	Raquel/take the forms	Raquel doesn't take the forms.
4.	Ms. Roberts/teach ESL	Ms. Roberts doesn't teach ESL.
5.	Some children/speak English	Some children don't speak English.

How Much and How Many?

Make a question with these words.

First, listen to the examples:

English/Ming speak	How much English does Ming speak? How many students does the ESL teacher have?
students/ESL teacher have	

Now it's your turn.

1. English/Ming speak	How much English does Ming speak?
2. students/ESL teacher have	How many students does the ESL teacher have?
3. time/you need	How much time do you need?
4. subjects/they study	How many subjects do they study?
5. students/are there	How many students are there?

Possessive Nouns, Adjectives, and Pronouns

Substitute the possessive noun with the adjective or pronoun.

First, listen to the example:

Ming's nephew	her nephew

Now it's your turn.

1. Ming's nephew	her nephew
2. Dr. John's office	his office
3. The children's desks	their desks
4. the cafeteria's doors	its doors

Again, listen to the example:

your computer	yours

Now it's your turn.

5. your computer   yours

6. my book   mine

7. our classroom   ours

8. the teacher's book   hers

Country–Nationality–Language

Listen to the country and say the nationality and language.

First, listen to the example:

Brazil   Brazilian   Portuguese

Now it's your turn.

1.	Brazil	Brazilian	Portuguese
2.	Cambodia	Cambodian	Cambodian
3.	China	Chinese	Chinese
4.	Dominican Republic	Dominican	Spanish
5.	France	French	French
6.	Mexico	Mexican	Spanish
7.	Russia	Russian	Russian
8.	Vietnam	Vietnamese	Vietnamese

Unit 3: A Job Interview

Vocabulary

Listen and repeat.

1. apple

2. banana

3. boss

4. bread

5. cereal

6. coworkers

7. department store

8. dime

9. diploma

10. discount

11. dollar

12. eggs

13. experience

14. few

15. interview

16. job

17. juice

18. little

19. lot

20. lunch break

21. many

22. milk

23. much

24. nickel

25. onion

26. pasta

27. paycheck

28. peach

29. penny

30. potato

31. quarter

32. raise

33. raspberry

34. register

35. rice

36. schedule

37. some

38. soup

39. supermarket

40. together

41. tomato

42. training

43. weekdays

44. weekends

45. working hours

Days of the Week

Monday

Tuesday

Wednesday

Thursday

Friday

Saturday

Sunday

Numbers

one	twelve	twenty-three	seventy
two	thirteen	twenty-four	eighty
three	fourteen	twenty-five	ninety
four	fifteen	twenty-six	one hundred
five	sixteen	twenty-seven	one hundred one
six	seventeen	twenty-eight	
seven	eighteen	twenty-nine	two hundred
eight	nineteen	thirty	one thousand
nine	twenty	forty	
ten	twenty-one	fifty	
eleven	twenty-two	sixty	

Singular and Plural

Make these words plural.

First, listen to the example:

apple   apples

Now it's your turn.

1. apple   apples
2. carrot   carrots
3. cherry   cherries
4. dollar   dollars
5. penny   pennies

Future Tense–Short Answers

Answer these questions.

First, listen to the example:

Will Elena work at the supermarket?	Yes, she will.

Now it's your turn.

1. Will Elena work at the supermarket? — Yes, she will.
2. Will Mr. Hart be her boss? — Yes, he will.
3. Will the other cashiers train her? — Yes, they will.
4. Will we be friendly and helpful? — Yes, we will.
5. Will the cash register work? — Yes, it will.

Future Tense–Negative Answers

Answer these questions.

First, listen to the example:

Will Jorge work at the supermarket?	No, he won't.

Now it's your turn.

1. Will Jorge work at the supermarket? — No, he won't.
2. Will Ming be a cashier? — No, she won't.
3. Will we earn $10 an hour? — No, we won't.
4. Will the other cashiers pay her? — No, they won't.

5. Will the cash register be broken?   No, it won't.

A *Little* or a *Few*?

Say the correct phrase.

First, listen to the examples:

bread   a little bread
peaches   a few peaches

Now it's your turn.

1. bread   a little bread

2. peaches   a few peaches

3. pasta   a little pasta

4. cereal   a little cereal

5. potatoes   a few potatoes

Telling Time

Say the time in a different way.

First, listen to the example:

It's a quarter past eight.   It's eight-fifteen.

Now it's your turn.

1. It's a quarter past eight.   It's eight-fifteen.

2. It's half past ten.   It's ten-thirty.

3. It's a quarter to twelve.   It's eleven-forty-five.

4. It's five past two.   It's two-o-five.

5. It's twenty past four.   It's four-twenty.

6. It's twenty-five to six.   It's five-thirty-five.

7. It's ten to nine.   It's eight-fifty.

8. It's ten past one.   It's one-ten.

Unit 4: Adult Education

Vocabulary

Listen and repeat.

1. aerobics
2. afternoon
3. bookkeeping
4. boring
5. business
6. calculus
7. catalog
8. course
9. degree
10. easy
11. engineering
12. equivalency
13. evening
14. fall
15. grades
16. hard
17. homework
18. instructor
19. interesting
20. manager

21. morning

22. next

23. night

24. register

25. registration form

26. schedule

27. sign up

28. spring

29. summer

30. test

31. winter

Months of the Year

January

February

March

April

May

June

July

August

September

October

November

December

Future with *Going to*–Affirmative Short Answers

Answer these questions.

First, listen to the example:

> Is Jorge going to register   Yes, he is.
> for a course?

Now it's your turn.

1. Is Jorge going to register for   Yes, he is.
   a course?

2. Is registration going to be in   Yes, it is.
   December?

3. Are classes going to start in   Yes, they are.
   January?

4. Is Ming going to sign up for   Yes, she is.
   bookkeeping?

5. Is she going to open a   Yes, she is.
   restaurant with her brother?

6. Are Elena and Raquel going   Yes, they are.
   to take aerobics?

7. Are we going to take a   Yes, we are.
   history class?

Future with *Going to*–Negative Short Answers

Answer these questions.

First, listen to the example:

> Is Ming going to   No, she's not.   No, she isn't.
> sign up for an
> exercise class?

Now it's your turn.

1. Is Ming going to sign up for an exercise class?	No, she's not.	No, she isn't.
2. Is Jorge going to study business?	No, he's not.	No, he isn't.
3. Are Elena and Raquel going to take cooking?	No, they're not.	No, they aren't.
4. Are you going to learn Russian?	No, I'm not.	No, I'm not.
5. Are we going to teach bookkeeping?	No, we're not.	No, we aren't.
6. Am I going to get a degree in computers?	No, you're not.	No, you aren't.
7. Is the computer going to be available?	No, it's not.	No it isn't.

Prepositions of Time–*In, On, At*

Make sentences with the correct prepositions.

First, listen to the example:

Jorge is going to take a course/evening

Jorge is going to take a course in the evening.

Now it's your turn.

1. Jorge is going to take a course/evening

Jorge is going to take a course in the evening.

2. Registration is going to be/December

Registration is going to be in December.

3. Classes are going to begin/January fifth

Classes are going to begin on January fifth.

4. The aerobics course is going to start/10:00

The aerobics course is going to start at 10:00.

5. Classes are going to end/May twelfth

Classes are going to end on May twelfth.

6. The U.S. History course is going to be/4:00 P.M.

The U.S. History course is going to be at 4:00 P.M.

Questions and Answers

Answer these questions.

First, listen to the example:

Who is going to take bookkeeping?

Ming is.

Now it's your turn.

1. Who is going to take bookkeeping?

Ming is.

2. Which course is Jorge going to register for?

U.S. History.

3. When is registration going to be?

In December.

4. Who is going to sign up for aerobics?

Elena and Raquel.

5. Where are they going to take courses?

At the college.

6. When are the courses going to begin?

In January.

Making Questions

Make questions from the sentences.

First, listen to the example:

> The tuition is going to be low.   Is the tuition going to be low?

Now it's your turn.

1. The tuition is going to be low.   Is the tuition going to be low?

2. The catalogs are going to be nice.   Are the catalogs going to be nice?

3. The homework is going to be easy.   Is the homework going to be easy?

4. The instructors are going to give an exam.   Are the instructors going to give an exam?

5. The students are going to come on time.   Are the students going to come on time?

6. The college is going to be open in the summer.   Is the college going to be open in the summer?

Unit 5: First Day on the Job

Work Vocabulary

Listen and repeat.

1. accident
2. assistant
3. customers
4. dental
5. directions
6. disability

7. medical

8. overtime

9. paycheck

10. policy

11. salary

12. shift

13. supervisor

14. time card

15. time clock

16. wages

17. weekly

Kitchen Vocabulary

1. boil

2. breakfast

3. chop

4. dinner

5. fish

6. fry

7. kitchen

8. lunch

9. meal

10. meat

11. pans

12. pots

13. refrigerator

14. serve

15. stove

16. wash

Affirmative Sentences

Make sentences from these words.

First, listen to the example:

| Ming/listen | Ming is listening. |

Now it's your turn.

1. Ming/listen	Ming is listening.
2. Ms. Chan/speak	Ms. Chan is speaking.
3. The waiters/take orders	The waiters are taking orders.
4. You and I/eat dinner	You and I are eating dinner.
5. I/order lunch	I am ordering lunch.

Negative Sentences

Make sentences from these words.

First, listen to the example:

| Ms. Chan/cook | Ms. Chan is not cooking. |

Now it's your turn.

1. Ms. Chan/cook	Ms. Chan is not cooking.
2. The assistants/serving dinner	The assistants are not serving dinner.
3. Chef Lee/washing dishes	Chef Lee is not washing dishes.
4. You and I/cleaning tables	You and I are not cleaning tables.
5. I/eating dinner	I am not eating dinner.

Yes and No Answers

Answer these questions.

First, listen to the example:

Is Ms. Chan supervising?	Yes, she is.
Is Chef Lee cleaning the kitchen?	No, he isn't.

Now it's your turn.

1. Is Ms. Chan supervising? — Yes, she is.

2. Are the waiters taking orders? — Yes, they are.

3. Is Chef Lee cleaning the kitchen? — No, he isn't.

4. Are the customers eating dinner? — Yes, they are.

5. Is Ming helping Chef Lee? — Yes, she is.

Object Pronouns

Substitute the noun with the pronoun.

First, listen to the example:

Ming is helping Chef Lee. — She is helping him.

Now it's your turn.

1. Ming is helping Chef Lee. — She is helping him.

2. Chef Lee is chopping vegetables. — He is chopping them.

3. The waiters are taking orders. — They are taking them.

4. I am eating with you and your family. — I am eating with you.

5. You and I are eating the rolls.   We are eating them.

Prepositions of Place—*In, On, At*

Make sentences with the correct prepositions.

First, listen to the example:

carrot/table   The carrot is on the table.

Now it's your turn.

1. carrot/table   The carrot is on the table.

2. glass/table   The glass is on the table.

3. meat/refrigerator   The meat is in the refrigerator.

4. rice/pot   The rice is in the pot.

5. pot/stove   The pot is on the stove.

Which?

Answer these questions.

First, listen to the examples:

Which rice does Ming cook?(white)   She cooks the white rice.

Which chef does she work with? (Lee)   She works with Chef Lee.

Now it's your turn.

1. Which rice does Ming cook? (white)   She cooks the white rice.

2. Which chef does she work with? (Lee)   She works with Chef Lee.

3. Which restaurant does she work at? (The Jade Palace)   She works at The Jade Palace Restaurant.

4. Which check does she get every week? (pay)

She gets a paycheck.

5. Which insurance does she have? (medical and dental)

She has medical and dental insurance.

Adverbs of Manner

Answer the questions with these words.

First, listen to the example:

How does Chef Lee cook? (well)

He cooks well.

Now it's your turn.

1. How does Chef Lee cook? (well)

He cooks well.

2. How does Sasha cook? (badly)

He cooks badly.

3. How does Ming chop vegetables? (slowly)

She chops slowly.

4. How does Jorge chop vegetables? (fast)

He chops fast.

5. How do the waiters work? (hard)

They work hard.

Unit 6: Getting a Driver's License and Buying a Car

Vocabulary

Listen and repeat.

1. bargain

2. car dealer

3. down payment

4. driver's education

5. driver's manual

6. installments

7. license

8. new car

9. offer

10. permit

11. photo

12. practice

13. Registry of Motor Vehicles

14. road test

15. safety

16. seat belt

17. test drive

18. used car

19. warranty

20. written test

Short Answers–Affirmative and Negative

Answer these questions.

First, listen to the example:

Can Jorge buy a new car?   No, he can't.

Now it's your turn.

1. Can Jorge buy a new car?   No, he can't.

2. Can Raquel go to the dealer   Yes, she can.
   with him?

3. Can he find very cheap cars?   No, he can't.

4. Can he bargain with the dealer?   Yes, he can.

5. Can he go for a test drive?   Yes, he can.

Questions and Long Answers

Answer these questions.

First, listen to the example:

Who can drive?   Jorge and Raquel can drive.

Now it's your turn.

1. Who can drive?   Jorge and Raquel can drive.

2. Who could pass the driver's test?   Jorge could pass the driver's test.

3. Where could Raquel go?   She could go to the car dealer.

4. What could Jorge look at?   He could look at used cars.

5. How much can Jorge spend?   He can spend less than $6,000.

Adjectives

Listen and repeat.

1. cheap

2. comfortable

3. expensive

4. fast

5. heavy

6. high

7. large

8. light

9. long

10. low

11. luxurious

12. new

13. old

14. pretty

15. short

16. simple

17. slow

18. small

19. ugly

20. uncomfortable

Comparative and Superlative

Say the comparative and superlative.

First, listen to the example:

| cheap | cheaper | cheapest |

Now it's your turn.

cheap	cheaper	cheapest
fast	faster	fastest
large	larger	largest
heavy	heavier	heaviest
pretty	prettier	prettiest

Again, listen to the example:

beautiful	more beautiful	most beautiful

Now it's your turn.

beautiful	more beautiful	most beautiful
comfortable	more comfortable	most comfortable
expensive	more expensive	most expensive
luxurious	more luxurious	most luxurious

Questions with *Which*

Answer these questions.

First, listen to the example:

Which car is faster, a Porsche or a Volkswagen?	A Porsche is faster than a Volkswagen.

Now it's your turn.

1. Which car is faster, a Porsche or a Volkswagen?

    A Porsche is faster than a Volkswagen.

2. Which car is more luxurious, a Rolls Royce or a Toyota?

    A Rolls Royce is more luxurious than a Toyota.

3. Which country is larger, Mexico or the Dominican Republic?

    Mexico is larger than the Dominican Republic.

4. Which country is smaller, Cuba or China?

    Cuba is smaller than China.

5. Which state in the U.S. is the largest?

    Alaska is the largest state.

Unit 7: Becoming a Citizen

Vocabulary

Listen and repeat.

1. alien
2. application
3. apply
4. birth certificate
5. citizenship
6. Constitution
7. court
8. dictation
9. employment authorization card
10. federal
11. fingerprints
12. government
13. green card
14. history
15. illegal
16. immigrant
17. interview
18. legal
19. marriage certificate
20. oral exam
21. presidents
22. registration card
23. residence

24. Revolutionary War

25. Social Security number

26. state

27. swearing-in ceremony

28. waiting period

29. written exam

Past Tense of Regular Verbs

Listen to the present tense and say the past tense.

The past tense of these verbs ends with a /t/ sound.

First, listen to the example:

    ask   asked

Now it's your turn.

1. ask   asked

2. announce   announced

3. help   helped

4. practice   practiced

5. talk   talked

The past tense of these verbs ends with a /d/ sound.

Listen to the example:

    apply   applied

Now it's your turn.

6. apply   applied

7. prepare   prepared

8. quiz   quizzed

| 9. receive | received |
| 10. study | studied |

The past tense of these verbs ends with an /ed/ sound.

Listen to the example:

| visit | visited |

Now it's your turn.

11. need	needed
12. start	started
13. submit	submitted
14. wait	waited
15. want	wanted

Questions and Answers

Answer these questions.

First, listen to the example:

| Who asked the questions? | Simon asked the questions. |

Now it's your turn.

1. Who asked the questions?	Simon asked the questions.
2. Who answered the questions?	Raquel answered the questions.
3. Who wanted to take an exam?	Raquel wanted to take an exam.
4. Who received a "green card"?	Sasha received a "green card."
5. What did Elena submit?	She submitted her papers.

Past Tense of Irregular Verbs

Listen to the present tense and say the past tense.

First, listen to the example:

begin   began

Now it's your turn.

1. begin   began
2. come   came
3. feel   felt
4. get   got
5. go   went
6. have   had
7. know   knew
8. read   read
9. say   said
10. see   saw
11. take   took
12. think   thought

Questions and Answers

Answer these questions.

First, listen to the example:

Who gave Raquel a quiz?   Simon gave her a quiz.

Now it's your turn.

1. Who gave Raquel a quiz?   Simon gave her a quiz.
2. How did Raquel feel?   She felt good.

3. Which test did Raquel take? She took the citizenship test.

4. Who went with her? Simon went with her.

5. How was the test? It wasn't difficult.

Short Answers

Answer these questions.

First, listen to the example:

Did Simon help Raquel? Yes, he did.

Now it's your turn.

1. Did Simon help Raquel? Yes, he did.

2. Did Elena take the test? No, she didn't.

3. Did Jorge and Sasha get their green cards? Yes, they did.

4. Did Raquel and Simon go to the ceremony? Yes, they did.

5. Were the classes expensive? No, they weren't.

How Long and How Often

Answer these questions.

First, listen to the example:

How long is the exam? (three hours long) It's three hours long.

How often are the classes? (every week) They're every week.

Now it's your turn.

1. How long is the exam? (three hours long) It's three hours long.

2. How often are the classes? (every week)   They're every week.

3. How long is the course? (six weeks long)   It's six weeks long.

4. How often are the exams? (every month)   They're every month.

5. How long are the interviews? (half an hour long)   They're half an hour long.

Health, Home, and Community

PART 3

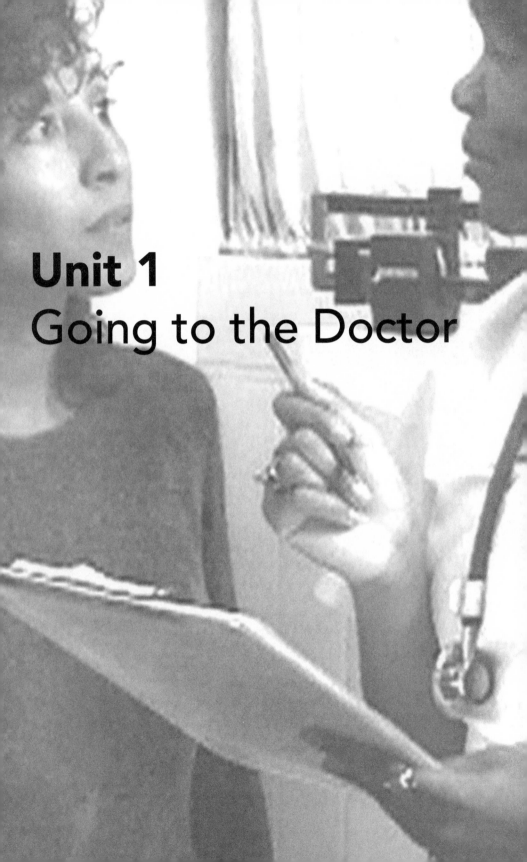

Unit 1
Going to the Doctor

A. What is it?

Fill in the missing vowels (A – E – I – O – U).

1. Symptoms:

H E A D A CH E

F __ V __ R

N __ __ S __ __

V __ M __ T __ NG

2. At the clinic:

__ PP __ __ NTM __ NT

N __ RS __

W __ __ T __ NG   R __ __ M

D __ CT __ R

3. Nurse's exam:

H __ __ GHT   W __ __ GHT

P __ LS __

T __ MP __ R __ T __ R __

BL __ __ D   PR __ SS __ R __

4. Doctor's exam:

__ __ RS   THR __ __ T

N __ S __

H __ __ RT

L __ NGS

5. At the lab:

BL __ __ D T __ ST

__ R __ N __ T __ ST

R __ S __ LTS

B. Verbs: Present Tense—*To Be*

Subject Pronouns

SINGULAR		PLURAL	

I

you

he

she

it

we

you

they

SINGULAR		PLURAL	
I	am	we	are
you	are	you	are
he	is	they	are
she	is	they	are
it	is	they	are

yesterday	today	tomorrow

present

Write the verbs in the sentences.

1. Simon and Raquel ___**are**___ at the International Center.

2. Raquel _____ Simon's wife.

3. Jorge and Elena _____ from Mexico.

4. Jorge _____ Elena's husband.

5. Ming _____ from China.

6. Sasha _____ from Russia.

7. The newspaper _____ on the table.

8. You _____ a teacher.

9. I _____ at home.

10. You _____ at school.

C. Contractions

I am = I'm	we are = we're
you are = you're	you are = you're
he is = he's	they are = they're
she is = she's	they are = they're
it is = it's	they are = they're

Write the contractions.

1. you are = _____   4. I am = _____

2. they are = _____   5. we are = _____

3. it is = _____   6. he is = _____

D. Negatives

Simon is a teacher.   He **is not** a nurse.

Raquel is a social worker.   She **is not** a doctor.

Elena is a cashier.   She **is not** a secretary.

I am not		**we are not**
you are not		**you are not**
he is not		**they are not**
she is not		**they are not**
it is not		**they are not**

Write the negative form of the verb.

1. I __**am not**__ at the International Center.

2. Simon and Raquel __**are not**__ at home.

3. Ming _____ nauseous.

4. Elena _____ well.

5. Sasha _____ from Mexico.

6. Jorge _____ at the doctor's office.

7. You _____ vomiting.

8. Elena and Jorge _____ from Russia.

9. We _____ in the waiting room.

10. The blood tests _____ ready.

E. Negative Contractions

I'm not	we're not / we aren't
you're not / you aren't	you're not / you aren't
he's not / he isn't	they're not / they aren't
she's not / she isn't	they're not / they aren't
it's not / it isn't	they're not / they aren't

Write the contractions.

1. he is not = __he isn't / he's not__

2. they are not = _____

3. we are not = _____

4. I am not = _____

5. you are not = _____

6. she is not = _____

F. Questions and Yes/No Answers

Jorge is at work. Is Jorge at work? Yes, he is.

Elena is at the clinic. Is Elena at home? No, she is not.

Write a short "yes" or "no" answer after the question.

1. Is Jorge at the clinic? __No, he is not.__

2. Is Elena at the clinic? __Yes, she is.__

3. Are Elena and Jorge from Mexico? _____

4. Is Sasha from China? _____

5. Is Simon from the United States? _____

Change the sentence to a question.

6. Raquel is with Elena.   **Is Raquel with Elena?**

7. You are at the center.   _____

8. Elena is with the doctor.   _____

9. They are in the lab.   _____

10. The results are ready.   _____

G. Short Answers

Who?

What?

Where?

Circle the correct short answer to the question.

1. **Who** is from China?   Ming is.

            Elena is.

2. **Where** are Jorge and Elena from?   From Venezuela.

            From Mexico.

3. **What** is in the lab?   The dogs are.

            The tests are.

4. **Where** is Simon from?   From the U.S.

            From the D.R.

5. **Who** is in the waiting room?   Sasha is.

            Raquel is.

6. **Where** is Jorge?   At the office.

                                           At home.

7. **What** is in the waiting room?   The lungs.

                                           The chairs.

8. **Who** is with Elena?   Simon is.

                                           Raquel is.

9. **Where** are the doctors?   At the clinic.

                                           At the center.

10. **Who** volunteers at the center?   Jorge and Elena.

                                           Simon and Raquel.

H. Question Words

*Write **Who**, **What**, or **Where** in the question.*

1. ____**Who**____ is at the International Center?
—Simon and Raquel are.

2. _____ is with Simon and Raquel?
—Jorge, Elena, Sasha, and Ming.

3. ____**What**____ is in the waiting room?
—The chairs are.

4. _____ is with you? —My friends are.

5. ____**Where**____ are the nurses? —At the clinic.

6. _____ does Sasha do? —He's a painter.

7. _____ are you? —At home.

8. _____ do you do? —I'm a student.

I. Parts of the Body

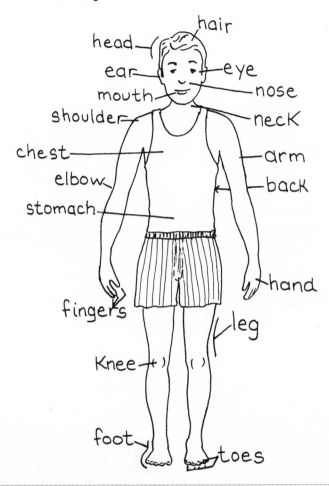

J. Verb Tense: Present Continuous

I	am ___ing	we	are ___ing
you	are ___ing	you	are ___ing
he	is ___ing	they	are ___ing
she	is ___ing	they	are ___ing
it	is ___ing	they	are ___ing

Remember the contractions: I am = I'm; you are = you're; etc.

yesterday   today   tomorrow

present continuous:
now
at the moment

Write the verbs in the sentences.

1. Elena __is feeling__ nauseous. (feel)

2. Raquel __is driving__ Elena to the clinic. (drive*)

3. They _____ about Elena's symptoms. (talk)

4. The nurse _____ Elena's temperature. (take*)

5. She _____ her about her blood pressure. (tell)

6. Elena _____ on the gown. (put*)

7. Dr. Summers _____ Elena questions. (ask)

8. He _____ to her answers. (listen)

9. Elena _____ with Raquel. (speak)

10. She _____ to the lab for tests. (go)

*Note: drive + ing = **driving**; take + ing = **taking**; put + ing = **putting**

K. Negatives

I	am not ___ing	we	are not ___ing
you	are not ___ing	you	are not ___ing
he/she/it	is not ___ing	they	are not ___ing

Write the negative form of the verb.

1. Elena __**is not working**__ today. (work)

2. Raquel _____ at the center. (stay)

3. Simon _____ a class at the center. (teach)

4. Jorge _____ at a restaurant. (eat)

5. The nurses _____ in the waiting room. (sit*)

6. I _____ now. (get up*)

7. You _____ dinner. (cook)

8. We _____ TV now. (watch)

9. The cat _____ on the chair. (sleep)

10. Raquel _____ for Ming. (wait)

*Note: sit + ing = **sitting**; get + ing = **getting**

L. Questions

Make the sentences from Exercise K into questions.

1. __**Is Elena working today?**__

2. _____

3. _____

4. _____

5. _____

6. _____

7. _____

8. _____

9. _____

10. _____

M. Yes/No Answers

Write a "yes" or "no" short answer after the question.

1. Is Elena talking to Raquel? **Yes, she is.**

2. Is Simon taking Elena to the clinic? **No, he isn't.**

3. Are Elena and Raquel sitting in the waiting room? **Yes,**

4. Is the nurse saying Raquel's name? **No,**

5. Is the nurse taking Elena's pulse? **Yes,**

6. Is the doctor examining Elena? **Yes,**

7. Is Jorge at the doctor's office? **No,**

8. Are the doctors waiting for Elena? **No,**

9. Is Elena going to the lab? **Yes,**

10. Are the test results coming in a few days? **Yes,**

N. Dialogue: Elena's News

Read the dialogue and choose the correct words.

Jorge: Hi, honey! Are _____**you**_____ feeling better?
         1. (you/they)

Elena: Yes, a little better. I went to the _____ with
         2. (center/clinic)
       Raquel today.

Jorge: What did the _____ say?
         3. (doctor/teacher)

Elena: He sent me to the _____ for some tests.
         4. (school/laboratory)

Jorge: What kind of _____ ?
5. (tests/classes)

Elena: _____ and urine tests.
6. (Blood/Heart)

Jorge: _____ wrong? Are you sick?
7. (Who's/What's)

Elena: I may be _____ .
8. (pregnant/vomiting)

Jorge: Really? You're going to have a _____ ?
9. (gown/baby)

Elena: Maybe. The test _____ are coming in a
10. (exams/results)
few days.

Jorge: I hope you _____ pregnant. I want to be a
11. (is/are)
_____ !
12. (father/mother)

O. Real People...Real Language

1. How often do you go to the doctor?

Underline the answer you hear.

a. once a month / <u>year</u>

b. very often / not very often

c. maybe once or twice a month / year

d. once a year / twice a year

2. Have you ever had an operation?

Circle the answer you hear.

a.   yes   (no)   tonsils

b.   yes   no   appendix

c.   yes   no   wisdom teeth

d.   yes   no   C-section (cesarean section)

3. Have you ever been in the hospital?

Circle the answer you hear.

a. (yes) no (broke my arm)

b. yes no had to get stitches

4. What kind of medical insurance do you have?

Underline the words you hear.

a. university heart/<u>health services</u>

b. medical/dental insurance

c. women's/workmen's compensation

d. Blue Cross–Blue Shield/blackbird co-payments are small

e. HMO/ANO $5.00 co-payment

VIDEO TRANSCRIPT

Watch and Listen

Raquel: So, how are you today, Elena?

Elena: I don't know...I don't feel very well.

Raquel: Oh, do you need to go to the clinic? I'm going right by there.

Elena: Yes, maybe I should.

Raquel: Come on. My car is right here. Come on.

Elena: This is so nice of you, Raquel.

Raquel: It's okay. Come on.

So, Elena, how long have you been feeling like this?

Elena: About a week. When I eat, I feel nauseous.

Raquel: Do you think it's a stomach virus?

Elena: No, I don't have a fever.

Raquel: Do you have a headache or any other symptoms?

Elena: No, and I only feel sick in the morning. Later in the day I feel fine.

Raquel: Well, I'm sure the doctor will know what's wrong.

(*At the doctor's office*)

Nurse: Elena Gonzalez?

Elena: Right here. I'll be back soon.

Nurse: Could you stand on the scale, please? I have to measure your height and your weight ...Okay, step back. You can sit down now. I have to take your temperature, your pulse, and your blood pressure.

Elena: How is my blood pressure?

Nurse: Oh, it's normal: one-ten over ninety. The doctor will be here in a few minutes. You can get undressed and put this gown on.

Doctor: Hello. I'm Dr. Summers.

Elena: Nice to meet you.

Doctor: So what seems to be the problem?

Elena: Well, I usually feel nauseous in the morning. Sometimes I try to eat breakfast, but I can't.

Doctor: Do you have any other symptoms—headache, fever, or vomiting?

Elena: Not really. I feel tired, but I work as a cashier, so I'm on my feet all day.

Doctor: Well, after I examine you, you can go to the lab for some tests. It doesn't sound too serious.

Raquel: Well, how did it go?

Elena: The doctor examined me.

Raquel: And...?

Elena: Well, he's not sure, but I may be pregnant.

Raquel: Oh, Elena, this is wonderful! What next?

Elena: Now I have to go for blood and urine tests.

Raquel: When will you get the test results?

Elena: In a few days.

Raquel: Oh, this is so exciting! After the tests, let's drive by Jorge's office.

Elena: He'll be so happy!

Raquel: Oh, I know.

Elena: I'd better get to the lab now.

Raquel: Congratulations! Isn't this wonderful? While I'm waiting for Elena, here are some phrases to remember from this lesson.

To introduce yourself, you say:

> **Hi, I'm** Raquel.   or
>
> **My name is** Raquel.

To answer, you say:

> **Nice to meet you.**   or
>
> **How do you do?**

Now let's listen to some people talk about going to the doctor.

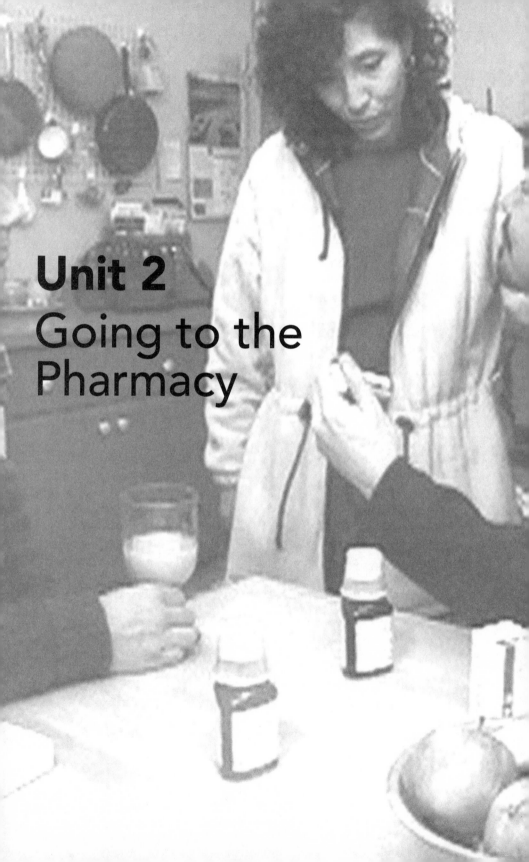

Unit 2
Going to the Pharmacy

A. What is it?

Write the illness below the picture.

1. _____ **cold** _____

2. _____

3. _____

4. _____

5. _____

6. _____

B. What is it used for?

Write the word below the picture.

1. To clean your teeth, you use ___**toothpaste**___.

2. To wash your hands, you use _____.

3. To wash your hair, you use
   _____ .

4. To make your hair soft,

   you use _____ .

C. Verbs: Present Simple

SINGULAR		PLURAL	
I	use	we	use
you	use	you	use
he/she/it	uses	they	use

yesterday   today   tomorrow

present
always
usually
sometimes
never

Also use the present simple tense with these words:

day	Mondays	March
every week	**on** weekends	**in** the winter
year	my birthday	the morning

319

Write the verbs in the sentences.

1. Elena _____ **needs** _____ to take some medicine. (need)

2. She _____ her medicine every day. (take)

3. The medicine _____ five dollars. (cost)

4. Cough syrup _____ your cough. (stop)

5. Nighttime cough syrup _____ you sleep. (help)

6. Jorge and Elena _____ dinner every night. (cook)

7. On weekends, they _____ with friends. (eat)

8. Sometimes, they _____ out to eat. (go)

9. Elena _____ in a supermarket. (work)

10. She _____ a discount on food. (get)

D. Negatives

I	do not ____	we	do not ____
you	do not ____	you	do not ____
he/she/it	does not ____	they	do not ____

Remember the contractions: I do not = I don't; he does not = he
doesn't; etc.

Write the negative form of the verb.

1. The pharmacist ___ **doesn't speak** ___ Spanish. (speak)

2. Sasha _____ in a pharmacy. (work)

3. Daytime cough syrup _____ you sleep. (help)

4. Jorge _____ shampoo and toothpaste. (buy)

5. Simon _____ a prescription filled. (get)

6. I _____ conditioner every day. (use)

7. Elena _____ any allergies. (have)

8. Simon _____ in the summer. (work)

9. Jorge _____ medicine every day. (take)

10. We _____ to take medicine. (need)

E. Questions and Yes/No Answers

Jorge works as an engineer.

Does Jorge **work** as an engineer?   Yes, he **does**.

Elena and her friends speak Spanish.

Do Elena and her friends **speak** Russian?   No, they **don't**.

Write a "yes" or "no" short answer after the question.

1. Does Elena work in a supermarket?   **Yes, she does.**

2. Do Jorge and Elena speak Chinese?   **No, they don't.**

3. Does Ming work at the center?   **No,** _____

4. Does Raquel work in an office?   **Yes,** _____

5. Does Simon teach English in high school?   **Yes,** _____

6. Does Sasha work in a restaurant?   **No,** _____

7. Does Ming work in a restaurant?   **Yes,** _____

8. Do Simon and Raquel eat lunch at home?   **No,** _____

9. Does Elena take her medicine every day?   **Yes,** _____

10. Do you watch the video before you write?   **Yes,** _____

F. Short Answers

Circle the correct answer.

1. Where is the pharmacy?   Near the center.

   Near the clinic.

2. Who needs a prescription filled?   Ming does.

   Elena does.

3. Who goes with Jorge?   Simon does.

   Raquel does.

4. What does Simon buy?   Toothpaste.

   Medicine.

5. Where do Jorge and Simon go?   To Simon's house.

   To Jorge's house.

6. Where do they sit?   In the kitchen.

   In the living room.

7. What does Simon drink?   Coffee.

   Juice.

8. Who comes home?   Elena does.

   Raquel does.

9. What does Jorge forget?   The medicine.

   Toothpaste and shampoo.

10. Who does Elena call?   Raquel.

    Sasha.

G. Questions

When?   How much?   How many?

*Write **When, How much,** or **How many** in the question.*

1. **When** is the pharmacy open? —From 8 A.M. to 10 P.M.

2. _____ tablets does Jorge get? —He gets fifty.

3. _____ tablets does Elena take? —Two each day.

4. _____ does she take them? —At breakfast and dinner.

5. _____ do the tablets cost? —Only $5.00.

6. _____ does Raquel arrive for dinner? —About six o'clock.

7. _____ do Simon and Raquel leave? —About eight o'clock.

8. _____ aspirin does Jorge take? —Two aspirin.

9. _____ does he take the cough medicine? —At night.

10. _____ spoonfuls of cough medicine does he take? —Only one.

H. Number Practice

Practice saying these numbers.

1 one	11 eleven	21 twenty-one	40 forty
2 two	12 twelve	22 twenty-two	50 fifty
3 three	13 thirteen	23 twenty-three	60 sixty
4 four	14 fourteen	24 twenty-four	70 seventy
5 five	15 fifteen	25 twenty-five	80 eighty
6 six	16 sixteen	26 twenty-six	90 ninety
7 seven	17 seventeen	27 twenty-seven	100 one hundred
8 eight	18 eighteen	28 twenty-eight	101 one hundred-one
9 nine	19 nineteen	29 twenty-nine	200 two hundred
10 ten	20 twenty	30 thirty	1,000 one thousand

A.M. *from 12:00 midnight to 12:00 noon*
P.M. *from 12:00 noon to 12:00 midnight*

I. Telling Time

Write the time in numbers.

What time is it?

1. __1:10__ 2. _____ 3. _____ 4. _____

What's the time?

5. _____ 6. _____ 7. _____ 8. _____

Do you have the time?

9. _____ 10. _____ 11. _____ 12. _____

Write the time in letters.

1. **It's one-ten.** _____ 7. _____

2. _____ 8. _____

3. _____ 9. _____

4. _____ 10. _____

5. _____ 11. _____

6. _____ 12. _____

J. Days of the Week

Say the days on the calendar.

APRIL						
SUNDAY	MONDAY	TUESDAY	WEDNESDAY	THURSDAY	FRIDAY	SATURDAY
			1	2	3	4
5	6	7	8	9	10	11
12	13	14	15	16	17	18
19	20	21	22	23	24	25
26	27	28	29	30		

4/2	3:30 Doctor's appointment—Elena
4/6	7:00 Dinner at Simon and Raquel's house
4/11	11:15 Dentist appointment—Jorge
4/22	2:00 Concert—"Sol y Luna"
4/30	6:45 Immigration meeting—International Center

Write the day and the time of the appointment.

1. When is Elena's doctor appointment?

   On **Thursday**, April second, at **3:30**.

2. When is dinner at Simon and Raquel's house?

   On ——————, April sixth, at ———.

3. When is Jorge's dentist appointment?

   On ——————, April eleventh, at ———.

4. When is the "Sol y Luna" concert?

   On ——————, April twenty-second at ———.

5. When is the Immigration meeting?

   On ——————, April thirtieth, at ———.

K. Dialogue: Dinner with Simon and Raquel

Read the dialogue and choose the correct words.

JORGE: I hear the doorbell. _____**Raquel**_____ is here.
1. (Raquel/Elena)

ELENA: _____ you let her in?
2. (Can/Do)

JORGE: Of course. Hi, Raquel! How are _____?
3. (she/you)

RAQUEL: Fine, _____, Jorge. And you?
4. (thanks/please)

JORGE: Just _____. Can I take your jacket?
5. (bad/fine)

RAQUEL: _____, please.
6. (Yes/No)

SIMON: Hi, honey. _____ was your day?
7. (What/How)

RAQUEL: Busy. A lot of people came to the _____.
8. (school/office)

SIMON: I had a busy day with my _____, too.
9. (students/teachers)

JORGE: _____ you like some beer or wine, Raquel?
10. (Do/Would)

RAQUEL: A glass of wine would be _____.
11. (good/bad)

JORGE: Here you are. _____ is almost ready.
12. (Lunch/Dinner)

RAQUEL: Thank _____ so much for inviting us.
13. (you/I)

JORGE: Don't mention it. _____ and I enjoy having you.
14. (Simon/Elena)

ELENA: Okay, dinner _____ ready!
15. (are/is)

JORGE: Come on, Simon and Raquel. Let's _____!
16. (eat/drink)

L. Real People...Real Language

1. Where do you get your prescriptions filled?

Draw a line under the word you hear.

a. at a   nearby/neighborhood pharmacy

b. at a   medicine /medical center pharmacy

c. at a   local/low-cost pharmacy

d. at a   local/low-cost drugstore

2. How often do you take medicine?

Check the answer you hear.

a. ( ) I take medicine every day   (✔) I don't take medicine

b. ( ) during spring and late summer ( ) during fall and late winter

c. ( ) every week   ( ) every day

d. ( ) only if I'm sick   ( ) only if I'm well

3. What do you usually buy at the pharmacy or drugstore?

Circle the words you hear.

a. (toothpaste)   shampoo   (nail polish)   conditioner

b. aspirin   cough medicine decongestant candy

c. film   soap   moisturizer   paper products

d. medication   toothbrushes   toothpaste   deodorant

e. hairspray   hair coloring cards   aspirin

f. cold drinks   cold remedies cough syrup   gum

4. Besides taking medicine, what else do you do when you're sick?

Underline the words you hear.

a. eat better, drink more/less tea, and more/less soup

b. stay at work / in bed

c. try to work/sleep, drink a little / a lot of orange juice, get as little/as much rest as I can

5. Some people don't believe in taking medicine. What do you think about that?

Check the answer you hear.

a. medicines can be very damaging (✔) to the body ( ) to the mind

b. the body naturally ( ) feels ( ) heals

c. taking medicine is ( ) important ( ) not important

d. I prefer ( ) homemade ( ) homeopathic remedies

VIDEO TRANSCRIPT

Watch and Listen

Jorge: Come on in, Simon. Have a seat.

Simon: Oh, thanks.

Jorge: Do you want some coffee or juice?

Simon: Oh, juice would be great.

Jorge: I'll be right there.

Simon: Okay, no hurry. Do you want me to take a look at Elena's medicine?

Jorge: Oh, yes, please do.

Simon: Oh, thank you. Let's see… one tablet twice a day with meals.

Jorge: When should Elena take it?

Simon: At breakfast and dinner.

Jorge: That's easy to remember.

Simon: How much did those capsules cost anyway?

Jorge: The copayment was only five dollars.

Simon: That's not much. Usually that medicine costs a lot more.

Jorge: I know, but my insurance is expensive. What did you get there?

Simon: Oh, some cough and cold remedies for Raquel.

Jorge: You know, I have a headache. I think I'm catching a cold, too.

Simon: Oh, here. Have some aspirin. That's good for headaches, muscle pain, and fever.

Jorge: What do you recommend for a cough?

Simon: Oh, this cough medicine is very good. It really stops the cough.

Jorge: What about this one?

Simon: Oh, no, that helps you sleep. You take that at night.

Jorge: This is probably what I need.

Simon: Oh, well, then take it. We have some at home.

Jorge: Oh, thank you.

Simon: You're welcome.

Jorge: I think Elena is coming. Elena, we're in the kitchen!

Elena: Oh, hi, Simon! Hi, honey.

Jorge: You know, we're back from the pharmacy. I just got your prescription filled. Here's your medicine.

Simon: The pharmacist says to take one capsule twice a day with meals.

Elena: Thanks, Simon. Did you remember to get my shampoo and toothpaste?

Jorge: I'm sorry, I forgot.

Elena: That's okay. I'll get them tomorrow.

Simon: Well, I'd better get going. It's my turn to make dinner tonight.

Jorge: Why don't you just join us for dinner?

Elena: I'll call Raquel and ask her to come over.

Jorge: And I'll start the salad.

Simon: Sounds good to me. While dinner's cooking, let's go over some phrases from this lesson.

When you offer something to someone, you say:

> **Can I get you some** juice?   or

> **Would you like some** coffee?

People might reply:

No, thanks.   or

Yes, please.   or

Juice **would be good.** or

Coffee **would be fine.**

When you need to say you're sorry, you say:

Sorry.   or

Pardon me.   or

Excuse me.

People might respond like this:

It's okay.   or

That's all right.   or

Don't worry about it.

Now let's listen to some other people talk about pharmacies or drugstores.

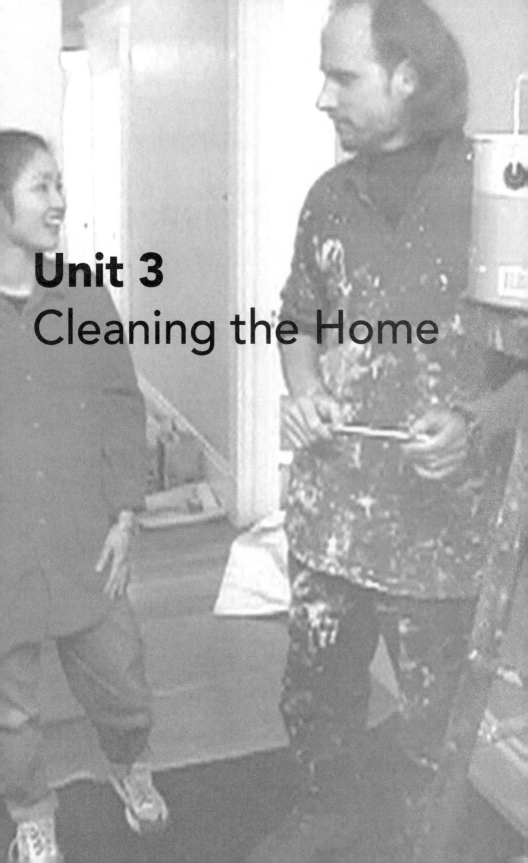

Unit 3
Cleaning the Home

A. Where do you use it?

Unscramble the words.

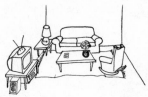

To paint the living room, you need _____ paint _____ ,
1. NTIPA

a _____ , and a _____ .
2. SNIBARTUPH   3. ELLROR

To clean the bathroom, you use _____ ,
4. CLAHEB

_____ cleaner, and a _____ .
5. LIET DNA BTU   6. GONEPS

To clean in the kitchen, you use dishwashing _____ ,
7. DILUIQ

oven _____ , and floor _____ .
8. NEARLEC   9. HOSPIL

334

B. What should you do?

Circle the correct answer.

1. If you inhale fumes, open the (window)/bottle.

2. Turn on the light/fan to blow out the vapors.

3. If you feel faint/paint or dizzy/busy call a doctor.

4. Use the television/telephone to call.

5. Read the label/results before you use cleaning products.

C. Verbs: Future with *Will/Won't*

I	will/won't	we	will/won't
you	will/won't	you	will/won't
he/she/it	will/won't	they	will/won't

Remember the contractions: will not = won't; will='ll.

yesterday   today   tomorrow

future:
tomorrow
next week/month/year
in a week/month/year

*Write **will** or **won't** in the sentences.*

1. Tomorrow, Elena _____ **will** _____ go to Ming's apartment to clean.

2. Jorge _____ **won't** _____ go to Ming's apartment to clean.

3. Sasha _____ help Ming, too.

4. First, he _____ paint the living room.

5. Then, he _____ paint the bedroom.

6. Ming _____ clean the kitchen.

7. She _____ clean the bathroom.

8. Elena _____ clean the bathroom.

9. She _____ clean the kitchen.

10. She _____ use oven cleaner for the stove.

D. Yes/No Answers

Write a "yes" or "no" short answer after the question.

1. Will Elena and Sasha help Ming? **Yes, they will.**

2. Will Raquel and Simon help Ming? **No,**

3. Will Elena clean the kitchen? **Yes,**

4. Will Ming clean the bathroom? **Yes,**

5. Will Sasha paint the apartment? **Yes,**

*Write **Will** in the question, and write a short answer.*

6. **Will** Jorge polish the floors? **No, he won't.**

7. _____ Elena inhale the vapors? **Yes,**

8. _____ she feel dizzy and faint? **Yes,**

9. _____ Ming call her doctor? **No,**

10. _____ Sasha take her home? **No,**

E. Questions

Draw a line to the correct affirmative or negative short answer.

1. Where will Sasha and Elena go today?   a. Ming.

2. Who will they help?   b. To Ming's apartment.

3. What kind of work will Sasha do?   c. Lie down on the bed.

4. What kind of work will Elena do?   d. She'll inhale the vapors.

5. What kind of work will Ming do?   e. Ming will.

6. Why will Elena faint?   f. Clean the kitchen.

7. Who will Sasha call?   g. In a few minutes.

8. What will Elena do?   h. He'll paint.

9. When will Jorge come?   i. Clean the bathroom.

10. Who will finish the oven?   j. Elena's doctor.

F. Plurals

Add "s" to a noun to make it plural: fan + s = fans.

 roller    rollers

 fan   fans

337

Give the plurals.

	Singular (=1)	Plural (>1)
1.	fan	**fans**
2.	room	
3.	sponge	
4.	window	
5.	bed	
6.	gown	
7.	ear	
8.	doctor	
9.	cleaner	
10.	oven	

G. More Question Words

Write the question words in the questions.

How much   money?   time?   work?

1. __**How much**__ money does Ming pay for rent?
—$800 a month.

2. _____ time does Sasha paint?
—Six hours.

3. _____ work does Elena do?
—Only a little.

How many   dollars?   hours?   years?

4. __**How many**__ dollars per hour does Sasha make?
—$8 per hour.

5. _____ hours does he work in the hardware store?
—12 hours on the weekends.

6. _____ years does he want to work there?

—2 years.

H. Money

  dollar   quarter   dime   nickel   penny

Sasha, Ming, and Elena went shopping at a hardware store. How much money did they spend?

1. Sasha

City Hardware	
• brushes	$ 5.97
• rollers	$ 7.59
• paint	$35.99
Subtotal	$49.55
10% disc. -	$ 4.96
Total	$44.59
Cash	$50.00

2. Ming

City Hardware	
• bleach	$ 1.59
• tile & tub	$ 2.79
• 3 sponges	$ 1.59
• 2 fans	$39.98
• floor polish	$ 2.99
Total	
Cash	$50.00

3. Elena

City Hardware	
• dish soap	$ 1.29
• oven cleaner	$ 2.99
• towels	$ 5.98
• detergent	$ 3.99
• lightbulbs	$ 1.99
Total	
Cash	$20.00

How much change did they get from the cashier?

4.  _____

5. _____

6.  _____

339

I. Count and Noncount Nouns

How many?   How much?

Here are some words to use with count and noncount nouns.

HOW MANY?		HOW MUCH?	
a	roller	_____	paint
some a few a lot of many	rollers	some a little a lot of much	paint
no not many	rollers	no not much	paint

Write the items from Sasha's, Ming's, and Elena's lists.

1. some/a few/a lot of/many:

brushes

rollers

_____

_____

_____

_____

_____

2. some/a little/a lot of/much:

paint

_____

_____

_____

_____

_____

_____

J. Questions and Answers

Underline the best answer.

1. How many brushes did Sasha buy? (4)

   <u>A few brushes.</u>   Many brushes.

2. How much oven cleaner did Elena inhale?

   A little oven cleaner.   A lot of oven cleaner.

3. How many fans did Ming buy? (2)

   A few fans.   A lot of fans.

4. How much money did Elena spend?

   A little money.   A lot of money.

5. How many sponges did Ming buy? (3)

   A few sponges.   Many sponges.

*Write **How much** or **How many** in the question. Underline the answer.*

6. ____**How much**____ paint did Sasha get?

   A little paint.   <u>A lot of paint.</u>

7. _____ bulbs did Elena buy?

   A few bulbs.   A lot of bulbs.

8. _____ cleaner did Ming get?

   Some cleaner.   A lot of cleaner.

9. _____ towels did Elena buy?

   A few towels.   Many towels.

10. _____ polish did Ming get?

   A little polish.   A lot of polish.

K. Real People...Real Language

1. What did you have to do when you moved into your new apartment?

Circle the answers you hear.

a. a little work (a lot of work) (paint and clean) floors and walls

b. very little   very much   apt. was clean   apt. was dirty

c. painting   cleaning   cleaning   a lot of
                     the walls   the floors   cleaning

d. cleaning   painting   arranging   nothing
                                       the furniture

2. How often do you clean your house?

Underline the answer you hear.

a. once a day   once a week   once a month

b. Fridays   Saturdays   Sundays

c. once every one or two weeks   once every one or two months

3. What products do you use to clean your house?

Circle the answers you hear.

a. tile cleaner in the   (bathroom/kitchen/hall

    mild soap on the floor in   bathroom/kitchen/bedroom

    glass cleaner on   glass/sink/shiny surfaces

b. disinfectant soap on   bathroom/kitchen/living room
    floors

c. Ajax and Lestoil on   bathroom/kitchen/dining room
    tiles

d. bleach on   counters/toilet/everything except floors

e. detergent with ammonia on   walls/floors

4. Have you or anyone you know been ill from those cleaners?

Underline the answer you hear.

a. yes   <u>no</u>

b. yes   no   use gloves   don't inhale fumes

c. yes   no

5. Where do you store cleaners and other chemical products?

Circle the answers you hear.

a. in a closet   (in a cabinet)   (with a child safety lock)

b. under the kitchen sink   under the table   under the bathroom sink

c. out of reach of son/daughter   put a lock on the door

VIDEO TRANSCRIPT

Watch and Listen

Ming: All set!

Sasha: Okay, great. I really like these colors, Ming. Your apartment will look great.

Ming: Oh, my cousin and I were lucky. My uncle's house was too small for all of us.

Elena: I'll clean the kitchen, okay?

Ming: Fine. I'll do the bathroom.

Sasha: And I'll paint the bedroom!

Elena: See, Ming— you're even getting a professional job.

Ming: Hey, Elena, how's it going?

Elena: I don't feel very well.

Ming: What's the matter?

Elena: I feel dizzy.

Ming: Sasha— can you come here?

Sasha: What's the matter?

Ming: Elena fainted. Maybe she inhaled the oven cleaner.

Sasha: What should we do?

Ming: Open the windows and turn on the fan. We need some fresh air.

Sasha: How is she?

Ming: I think she's all right now.

Elena: What happened?

Ming: You fainted. There wasn't enough ventilation in the kitchen.

Sasha: These cleaning products may be dangerous. See? Some of them are poisonous.

Ming: Yes, we should have read the label first.

Sasha: Should we take Elena to the emergency room?

Ming: No, I think she's all right, but let's give her doctor a call.

Elena: No, no. I'm all right now. I'm okay.

Ming: But you're pregnant and these vapors are not good for you—or the baby.

Sasha: She's right, Elena. Let's just call and see what he says, okay?

Elena: You're right. I want to make sure my baby is all right.

Sasha: Where's the number?

Elena: The doctor's number is in my bag. And maybe you could call Jorge, too.

Sasha: The doctor says you should go home and rest, Elena, but if you feel dizzy again, you should call him. And Jorge is coming right over to pick you up.

Elena: Okay.

Ming: Please take care of yourself, Elena.

Elena: I will. I promise.

Sasha: Why don't you go lie down until Jorge gets here?

Elena: Okay.

Raquel: Don't worry—Elena is fine now. Here are some phrases to remember from this lesson.

When something could happen, you can say:

> You **may** feel dizzy if you don't open the windows.   or

> Elena **might** feel better if she rests.

When something will probably happen, you can say:

> Jorge's office **must** be close. He came over right away.   or

> Sasha **must** be a good painter. Ming's apartment looks beautiful.

Now let's listen to some other people talk about their houses or apartments.

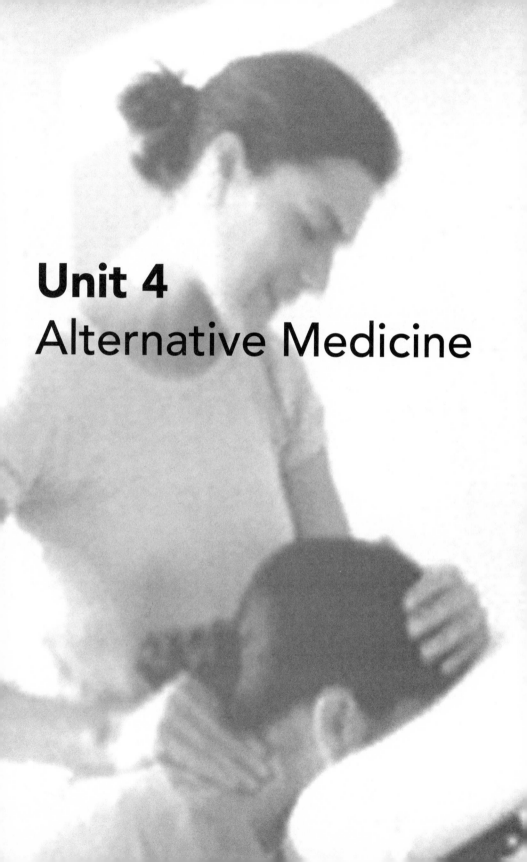

Unit 4
Alternative Medicine

A. What is it?

Unscramble the letters and write the missing word.

RSESTS

1. Some people feel _____**stress**_____ in their lives.

GOAY

2. _____ eases tension.

SAMESAG

3. _____ relaxes the muscles.

TIED

4. A good _____ is also helpful.

TANREEGVIA

5. A _____ eats vegetables, fruits, and grains.

HATLEH

6. _____ food keeps us healthy.

PACUTUNECRU

7. _____ is part of Chinese medicine.

B. Verbs: Present Tense—*Can/Can't*

He **can lift** the suitcase.   She **can't lift** the suitcase.

I	can/can't	we	can/can't
you	can/can't	you	can/can't
he/she/it	can/can't	they	can/can't

Remember the contraction: cannot = **can't**.

yesterday   today   tomorrow

present

Write can or can't in the sentences.

1. Dr. Huang ____can____ give acupuncture treatments.

2. Ming ____can't____ give acupuncture treatments.

3. Dr. Huang _____ see Simon and Sasha today.

4. She _____ explain the chart to them.

5. They _____ stay for a treatment.

6. Sasha _____ paint houses.

7. He _____ teach English.

8. Simon _____ teach English.

9. He _____ teach Russian.

10. He _____ lift heavy boxes because he hurt his back.

C. Questions: *Can/Can't*

Sasha **can paint** houses.   **Can** Sasha **paint** houses?
Yes, he **can**.

Simon **can't teach** Russian.   **Can** Simon **teach** Russian?
No, he **can't**.

Write Can in the questions. Give short "yes" or "no" answers.

1. _____ Elena work as a cashier?   **Yes,** _____

2. _____ she work as an engineer?   **No,** _____

3. _____ Jorge work as an engineer?   **Yes,** _____

4. _____ Dr. Huang help people?   **Yes,** _____

5. _____ you do yoga?   **No,** _____

D. Question Words: *What kind/type/sort of?*

What kind of food does Ming cook? —**Chinese** food.

Draw a line from the question to the answer.

1. What kind of food
   does Raquel cook?   Clean needles.

2. What type of work
   does Jorge do?   Social work.

3. What sort of medicine
   does Dr. Huang practice?   Light exercise.

4. What kind of needles
   does she use?   Dominican food.

5. What type of remedies
   does she advise?   He's an engineer.

6. What sort of exercise
   does Simon do?   Engineering classes.

7. What kind of classes
   does Ming take?   He's an English teacher.

8. What type of classes
   does Jorge take?   Bookkeeping classes.

9. What sort of work
   does Raquel do?   Alternative medicine.

10. What kind of work
    does Simon do?   Herbal remedies.

E. Adjectives: Opposites

cheap	≠	expensive
($1.50)	≠	($1,500)
clean	≠	dirty
fast	≠	slow
funny	≠	serious
healthy	≠	unhealthy
large	≠	small
light	≠	heavy
new	≠	old
relaxed	≠	tense
same	≠	different
short	≠	tall

Draw a line through the words that are not correct.

1. Ming is   short.   ~~tall.~~

2. Her apartment is   new.   old.

3. It is   dirty.   clean.

4. The rent is   cheap.   expensive.

5. Sasha is   short.   tall.

6. He is a   fast   slow   painter.

7. He can lift   light   heavy   boxes.

8. He usually eats   healthy   unhealthy   food.

9. Simon usually eats   healthy   unhealthy   food.

10. He is usually   relaxed.   tense.

F. Adjectives: Comparative and Superlative

| Superlative | Comparative | Adjective | Comparative | Superlative |

least   less   more   most
-est   -er   -er   -est

Use the **comparative** when comparing **two** things or people.
Use the **superlative** when comparing **three or more** things or people.

Jorge is taller than Ming.   Sasha is taller than Jorge.

Sasha is tallest of the three.

Fill in the chart with the comparative and superlative forms.

	ADJECTIVE	COMPARATIVE (+/-)	SUPERLATIVE (+++/- - -)
1.	cheap	cheaper	cheapest
2.	clean		
3.	new		
4.	old		
5.	healthy*	healthier	healthiest
6.	heavy*		
7.	funny*		
8.	expensive $$$	more expensive $$$$ less expensive $$	most expensive $$$$$ least expensive $
9.	relaxed		
10.	serious		

*y + er = ier; y + est = iest
Note: good → better → best; bad → worse → worst

G. Sentences with Comparatives

Sasha wants to eat lunch. Which restaurant will he choose?

Veggie Delight

Burger World

Pasta di Roma

- Est. 1999
- $8.25
- small
- healthy
- relaxed

- Est. 1972
- $10.00
- large
- unhealthy
- relaxed

- Est. 1993
- $14.95
- medium
- healthy
- serious

Write the comparative in the sentences.

1. Burger World is _____**older**_____ than Veggie Delight.
   (old)

2. Veggie Delight is _____ than Burger World.
   (new)

3. Burger World is _____ than Veggie Delight
   and Pasta di Roma. (large)

4. Veggie Delight is _____ than Pasta di Roma.
   (small)

5. Burger World is **more expensive** than Veggie Delight,
   but **less expensive** than Pasta di Roma. (expensive)

6. Veggie Delight is _____ than Burger World.
   (cheap)

7. The food at Veggie Delight is _____ than
   the food at Burger World. (healthy)

8. The food at Burger World is _____ than the
   food at Pasta di Roma. (healthy)

9. The atmosphere at Pasta di Roma is _____ than at Veggie Delight. (relaxed)

10. The waiters at Pasta di Roma are _____ than the waiters at Burger World. (serious)

H. Sentences with Superlatives

Write the superlative in the sentences.

1. Veggie Delight is the ___**newest**___ restaurant of all. (new)

2. Pasta di Roma is the _____ one of all. (expensive)

3. Burger World is the _____ one of all. (large)

4. Burger World is the _____ one of all. (unhealthy)

5. Veggie Delight is the _____ one of all. (small)

I. Questions: *Which/Which one*

The **fast-food restaurant** is old.	The **vegetarian one** is new.
Which restaurant is the oldest?	The **fast-food one.**
Which one is the newest?	The **vegetarian one.**

(restaurant = one)

*Write **Which** or **Which one** in the question.*

1. ___**Which**___ restaurant is the least expensive?

2. ___**Which one**___ is the most expensive?

3. _____ restaurant is newer?

4. _____ is older?

5. _____ restaurant is cleaner?

6. _____ is dirtier?

7. _____ restaurant has the heaviest food?

8. _____ has the lightest food?

9. _____ restaurant is larger?

10. _____ is smaller?

J. Sasha's New Diet: Veggie Stir-Fry

Add vowels (A-E-I-O-U-) to the words in Sasha's recipe.

1. a cup of P **A** S T **A**   5. one C __ R R __ T

2. 4 cups of W __ T __ R   6. a small __ N __ __ N

3. some red and green P __ P P __ RS 7. a little G __ R L __ C

4. a little olive __ __ L   8. some S __ L T and P __ P P __ R

• Cut the carrot, peppers, onion, and garlic into small pieces.

• Boil the water in a pot. Add the pasta and boil for ten minutes.

• Heat the frying pan and pour in the oil.

• Fry the carrot first, then add peppers, onion, and garlic.

• Stir the vegetables in the pan for a few minutes.

• Drain the pasta and put on a plate. Put the vegetables on top of the pasta.

• Add cheese and salt and pepper to taste. (optional)

• Enjoy your veggie stir-fry!

K. Dialogue: On the Telephone

Write the correct word.

MING: Hello?

SASHA: Hello, Ming. This is ___**Sasha**___ .
1. (Sasha/Simon)

MING: Oh, hi, Sasha!

SASHA: Thank _____ for telling me about
2. (me/you)
your aunt.

MING: Did you go to her _____ ?
3. (office/house)

SASHA: Yes, I went with Simon last _____ .
4. (year/week)

MING: _____ did you do there?
5. (Who/What)

SASHA: First your _____ asked us questions.
6. (aunt/uncle)
Then we had a treatment.

MING: To stop _____ ?
7. (drinking/smoking)

SASHA: Yes, and Simon had one for his _____ .
8. (headache/backache)

MING: That's great. How do you _____ ?
9. (feel/do)

SASHA: I haven't smoked any cigarettes since the

_____ .
10. (interview/treatment)

MING: Really?

SASHA: And I'm eating better, too. I'm learning to

_____ .
11. (cook/shop)

MING: _____ learning to cook? I can't believe it!
12. (I'm/You're)

SASHA: Yes, I'll invite you and your cousin to

_____ some day.
13. (dinner/a movie)

MING: Great! Well, I have to go to work _____.
14. (later/now)

SASHA: Okay. _____ you soon.
15. (See/Hear)

MING: _____, Sasha!
16. (Bye/Hi)

L. Real People...Real Language

1. Are you a healthy person?

Circle the words you hear.

a. (very healthy)   not so healthy

b. as healthy as I'd like to be   not as healthy as I'd like to be

c. healthy but underweight   healthy but overweight

d. I'm a healthy person   I'm an unhealthy person

2. What kind of food do you eat?

Underline the words you hear.

a. food that doesn't contain a lot of   fat   catfish

b. a lot of vegetables and   fresh meat   fresh fruit

c. a lot of rice and beans with seafood, poultry   pasta

d. I eat fresh vegetables,   fish   tofu

e. I limit my intake of   cheese   fatty
                                                     products

3. Do you exercise?

Cross out the words you don't hear.

a. step aerobics   weight training   jogging

b. run to work   walk to work

c. run   work out in the gym   play basketball

d. walk   swim   practice karate

e. jog once a week   gym three times a week

4. Have you ever tried acupuncture or another form of alternative medicine?

*Circle **no** or **yes** and the alternative treatment you hear.*

a. (no)   yes   shiatsu   Jacuzzi

b. no   yes   technology   reflexology

c. no   yes   tai chi   tae kwon do

d. no   yes   acupuncture   chiropractor

e. no   yes   massage   acupuncture

5. Have you ever done yoga or meditation?

*Underline **yes** or **no** and the words you hear.*

a. no   yes   yoga   meditation   self-hypnosis

b. no   yes   yoga   meditation   self-hypnosis

c. no   yes   yoga   meditation   self-hypnosis

d. no   yes   yoga   meditation   self-hypnosis

VIDEO TRANSCRIPT

Watch and Listen

Simon: Dr. Huang, I'm Simon Bradford. And this is Sasha Tarlovsky. Ming sent us to see you.

Sasha: How do you do, Doctor?

Dr. Huang: Nice to meet you both. Ming has told me a lot about you and your wife at the International Center. And you painted Ming's apartment. Thank you.

Sasha: It was nothing.

Dr. Huang: So, what brings you here?

Simon: Well, when I was helping Ming move, I hurt my back lifting some heavy boxes. She said you could help me.

Sasha: And I'd like to try to quit smoking. Ming said there's an acupuncture treatment for that.

Dr. Huang: There's a treatment for everything. This chart explains the procedure.

Simon: So you put needles into the body to help people feel better.

Dr. Huang: Exactly. A treatment can last for a month or longer.

Sasha: So I can stop smoking if I get acupuncture?

Dr. Huang: Yes, I'll also tell you what to eat and what else to do. What kind of food do you eat?

Sasha: Well, when I'm working, I usually eat fast food. I know it's not good for me.

Dr. Huang: No, it's not.

Sasha: But my mother cooks me good food on weekends.

Dr. Huang: How is your diet, Simon?

Simon: We have lots of great Dominican food—rice, beans, and vegetables. We usually have fish instead of meat.

Dr. Huang: That's good. What type of medicine do you take when you're sick?

Simon: I usually get something from the drugstore.

Dr. Huang: Well, I recommend herbs. There are herbs for all sorts of illnesses— coughs, colds, and fevers.

Simon: I see.

Dr. Huang: Do you get much exercise?

Sasha: I paint houses, so I get lots of exercise.

Simon: I have to admit I don't get that much.

Dr. Huang: Exercise and relaxation like yoga or meditation are good.

Simon: Well, I'd like to try acupuncture for my back.

Sasha: And I'd like to try it to quit smoking.

Dr. Huang: All right. I can give you the first treatment now if you have time.

Simon: I do. What about you, Sasha?

Sasha: Me, too.

Dr. Huang: You can go in there and change.

Simon: While Sasha's changing, here are a few phrases to remember from this lesson.

To talk about where to go for health care, you can say:

> **There is** an acupuncturist near my house. **Is there** one near yours?

> or

> **There are** seven hospitals in my city. **Are there** many in yours?

To get information, you can ask:

> **What kind** of food do you eat?   or

> **What type** of medicine do you take?   or

> **What sort** of exercise do you recommend?

You might hear answers like these:

> I eat **all kinds of food.**   or

> I take **homeopathic medicine.**   or

> I recommend **biking.**

Now let's listen to some people talk about their health.

Unit 5
Reporting a Crime

A. What is it?

Write the word.

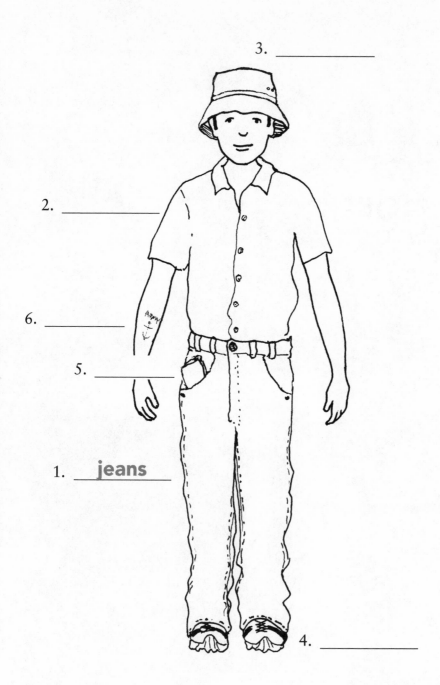

3. _____

2. _____

6. _____

5. _____

1.   **jeans**   _____

4. _____

B. Odd One Out

Cross out the word that does not go with the other words.

1. tall   thin   old   sign
2. jeans   bank card   T-shirt   dress
3. wallet   cash   paycheck   sneakers
4. subway   train   young   token
5. license   short   credit card bank card
6. steal   crime   suit   mugged
7. young   short   fat   cash
8. sneakers   tattoo   hat   shirt
9. police   station   subway   report
10. suit   jacket   pants   help

C. Verbs: Simple Past—Regular

_____+ed

I	reported	we	reported
you	reported	you	reported
he/she/it	reported	they	reported

yesterday   today   tomorrow

past:
yesterday
last week/month/year
a long time ago
in 1960

Write the verbs in the past tense.

1. cancel __**canceled**__

2. describe* _____

3. grab* _____

4. happen _____

5. look _____

6. offer _____

7. remember _____

8. sign _____

9. stop* _____

10. talk _____

*Note: describe + ed = **described**;

grab + ed = **grabbed**;

stop + ed = **stopped**

Now write the verbs in the sentences.

1. Jorge's boss __**canceled**__ his paycheck.

2. Jorge _____ the man to the police officer.

3. The man _____ Jorge's wallet.

4. This _____ in the subway station.

5. Jorge _____ for Raquel at the center.

6. Raquel _____ to take him to the police station.

7. Jorge _____ the man's tattoo.

8. He _____ the police report.

9. Raquel _____ at the ATM to get money for Jorge.

10. She _____ to Jorge about the crime.

D. Negatives

I	did not ___	we	did not ___
you	did not ___	you	did not ___
he/she/it	did not ___	they	did not ___

Remember the contraction: did not = **didn't.**

Write the subject pronouns and the negative form of the verbs in Exercise C.

1. _____ **He didn't cancel** _____ Jorge's driver's license.

2. _____ the man to Raquel.

3. _____ Jorge's passport.

4. _____ at the bus station.

5. _____ for Raquel at her office.

6. _____ to take him to the fire station.

7. _____ the man's face.

8. _____ his paycheck.

9. _____ at the supermarket to get food.

10. _____ to Jorge about the news.

E. Questions and Yes/No Answers

A man **grabbed** Jorge's wallet.

Did a man **grab** Jorge's wallet?   Yes, he **did.**

Did a woman **grab** Jorge's wallet? No, she **didn't.**

Circle the correct short answer for the questions.

1. Did people try to stop the man?

   (Yes, they did.)   No, they didn't.

2. Did the man run away?

   Yes, he did.   No, he didn't.

3. Did Jorge get his wallet from the man?

   Yes, he did.   No, he didn't.

4. Did he go to the International Center?

   Yes, he did.   No, he didn't.

5. Did he talk to Simon?

   Yes, he did.   No, he didn't.

6. Did Raquel take him to the police station?

   Yes, she did.   No, she didn't.

7. Did the police officer give Jorge his wallet?

   Yes, he did.   No, he didn't.

8. Did he write a report?

   Yes, he did.   No, he didn't.

9. Did he ask Jorge questions?

Yes, he did. No, he didn't.

10. Did he give Raquel a copy of the report?

Yes, he did. No, he didn't.

F. Verbs: Simple Past—Irregular

drive	drove	speak	spoke
get	got	steal	stole
give	gave	take	took
go	went	tell	told
run	ran	wear	wore
see	saw	write	wrote

To be: am/is → was; are → were
To have → has → had

Write the past tense in the sentences.

1. Jorge **took** his wallet out of his pocket. (take)

2. A man _____ it from him. (steal)

3. He _____ the man. (see)

4. The man _____ a T-shirt and jeans. (wear)

5. Jorge _____ to the center. (run)

6. He _____ Raquel about the man. (tell)

7. Raquel _____ Jorge to the police station. (drive)

8. Jorge _____ to the officer about the crime. (speak)

9. The officer _____ a report. (write)

10. He _____ Jorge a copy of the report. (give)

11. Raquel _____ to an ATM. (go)

12. She _____ money for Jorge. (get)

G. Question Words

Underline the correct question word and draw a line to the correct answer.

1. Where/When did Jorge go the next day?   A new paycheck.

2. How/Who did he talk to?   A new wallet.

3. When/What did his boss do?   To his office.

4. What/When did his boss give him?   At the Registry.

5. How/Where did he go later?   To his boss.

6. What/When did he ask for at the bank?   To the bank.

7. Who/Where did he get a new license?   Cancel the stolen check.

8. What/When did Elena buy him?   A new bank card.

H. Verbs in Questions

When **did** the crime **happen**?   It **happened** last week.

Write verbs in the questions.

1. Where ____did____ Jorge ____go____ the next day? (go)

2. Who _____ he _____ to? (talk)

3. What _____ his boss _____? (do)

4. What _____ his boss _____ him? (tell)

5. Where _____ Jorge _____ later? (go)

6. What _____ he _____ for at the bank? (ask)

7. Where _____ he _____ a new license? (get)

8. What _____ Elena _____ him? (buy)

I. *How much?/How long?*

*Write **How much** or **How long** in the question.*

1. __How much__ cash did Jorge lose? —About $20.00.

2. _____ was his paycheck? —About $350.00.

3. _____ is a new license? —$30.00.

4. _____ is a new wallet? —About $15.00.

5. __How long__ was Raquel at the center?
   —Until 8:00 P.M.

6. _____ was Jorge at the police station?
   —Twenty minutes.

7. _____ was he at the bank? —Half an hour.

8. _____ was he at the Registry? —Two hours.

J. Possessives: Nouns and Adjectives

Write the possessive noun.

1. Raquel is __Simon's__ wife.　　4. Jorge is _____ husband.

2. Simon is _____ husband.　　5. Ming is _____ friend.

3. Elena is _____ wife.　　6. Sasha is _____ friend.

ADJECTIVE + NOUN	PRONOUN	ADJECTIVE + NOUN	PRONOUN
my license	mine	our money	ours
your paycheck	yours	your report	yours
his wallet	his	their T-shirts	theirs
her car	hers	their jeans	theirs
its ATM	—	their hats	theirs

Al   Burt   Charles

7. __Al's__ jeans are blue. __His__ T-shirt is black. __His__ hair is blond.

8. _____ suit is gray, _____ tie is red, and _____ beard is brown.

9. _____ sweater is green, _____ pants are beige, and _____ hat is yellow.

10. Which man stole Jorge's wallet? _____

11. Raquel and Simon have a car. _____ car is dark blue.

12. Ming has a cat. _____ cat is orange. _____ milk is on the floor.

13. Jorge has a new wallet. _____ wallet is black.

14. Elena has a new dress. _____ dress is red.

15. Jorge and Elena have new bank cards. _____ bank cards are green.

16. Raquel has a new skirt. _____ skirt is pink.

K. Possessives: Pronouns

Cross out the possessive adjective + noun and write the possessive pronoun.

1. Where are the bank cards?

    Mine   **yours**
    ~~My bank card~~ is on the table and ~~your bank card~~ is on the desk.

2. Where are the reports?

    His report is on the desk, and *her report* is on her table.

3. Where is the dog's food?

    Its food is on the floor.

4. Where is your office?

    Our office is near *your office*—on the same street.

5. Where are the cars?

    Their car is in the parking lot, and *our car* is on the street.

L. Object Pronouns

<u>Raquel</u> took <u>Jorge</u> to the police station.
 Subject   Object

<u>She</u> took <u>him</u> to the police station.
 Subject   Object

SUBJECT	OBJECT	SUBJECT	OBJECT
I	me	we	us
you	you	you	you
he	him		
she	her	they	them
it	it		

Write the sentence with the object pronoun.

1. Jorge met <u>Raquel</u> at the center.

   Jorge met her at the center.

2. Raquel took <u>Jorge</u> to the police station.

   _____

3. Jorge told <u>the officer</u> about the crime.

   _____

4. The officer asked <u>Jorge</u> questions.

   _____

5. Jorge answered <u>the questions</u>.

   _____

6. The officer gave <u>the report</u> to Jorge.

   _____

7. Raquel drove <u>Jorge</u> home.

   _____

8. She lent <u>some money</u> to Jorge.

   _____

9. Jorge told <u>Elena</u> about the crime.

   _____

10. Elena bought <u>a new wallet</u> for Jorge.

   _____

M. Conjunctions: *And* Versus *Or*

The man stole Jorge's bank card and driver's license.

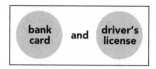

Was the man tall or short?

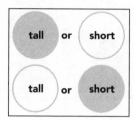

The people did not see or catch the thief.

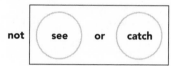

*Write **and** or **or** in the sentences.*

1. Jorge lost his paycheck _____ his bank card.

2. He didn't have money _____ a token to get home.

3. Raquel drove him to the police station _____ home.

4. He got a new paycheck _____ a new bank card.

5. Elena bought him a new wallet. Was it black _____ brown?

N. Conjunctions: *And* Versus *But*

+	−
fast	slow
new	old
easy	difficult
nice	rude
calm	upset

375

AND: (+/+) or (-/-)

BUT: (+/-) or (-/+)

Getting a new bank card was easy and fast. (+/+)

Getting a new driver's license was easy but slow. (+/-)

The police officer was slow but nice. (-/+)

*Write **and** or **but** in the sentences.*

1. Catching a thief is slow _____ difficult.

2. The thief was tall _____ thin.

3. He was old _____ fast.

4. Jorge was upset _____ not hurt.

5. Raquel was nice _____ calm.

O. Real People...Real Language

1. Has anyone ever stolen anything from you?

Underline the words you hear.

a. my car   <u>my car stereo</u>

b. an automobile   an automobile phone

c. a couple of bicycles   a truck

   a car   a variety of small items

d. No, I've been lucky.   No, I've been unlucky.

2. Have you ever been mugged?

Circle yes or no.

a. yes   (no)

b. yes   no

c. yes   no

d. yes   no

3. Have you ever been involved in a serious crime?

Cross out the words you don't hear.

a. ~~yes~~   no

b. yes   no

c. yes   no

d. yes   no

e. yes   no

4. Have you ever had to go to a police station?

Underline the words you hear.

a. car/train accident   kind and thoughtful/unkind and thoughtless

b. <u>car</u>/truck stolen   <u>helpful/unhelpful</u>

c. car/bicycle stolen   accident

d. car/bus accident

5. Have you ever had a wallet stolen?

Cross out the words you don't hear.

a. ~~yes~~   no

b. yes   no   purse/briefcase   pickpocketed

c. yes   no

d. yes   no   wallet/suitcase   stolen

VIDEO TRANSCRIPT

Watch and Listen

Jorge: Raquel, thank God you're still here!

Raquel: Jorge, you're back!

Jorge: Someone stole my wallet!

Raquel: Oh, no! What happened?

Jorge: I was at the subway buying a token, when all of a sudden, someone took my wallet and ran!

Raquel: You were mugged! What did you do?

Jorge: I ran after him. Some people tried to stop him, but he got away. He took everything! He took my money, my bank card, my driver's license—I just got my paycheck!

Raquel: Let's go to the police station and report the crime. It's okay. Come on.

At the police station.

Officer: Hello, I'm Officer Andrews. I'm here to take your report. When and where did this crime happen?

Jorge: About 3:45 at the Main Street subway station.

Officer: Tell me exactly what happened.

Jorge: Well, I took my wallet out to buy a token, and a man grabbed it and ran away.

Officer: Did you get a good look at him?

Jorge: It happened so fast.

Officer: Can you remember what he was wearing?

Jorge: A black T-shirt and a pair of jeans.

Officer: Can you describe him?

Jorge: He was tall and thin.

Officer: How tall?

Jorge: About 1 meter 80 centimeters, under 100 kilos.

Raquel: That means he was a little over 6 feet—and under 220 pounds.

Officer: Anything else you can tell us?

Jorge: He was blond and had a tattoo on his right arm.

Officer: Thank you. We'll see what we can do. Sign here, please. This is your copy. Are you okay?

Jorge: Yeah.

Raquel: Thank you. Okay, Jorge, let me drive you home. You know, I can lend you some money until you get a new paycheck.

Jorge: Thanks, Raquel. I'm so glad you were still at the center. I don't know what I would have done without you.

Raquel: No problem. Come on.

Raquel: Jorge got a new license and a new bank card. His boss canceled his stolen paycheck and gave him a new one, so he didn't lose that much money. Now let's look at some useful phrases.

To describe someone, you can say:

> She was **tall and thin.**   or
>
> He was **short and heavy.**   or
>
> They had **light skin and dark hair.**

To offer to help someone, you can say:

> **Let me** drive you home.   or
>
> **Why don't I** lend you some money?   or
>
> **How about if I** take you to the police station?

Now let's listen to other people talk about crime.

Unit 6
Getting Things Fixed

A. Who can fix it?

Write the words. Draw a line to the person who can fix it.

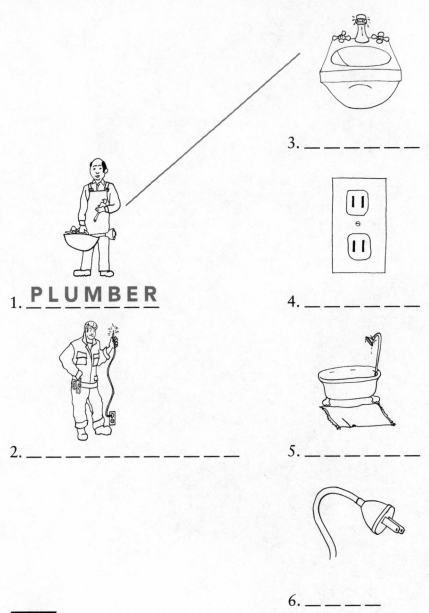

1. P L U M B E R

2. _ _ _ _ _ _ _ _ _ _ _

3. _ _ _ _ _ _ _ _

4. _ _ _ _ _ _ _

5. _ _ _ _ _ _ _ _

6. _ _ _ _ _

B. Verbs: Past Tense—*Could/Couldn't*

I	could/couldn't	we	could/couldn't
you	could/couldn't	you	could/couldn't
he/she/it	could/couldn't	they	could/couldn't

yesterday	today	tomorrow

past:
could

present:
can

*Write **could** or **couldn't** in the sentences.*

1. Simon ___could___ smell something strange.

2. Ming _____ smell it, too.

3. She _____ find the number of the gas company.

4. They _____ send a service representative to check it.

5. Simon _____ help Ming open the windows.

6. Ming _____ fix the dripping faucet or shower.

7. A plumber _____ fix them.

8. Simon _____ fix the electrical outlet in the kitchen.

9. An electrician _____ fix it.

10. Ming _____ make a list of repairs for the landlord.

C. Questions

> **Could** Ming paint her apartment? No, she **couldn't.**
>
> **Could** Sasha paint it?   Yes, he **could.**

*Write **Could** in the questions. Write short "yes" or "no" answers.*

1. __Could__ Jorge help Sasha paint? __No, he couldn't.__
2. _____ Ming lift the heavy boxes? __No,__
3. _____ Simon lift them? __Yes,__
4. _____ Elena help Ming clean? __Yes,__
5. _____ Raquel help her clean? __No,__

D. Can/Can't or Could/Couldn't

Circle the correct verb in the sentence.

1. Ming (could) / couldn't   find a nice apartment.
2. Sasha   could / couldn't   help her paint it.
3. Jorge   could / couldn't   help her paint it.
4. Elena   could / couldn't   help her clean it.
5. Raquel   could / couldn't   help her clean it.
6. Ming   can / can't   fix the gas leak.
7. The gas company   can / can't   fix it.
8. Simon   can / can't   repair the dripping shower.
9. The plumber   can / can't   repair it.
10. The landlord   can / can't   pay for the repairs.

E. Short Answers

Write a short "yes" or "no" answer after the question.

1. Can you speak Chinese? __No, I can't.__

2. Could Ming speak English ten years ago?
   __No, she couldn't.__

3. Can horses run fast? __Yes,__

4. Could Raquel help Jorge report a crime?
   __Yes,__

5. Could Ming rent an expensive apartment?
   __No,__

6. Can you understand the video? __Yes,__

7. Can we use an ATM at night? __Yes,__

8. Could you write in English last year? __No,__

9. Can you ask your landlord to fix things?
   __Yes,__

10. Could Simon and Sasha get acupuncture treatments?
    __Yes,__

F. *There is.../There are...*

There is	an outlet in the kitchen. a light on the ceiling. a radiator in the bedroom.	There are	outlets on the walls. lights in the rooms. radiators in the house.

*Write **There is** or **There are** in the sentences.*

1. __There are__ many electricians in the city.

2. _____ some extension cords in the closet.

3. _____ a toilet in the bathroom.

4. _____ ten outlets in the apartment.

5. _____ a stove in the kitchen.

6. _____ a furnace in the basement.

7. _____ two windows in the bedroom.

8. _____ many repairs on the list.

9. _____ a gas leak in Ming's apartment.

10. _____ two windows in the bedroom.

G. Prepositions of Place: *In/On/At*

in   on   at

in	the bathroom/the city/Boston
on	the wall/the stove/Center Street/the bus/the train
at	the desk/the bus stop/715 Elm Avenue/home

Cross out the incorrect preposition.

1. Ming's apartment is on/in the corner.

2. The stove is on/in the kitchen.

3. The picture is at/on the wall.

4. The furnace is in/on the basement.

5. The telephone book is in/on the table.

6. The plumber is on/at Ming's apartment.

7. He is in/on the bathroom.

8. He is standing in/at the sink.

9. The gas company is on/in Park Street.

10. The service rep is in/on his office.

H. Clauses with Imperatives: Home Safety

If there is a fire,

- **call** the fire department, (Yes)
- **don't stay** in the house, (No)
- **leave** the house quickly. (Yes)

Write the missing word.

1. If there is a strange smell,

_____ **call** _____ the gas company, (*call/don't call*)

_____ the windows, (*open/don't open*)

_____ in the house, (*smoke/don't smoke*)

_____ for the service rep to come. (*wait/don't wait*)

2. If you have a dripping faucet,

_____ a plumber, (*phone/don't phone*)

_____ at home while he works, (*stay/don't stay*)

_____ him to check for other water problems. (*ask/don't ask*)

3. If you have a broken outlet,

_____ it, (*use/don't use*)

_____ an electrician, (*call/don't call*)

_____ him to check the other outlets. (*get/don't get*)

4. If you have no heat or hot water,

_____ your landlord, (*phone/don't phone*)

_____ him about the problem, (*tell/don't tell*)

_____ him to fix it right away. (*ask/don't ask*)

5. If your doors or windows are broken,

_____ your landlord, (*call/don't call*)

_____ him about the doors or windows,
(*tell/don't tell*)

_____ him to fix them as soon as possible.
(*ask/don't ask*)

If your landlord doesn't fix things, call your city housing authority
and report the problem.

I. Dialogue: What is the problem?

Write the words in the dialogue.

PLUMBER: _____**What**_____ is the problem?
          1. (What/Who)

MING: The _____ and the faucet drip.
              2. (toilet/shower)

PLUMBER: Oh, that's _____ to fix.
                    3. (easy/difficult)

MING: Oh, good. Can you fix them _____ ?
                                       4. (yesterday/today)

PLUMBER: I can _____ them in half an hour.
               5. (fix/list)

MING: Great. Do you need _____ for anything?
                               6. (him/me)

PLUMBER: No, I'll tell you when I'm _____ .
                                    7. (finished/hungry)

MING: I'll be in the _____ .
                           8. (supermarket/kitchen)

Half an hour later...

PLUMBER: Everything _____ in working order.
                    9. (is/are)

MING: _____ I see?
            10. (Am/Can)

PLUMBER: Sure. The shower and the sink don't _____
         anymore.   11. (drip/slip)

MING: Great! Could you check the kitchen _____ ,
            too?   12. (stove/sink)

PLUMBER: Good idea... It looks _____ to me.
                               13. (dirty/fine)

MING: Okay. I guess that's all. My _____ will pay
            the bill, right?   14. (landlord/aunt)

PLUMBER: Yes. Could you sign it here? I'll leave you a

         _____ .
         15. (copy/money)

MING: _____ a lot.
            16. (Eat/Thanks)

PLUMBER: Have a _____ day!
                17. (good/bad)

MING: _____ , too. Bye!
            18. (Me/You)

J. Real People...Real Language

1. Have you had any problems in your apartment lately?

Underline the words you hear.

a.   The <u>bathroom</u> / bedroom is old and needs work.

b. Yes / No

c. Yes / No

d. A leak from a radiator made a stain on the wall / ceiling.

2. How often do you have to have things repaired?

Circle the words you hear.

a. Leaky faucet repaired once a month / (year.)

b. Utilities and appliances are up to date / up for repair.

c. Once a month / year.

3. Do you know how to fix things around the house on your own?

Underline the words you hear.

a. I fix things by myself or with friends / children.

b. I fix things in my house / on my own.

c. I can tighten a washer on a sink / stove and replace light bulbs.

d. I replace broken door / window hinges and locks, doors / windows that have the glass cracked.

4. Do you have to pay for your own repairs?

Write the words you hear.

a. I do ____**minor**____ repairs.

The landlord does _____ repairs.

b. _____ do the repairs in my house.

c. The _____ does that.

5. Do you have a good repairman you trust?

Circle "yes" or "no" according to what you hear.

a. (Yes) / No

b. Yes / No

c. Yes / No

d. Yes / No

VIDEO TRANSCRIPT

Watch and Listen

Ming: Hi, Simon! Thanks for stopping by.

Simon: Hi, Ming. How's everything going?

Ming: Oh, fine. My cousin and I love our new apartment. It's clean and painted, and most of the boxes are unpacked.

Simon: Hey—what's that strange smell?

Ming: Oh, I noticed it, too. I'm not sure.

Simon: Ming, I think you have a gas leak.

Ming: Oh, no. What should I do?

Simon: Where's your phone book?

Ming: Oh, here it is.

Simon: You have to call the gas company; there's the number.

Ming: You mean I have to report it?

Simon: Yes, it could be dangerous. They'll send a representative to check it out.

Ming: Okay.

City Gas: You've reached the City Gas Emergency Leak Center. To ensure quality service, your call is being recorded. Please remain on the line, and your call will be answered by the next available representative.

Ming: Hello? Yes, I think I have a gas leak... 142 Summer Street, Apartment 6. Open the windows? Okay. Yes, I'll be here. Okay, thank you. Good-bye.

Simon: Okay, I'll help you open all the windows.

Ming: Okay.

Simon: I see your faucet is dripping.

Ming: Yes, and the shower drips, too.

Simon: Oh, that wastes a lot of water. You should ask your landlord to call a plumber.

Ming: Oh, and one of the electrical outlets in the kitchen doesn't work.

Simon: Make a list of repairs and call your landlord.

Ming: Does that mean that we have to pay for the repairs?

Simon: No, he does. It's his apartment.

Ming: Oh, I'll make a list now.

Simon: I'll help you if you'd like.

Ming: Okay. I'll get a piece of paper and a pen.

Simon: While Ming's getting some paper, let's review some important expressions from this lesson.

To give directions, you can use phrases like this:

Call the gas company.   or

Open the window.   or

Don't smoke in the house.   or

Don't use broken electrical outlets.

To ask for clarification, you can say this:

Does that mean I have a gas leak?   or

Are you saying I have to call the gas company?

In response, you might hear:

That's correct.   or

That's right.

Now let's listen to people talk about repairs.

Unit 7
Social Services

A. People who...

Write the words in the blanks.

1. People who can't see are b l i n d.

2. People who can't hear are d _ _ _.

3. People who can't walk are d _ _ _ _ _ _ _ _.

4. People who don't have homes are h _ _ _ _ _ _ _.

5. People who drink too much a _ _ _ _ _ _ _ are alcoholics.

6. People who take illegal d _ _ _ _ are drug addicts.

B. Verbs: Future with *Going To*

I	am going to __	we	are going to __
you	are going to __	you	are going to __
he/she/it	is going to __	they	are going to __

yesterday   today   tomorrow

← ═══════════════════════════════ →

future:
tomorrow
next week
next month
next year

Write the verbs in the sentences.

1. Raquel **is going to see** Sasha and Elena. (see)

2. Sasha _____ Raquel about his job situation.
   (tell)

3. Raquel _____ him advice about unemployment.
   (give)

4. Sasha _____ for unemployment benefits. (apply)

5. He _____ an application at the
   unemployment office. (fill out)

6. Elena _____ to Raquel about her pregnancy.
   (talk)

7. Raquel _____ Elena about Medicare. (advise)

8. Elena _____ home an application. (take)

9. She _____ it with Jorge. (read)

10. She _____ it back soon. (bring)

C. Negatives

I	am not going to __	we	are not going to __
you	are not going to __	you	are not going to __
he/she/it	is not going to __	they	are not going to __

Remember the contractions: I am = I'm; you are = you're; he is = he's
or: are not = aren't; is not = isn't.

Write the subject pronoun and the contracted negative form of the verb.

1. __He's not going to__ work for the painting company.
    (Sasha)

2. _____ get any more paychecks. (Sasha)

3. _____ find Sasha another job. (Raquel)

4. _____ tell him about Medicare. (Raquel)

5. _____ stop by the International Center
    today. (Sasha)

6. _____ be a cashier at the supermarket next
    month. (Elena)

7. _____ have triplets (three babies at once).
    (Elena)

8. _____ get his engineering degree next
    month. (Jorge)

9. _____ have much money. (Elena and Jorge)

10. _____ apply for Medicare. (Jorge)

D. Questions and Yes/No Answers

Raquel **is going to** help Elena.

Is Raquel **going to** help Elena?

Yes, she is.
No, she isn't.

Circle the correct answer.

1. Is Raquel going to give Sasha some advice?   Yes, she is.
   No, she isn't.

2. Is Sasha going to listen to her advice?   Yes, he is.
   No, he isn't.

3. Is he going to apply for Medicare?   Yes, he is.
   No, he isn't.

4. Is Raquel going to fill out his application?   Yes, she is.
   No, she isn't.

5. Is Elena going to apply for unemployment   Yes, she is.
   benefits?   No, she isn't.

6. Is she going to work until the twins   Yes, she is.
   are born?   No, she isn't.

7. Is Jorge going to apply for Medicare?   Yes, he is.
   No, he isn't.

8. Is Elena going to get free baby supplies?   Yes, she is.
   No, she isn't.

E. Short Answers

Draw a line to the correct answer.

1. Who visited Raquel's office?

2. What kind of work does Raquel do?

3. What sort of work does Sasha do?

4. What type of work does Elena do?

5. Where is Sasha going next?

6. What is Sasha going to do there?

7. How many babies is Elena going to have?

8. How long can she work in the supermarket?

9. Which application is she going to fill out?

10. What kind of help is she going to get?

She's a cashier.

To the Unemployment Office.

Two babies.

Sasha and Elena.

A few more weeks.

A Medicare application.

Vouchers for baby supplies.

Social work.

Fill out an application.

He's a painter.

F. Question Words: Review

Write Who, Where, What, When, or How in the questions.

1. __Who__ is a social worker? —Raquel is.

2. _____ does she work? —In an office.

3. _____ came to see her? —Sasha and Elena.

4. _____ did Sasha tell her? —About his layoff.

5. _____ did she tell him to go? —To the Unemployment Office.

6. _____ is he going to get there? —An application for unemployment benefits.

7. _____ did Elena talk about? —Her pregnancy.

8. _____ is she going to stop working? —Soon.

9. _____ can she get help? —By applying for Medicare.

10. _____ is she going to give her application to? —Raquel.

G. How often?

How often?

*Write **How often** in the questions.*

1. **How often** does Raquel work in her office? —Three days a week.

2. _____ did Sasha paint houses? —Every day.

3. _____ does Elena work at the supermarket? —Five days a week.

4. _____ does Raquel work at the International Center? —On Monday and Friday.

5. _____ does Jorge take classes? —Every semester.

6. _____ does Sasha see his family? —Every week.

7. _____ does Raquel visit families? —Twice a week.

8. _____ does Elena go to the doctor? —Every two weeks.

H. Adverbs of Frequency

100%	always	Elena always goes to the supermarket on Saturday.
80%	usually	Raquel usually cooks dinner in the evening.
60%	often	Sasha often paints apartments.
40%	sometimes	Jorge sometimes cooks dinner for Elena.
20%	rarely	Simon rarely comes home late.
0%	never	Ming never works in the restaurant on Sunday.

Write the missing adverb.

1. People can ___**always**___ visit the International Center. (every day)

2. Raquel's office is ___**usually**___ open from 8:00 A.M. to 6:00 P.M. (Monday to Friday)

3. Sasha _____ deposits his paycheck into his account on Friday. (every Friday)

4. The government _____ approves unemployment applications. (4 out of 10 times)

5. It _____ snows in Russia in winter. (0°–40° F)

6. It _____ snows in the Dominican Republic. (70°–90° F)

7. Raquel _____ works on Sunday. (three times a year)

8. Elena _____ walks to work. (four times a week)

9. Jorge and Elena _____ speak Spanish with each other. (not always)

10. They _____ speak English with Simon.

I. Questions: *How long?* and *How far?*

How long is Jorge's class?
—Three hours.

How far is the hospital?
—Two miles.

*Write **How long** or **How far** in the questions.*

1. __How long__ was Sasha talking to Raquel? —Only ten minutes.

2. __How far__ is the unemployment office? —A few blocks.

3. _____ is Sasha's apartment? —Four subway stops.

4. _____ was Elena with Raquel? —Not very long.

5. _____ can she work as a cashier? —A few more weeks.

6. _____ is the supermarket? —About a mile.

7. _____ will Jorge study? —For another year.

8. _____ will Elena receive Medicare? —For about a year.

9. _____ is Raquel's apartment? —Ten blocks.

10. _____ is the International Center? —Less than a mile.

J. *Too* and *Enough*

A truck is **too expensive.**   Sasha doesn't have **enough money.**

*Write **too** or **enough** in the sentences.*

1. Can Sasha buy a truck now?

   No, he can't. A truck is _____ **too** _____ expensive.

2. Can he get unemployment benefits?

   Yes, he can. He has _____ **enough** _____ time with the company.

3. Can Elena work as a cashier?

   No, she can't. It's _____ hard.

4. Can Jorge get his degree soon?

   No, he can't. The classes are _____ expensive.

5. Can Ming fix a gas leak?

   No, she can't. She doesn't have _____ knowledge.

K. *If* Clauses: Advice

If it rains, you'll get wet.   If you take your umbrella, you won't get wet.

Write the missing word.

1. If you lose your job, you can apply for unemployment
   benefits .
   (benefits/breakfasts)

2. If your application is approved, you'll get _____
   every two weeks. (money/papers)

3. If you find another _____ , you won't get benefits
   anymore. (office/job)

4. If Sasha saves his money, he can _____ a truck.
   (wash/buy)

5. If you spend your money, the _____ in your bank
   account will go down. (balance/bills)

6. If Elena has twins, she and Jorge will be very _____ .
   (bored/busy)

7. If Elena gets Medicare, she'll have _____ diapers
   for the babies. (free/four)

8. If your faucet drips, a _____ will fix it.
   (painter/plumber)

L. Dialogue: Help is on the way.

Put the sentences in order.

1.

a. __1__ JORGE: Hi, honey! How was your day?

b. ____ ELENA: She said I should apply for Medicare.

c. __3__ JORGE: What did she say?

d. ____ ELENA: Medical aid the government gives you.

e. __2__ ELENA: Pretty good. I went to see Raquel.

f. ____ JORGE: Really? What's that?

2.

a. ____ JORGE: How do you get it?

b. ____ ELENA: When I stop working.

c. ____ JORGE: Oh, that's easy. When should you do it?

d. ____ ELENA: The doctor said to stop in a few weeks.

e. ____ ELENA: You fill out an application.

f. ____ JORGE: When will that be?

3.

a. ____ JORGE: You can stop now if you want.

b. ____ JORGE: Me, too. And I want them to have a healthy mother!

c. ____ ELENA: I'm a little tired, but I can work a little longer.

d. ____ ELENA: Don't worry, I will. I want to have healthy babies.

e. ____ JORGE: Okay, but I want you to stop if you don't feel well.

M. Real People...Real Language

1. Have you ever used any social services?

Circle "Yes" or "No."

a.   Yes / No   but I know people who have.

b.   Yes / No   unemployed / housing / food /clothing

c.   Yes / No   mother in an assisted living situation

2. Do you know of anyone who has lived in a shelter?

Underline what you hear.

a.   Yes / No

b.   Yes / No   my aunt's husband / my husband's aunt

c.   Yes / No   a girl / a boy who lived in a shelter

d.   Yes / No

e.   Yes / No   a childhood friend / a friend's child

3. Have you ever thought of adopting a child?

Write "Yes" or "No."

a.   _____**No**_____ , I'm not ready for children right now.

b.   _____ , I might adopt sometime in the future.

c.   _____ , I adopted a child fourteen years ago.

4. Do you do any volunteer work?

Circle the words you hear.

a.   a detox program with Hispanic / Asian women

b.   volunteer coach with a girls' basketball / softball team

c.   once a month / once a year fund-raising activities

d.   in detox centers to help people recover from alcoholism / drug addiction

VIDEO TRANSCRIPT

Watch and Listen

Raquel: Hi! What are you two doing here?

Sasha: I lost my job, Raquel, and I don't know what to do.

Raquel: Oh, that's too bad, Sasha. Well, come on in, and we'll talk.

Sasha: Thank you. I'm sorry for this.

Raquel: So, what happened?

Sasha: Most people want their houses painted in the summer. The company has less work now, so they laid off three painters.

Raquel: Oh, I'm sorry to hear that. I'll tell you what your options are. You may be able to apply for unemployment benefits. How long have you been working there?

Sasha: Eight months.

Raquel: That means you can get money from the government while you're looking for work.

Sasha: Really? I didn't know that.

Raquel: The application process takes about two weeks. But then you can get benefits until you find a job—for up to six months.

Sasha: I just fill out an application?

Raquel: No, it has to be approved, but it sounds like you have a good case.

Sasha: Should I do that here?

Raquel: No, you should go to the Unemployment Office. It's not far. This is their address. They may still be open.

Sasha: Okay. I'll go there right now and talk to someone. Thanks a lot, Raquel.

Raquel: Sure, you're welcome. Good luck! Elena, come on in.

Elena: Thanks. It's too bad that Sasha lost his job.

Raquel: Yes, I know. But what brings you here?

Elena: The doctor said I'm going to have twins.

Raquel: Twins! Wow! You and Jorge are going to be busy.

Elena: Yes, but she also said that I shouldn't work any more.

Raquel: Why?

Elena: Because there could be complications.

Raquel: Oh, no.

Elena: And Jorge doesn't earn very much now. He's still trying to get his equivalency degree in engineering.

Raquel: He has to take a few more courses, right?

Elena: Right. We don't have much money, and with twins...

Raquel: Maybe you can apply for Medicare.

Elena: What does that mean?

Raquel: You fill out an application, and if it's approved, you get free prenatal care.

Elena: So I wouldn't have any doctor's bills?

Raquel: That's right. And when the babies are born, you get free vouchers for baby food, milk, diapers, and things like that.

Elena: That sounds perfect!

Raquel: Here's an application. Take it home, look at it, and when you stop working, fill it out and bring it in.

Elena: Oh, Raquel, this is wonderful. We were so worried.

Raquel: Well, you have enough to worry about right there.

Elena: Thanks, Raquel. See you tomorrow at the center.

Raquel: Okay. Take care.

Everyone goes through hard times, and social services can help. Here are some useful phrases to remember.

When you need to ask for advice or help, you say:

> **What can** Elena **do**?   or
>
> **What do you think** Sasha **should do**?

People might respond like this:

> She **can** apply for Medicare.   or
>
> He **should** apply for unemployment benefits.

Now let's listen to other people talk about social services.

Answer Key:
Health, Home, and Community

Unit 1: Going to the Doctor

A. What is it?
1. headache, fever, nausea, vomiting
2. appointment, nurse, waiting room, doctor 3. height, weight, pulse, temperature, blood pressure 4. ears, throat, nose, heart, lungs 5. blood test, urine test, results

B. Verbs: Present Tense—To Be
1. are 2. is 3. are 4. is 5. is 6. is
7. is 8. are 9. am 10. are

C. Contractions
1. you're 2. they're 3. it's 4. I'm
5. we're 6. he's

D. Negatives
1. am not 2. are not 3. is not 4. is not
5. is not 6. is not 7. are not
8. are not 9. are not 10. are not

E. Negative Contractions
1. he isn't/he's not 2. they aren't/
they're not 3. we aren't/we're not
4. I'm not 5. you aren't/you're not
6. she isn't/she's not

F. Questions and Yes/No Answers
1. No, he is not. 2. Yes, she is. 3. Yes, they are. 4. No, he is not. 5. Yes, he is. 6. Is Raquel with Elena? 7. Are you at the center? 8. Is Elena with the doctor? 9. Are they in the lab?
10. Are the results ready?

G. Short Answers
1. Ming is. 2. From Mexico. 3. The tests are. 4. From the U.S. 5. Raquel is. 6. At the office. 7. The chairs.
8. Raquel is. 9. At the clinic.
10. Simon and Raquel.

H. Question Words
1. Who 2. Who 3. What 4. Who
5. Where 6. What 7. Where
8. What

I. Parts of the Body
No answers

J. Verb Tense: Present Continuous
1. is feeling 2. is driving 3. are talking
4. is taking 5. is telling 6. is putting
7. is asking 8. is listening
9. is speaking 10. is going

K. Negatives
1. is not working 2. is not staying
3. is not teaching 4. is not eating
5. are not sitting 6. am not getting up
7. are not cooking 8. are not watching
9. is not sleeping 10. is not waiting

L. Questions
1. Is Elena working today? 2. Is Raquel staying at the center? 3. Is Simon teaching a class at the center?
4. Is Jorge eating at a restaurant? 5. Are the nurses sitting in the waiting room? 6. Are you getting up now?

7. Am I cooking dinner? 8. Are we watching TV now? 9. Is the cat sleeping on the chair? 10. Is Raquel waiting for Ming?

M. Yes/No Answers
1. Yes, she is. 2. No, he isn't. 3. Yes, they are. 4. No, she isn't. 5. Yes, she is. 6. Yes, he is. 7. No, he isn't. 8. No, they aren't. 9. Yes, she is. 10. Yes, they are.

N. Dialogue: Elena's News
1. you 2. clinic 3. doctor 4. laboratory 5. tests 6. Blood 7. What's 8. pregnant 9. baby 10. results 11. are 12. father

O. Real People...Real Language
1. a. once a year b. not very often c. maybe once or twice a year d. once a year
2. a. no b. yes, appendix c. yes, wisdom teeth d. yes, C-section
3. a. yes, broke my arm b. yes, had to get stitches
4. a. health b. medical c. workmen's d. Blue Cross/Blue Shield e. HMO

Unit 2: Going to the Pharmacy

A. What is it?
1. cold 2. sore throat 3. headache 4. earache 5. stomachache 6. backache

B. What is it used for?
1. toothpaste 2. soap 3. shampoo 4. conditioner

C. Verbs: Present Simple
1. needs 2. takes 3. costs 4. stops 5. helps 6. cook 7. eat 8. go 9. works 10. gets

D. Negatives
1. doesn't speak 2. doesn't work 3. doesn't help 4. doesn't buy 5. doesn't get 6. don't use 7. doesn't have 8. doesn't work 9. doesn't take 10. don't need

E. Questions and Yes/No Answers
1. Yes, she does. 2. No, they don't. 3. No, she doesn't. 4. Yes, she does. 5. Yes, he does. 6. No, he doesn't. 7. Yes, she does. 8. No, they don't. 9. Yes, she does. 10. Yes, I do.

F. Short Answers
1. Near the clinic. 2. Elena does. 3. Simon does. 4. Medicine. 5. To Jorge's house. 6. In the kitchen. 7. Juice. 8. Elena does. 9. Toothpaste and shampoo. 10. Raquel.

G. Questions
1. When 2. How many 3. How many 4. When 5. How much 6. When 7. When 8. How many 9. When 10. How many

H. Number Practice
No answers

I. Telling Time
1. 1:10, It's one-ten. 2. 2:25, It's two-twenty-five. 3. 12:15, It's twelve-fifteen. 4. 8:55, It's eight-fifty-five. 5. 9:30, It's nine-thirty. 6. 7:05, It's seven-o-five. 7. 4:35, It's four-thirty-five. 8. 6:50, It's six-fifty. 9. 11:00, It's eleven o'clock. 10. 10:40, It's ten-forty. 11. 7:20, It's seven-twenty. 12. 11:45, It's eleven-forty-five.

J. Days of the Week
1. Thursday, 3:30 2. Monday, 7:00 3. Saturday, 11:15 4. Wednesday, 2:00 5. Thursday, 6:45

K. Dialogue: Dinner with Simon and Raquel
1. Raquel 2. Can 3. you 4. thanks
5. fine 6. Yes 7. How 8. office
9. students 10. Would 11. good
12. Dinner 13. you 14. Elena 15. is
16. eat

L. Real People...Real Language
1. a. neighborhood pharmacy
b. medical center pharmacy c. local
pharmacy d. local drugstore
2. a. I don't take medicine b. during
spring and late summer c. every day
d. only if I'm sick
3. a. toothpaste, nail polish b. aspirin,
decongestant, candy c. soap,
moisturizer, paper products
d. medication, toothpaste, deodorant
e. hair coloring, aspirin f. cold
remedies, cough syrup
4. a. eat better, more tea, more soup
b. stay in bed c. try to sleep, drink a
lot of orange juice, get as much rest as
I can
5. a. to the body b. heals c. important
d. homeopathic

Unit 3: Cleaning the Home

A. Where do you use it?
1. paint 2. paintbrush 3. roller
4. bleach 5. tile and tub 6. sponge
7. liquid 8. cleaner 9. polish

B. What should you do?
1. window 2. fan 3. faint, dizzy
4. telephone 5. label

C. Verbs: Future with *Will/Won't*
1. will 2. won't 3. will 4. will 5. will
6. won't 7. will 8. won't 9. will
10. will

D. Yes/No Answers
1. Yes, they will. 2. No, they won't.
3. Yes, she will. 4. Yes, she will.
5. Yes, he will. 6. Will/No, he won't.
7. Will/Yes, she will. 8. Will/Yes, she
will. 9. Will/No, she won't.
10. Will/No, he won't.

E. Questions
1. b 2. a 3. h 4. f 5. i 6. d 7. j 8. c
9. g 10. e

F. Plurals
1. fans 2. rooms 3. sponges
4. windows 5. beds 6. gowns 7. ears
8. doctors 9. cleaners 10. ovens

G. More Question Words
1. How much 2. How much 3. How
much 4. How many 5. How many
6. How many

H. Money
1. $44.59 2. $48.94 3. $16.24
4. $5.41 5. $1.06 6. $3.76

I. Count and Noncount Nouns
1. brushes, rollers, sponges, fans,
towels, lightbulbs 2. paint, bleach, tile
& tub cleaner, floor polish, dish soap,
oven cleaner, detergent

J. Questions and Answers
1. A few brushes. 2. A lot of oven
cleaner. 3. A few fans. 4. A little
money. 5. A few sponges. 6. How
much/A lot of paint. 7. How many/A
few bulbs. 8. How much/Some
cleaner. 9. How many/A few towels.
10. How much/A little polish.

K. Real People...Real Language
1. a. a lot of work/paint and clean
b. very little/apartment was clean

c. painting/cleaning the floors/a lot of cleaning d. arranging furniture
2. a. once a week b. Saturdays c. once every one or two weeks
3. a. bathroom/kitchen, kitchen, sink/shiny surfaces b. bathroom/kitchen
c. bathroom/kitchen
d. counters/toilet/everything except floors e. floors
4. a. no b. no/use gloves/don't inhale fumes c. yes
5. a. in a cabinet/ with a child safety lock b. under the kitchen sink/under the bathroom sink c. out of reach of son/put a lock on the door

Unit 4: Alternative Medicine

A. What is it?
1. stress 2. Yoga 3. Massage 4. diet
5. vegetarian 6. Health
7. Acupuncture

B. Verbs: Present Tense— Can/Can't
1. can 2. can't 3. can 4. can 5. can
6. can 7. can't 8. can 9. can't
10. can't

C. Questions: Can/Can't
1. Can/Yes, she can. 2. Can/No, she can't. 3. Can/Yes, he can. 4. Can/Yes, she can. 5. Can/No, I can't.

D. Question Words: What kind/type/sort of?
1. Dominican food. 2. He's an engineer. 3. Alternative medicine.
4. Clean needles. 5. Herbal remedies.
6. Light exercise. 7. Bookkeeping classes. 8. Engineering classes.
9. Social work. 10. He's an English teacher.

E. Adjectives: Opposites
(crossed out)
1. tall. 2. old. 3. dirty. 4. cheap.
5. short. 6. slow 7. light 8. healthy
9. unhealthy 10. tense.

F. Adjectives: Comparative and Superlative
1. cheaper, cheapest 2. cleaner, cleanest 3. newer, newest 4. older, oldest 5. healthier, healthiest
6. heavier, heaviest 7. funnier, funniest
8. more/most expensive, less/least expensive 9. more/most relaxed, less/least relaxed 10. more/most serious, less/least serious

G. Sentences with Comparatives
1. older 2. newer 3. larger 4. smaller
5. more expensive/less expensive
6. cheaper 7 healthier 8. less healthy
9. less relaxed 10. more serious

H. Sentences with Superlatives
1. newest 2. most expensive 3. largest
4. unhealthiest 5. smallest

I. Questions: Which/Which one
1. Which 2. Which one 3. Which
4. Which one 5. Which 6. Which one
7. Which 8. Which one 9. Which
10. Which one

J. Sasha's New Diet: Veggie Stir-Fry
1. pasta 2. water 3. peppers 4. oil
5. carrot 6. onion 7. garlic 8. salt, pepper

K. Dialogue: On the Telephone
1. Sasha 2. you 3. office 4. week
5. What 6. aunt 7. smoking
8. backache 9. feel 10. treatment
11. cook 12. You're 13. dinner
14. now 15. See 16. Bye

L. Real People...Real Language
1. a. very healthy b. not as healthy as I'd like to be c. healthy but overweight d. I'm a healthy person
2. a. fat b. fresh fruit c. poultry, pasta d. fish, tofu e. fatty products
3. (crossed out) a. jogging b. run to work c. play basketball d. practice karate e. jog once a week
4. a. no b. yes/reflexology c. yes/tai chi d. yes/acupuncture/chiropractor e. yes/acupuncture
5. a. yes/yoga b. yes/yoga c. yes/meditation/self-hypnosis d. yes/yoga/meditation

Unit 5: Reporting a Crime

A. What is it?
1. jeans 2. shirt 3. hat 4. sneakers 5. wallet 6. tattoo

B. Odd One Out
(crossed out) 1. sign 2. bank card 3. sneakers 4. young 5. short 6. suit 7. cash 8. tattoo 9. subway 10. help

C. Verbs: Simple Past—Regular
1. canceled 2. described 3. grabbed 4. happened 5. looked 6. offered 7. remembered 8. signed 9. stopped 10. talked

D. Negatives
1. He didn't cancel 2. He didn't describe 3. He didn't grab 4. It didn't happen 5. He didn't look 6. She didn't offer 7. He didn't remember 8. He didn't sign 9. She didn't stop 10. She didn't talk

E. Questions and Yes/No Answers
1. Yes, they did. 2. Yes, he did. 3. No, he didn't. 4. Yes, he did. 5. No, he didn't. 6. Yes, she did. 7. No, he didn't. 8. Yes, he did. 9. Yes, he did. 10. No, he didn't.

F. Verbs: Simple Past—Irregular
1. took 2. stole 3. saw 4. wore 5. ran 6. told 7. drove 8. spoke 9. wrote 10. gave 11. went 12. got

G. Question Words
1. Where/To his office. 2. Who/To his boss. 3. What/Cancel the stolen check. 4. What/A new paycheck. 5. Where/To the bank. 6. What/A new bank card. 7. Where/At the Registry. 8. What/A new wallet.

H. Verbs in Questions
1. did/go 2. did/talk 3. did/do 4. did/tell 5. did/go 6. did/ask 7. did/get 8. did/buy

I. How much?/How long?
1. How much 2. How much 3. How much 4. How much 5. How long 6. How long 7. How long 8. How long

J. Possessives: Nouns and Adjectives
1. Simon's 2. Raquel's 3. Jorge's 4. Elena's 5. Sasha's 6. Ming's 7. Al's/His/His 8. Burt's/his/his 9. Charles's/his/his 10. Al did. 11. Their 12. Her/Its 13. His 14. Her 15. Their 16. Her

K. Possessives: Pronouns
1. Mine/yours 2. His/hers 3. Its 4. Ours/yours 5. Theirs/ours

L. Object Pronouns
1. Jorge met her at the center.
2. Raquel took him to the police station. 3. Jorge told him about the crime. 4. The officer asked him questions. 5. Jorge answered them.
6. The officer gave it to Jorge.
7. Raquel drove him home. 8. She lent it to him. 9. Jorge told her about the crime. 10. Elena bought it for Jorge.

M. Conjunctions: *And* Versus *Or*
1. and 2. or 3. and 4. and 5. or

N. Conjunctions: *And* Versus *But*
1. and 2. and 3. but 4. but 5. and

O. Real People...Real Language
1. a. my car stereo b. an automobile c. a couple of bicycles, a truck, a car, a variety of small items d. No, I've been lucky.
2. a. no b. no c. yes d. no
3. (crossed out) a. yes b. no c. yes d. yes e. no
4. a. car/kind and thoughtful b. truck stolen/helpful c. car stolen/accident d. car accident
5. (crossed out) a. yes b. no/briefcase pickpocketed c. no d. yes/wallet stolen

---

Unit 6: Getting Things Fixed

A. Who can fix it?
1. plumber 2. electrician 3. faucet
4. outlet 5. shower 6. plug

B. Verbs: Past Tense—*Could/ Couldn't*
1. could 2. could 3. couldn't 4. could
5. couldn't 6. couldn't 7. could
8. couldn't 9. could 10. could

C. Questions
1. Could/No, he couldn't.
2. Could/No, she couldn't.
3. Could/Yes, he could. 4. Could/Yes, she could. 5. Could/No, she couldn't.

D. *Can/Can't or Could/Couldn't*
1. could 2. could 3. couldn't 4. could
5. couldn't 6. can't 7. can
8. can't 9. can 10. can

E. Short Answers
1. No, I can't. 2. No, she couldn't.
3. Yes, they can. 4. Yes, she could.
5. No, she couldn't. 6. Yes, I can.
7. Yes, we can. 8. No, I couldn't.
9. Yes, I can. 10. Yes, they could.

F. *There is.../There are...*
1. There are 2. There are 3. There is
4. There are 5. There is 6. There is.
7. There are 8. There are 9. There is
10. There are

G. Prepositions of Place: *In/On/At*
(crossed out) 1. in 2. on 3. at 4. on
5. in 6. on 7. on 8. in 9. in 10. on

H. Clauses with Imperatives: Home Safety
1. call, open, don't smoke, wait
2. phone, stay, ask 3. don't use, call, get 4. phone, tell, ask 5. call, tell, ask

I. Dialogue: What is the problem?
1. What 2. shower 3. easy 4. today
5. fix 6. me 7. finished 8. kitchen
9. is 10. Can 11. drip 12. sink
13. fine 14. landlord 15. copy
16. Thanks 17. good 18. You

J. Real People...Real Language
1. a. bathroom b. no c. no d. ceiling
2. a. once a year b. up to date c. once a month
3. a. friends b. on my own c. washer on a sink d. door hinges, windows
4. a. minor/major b. Repairmen c. landlord
5. a. Yes b. Yes c. Yes d. No

Unit 7: Social Services

A. People who...
1. blind 2. deaf 3. disabled
4. homeless 5. alcohol 6. drugs

B. Verbs: Future with *Going To*
1. is going to see 2. is going to tell
3. is going to give 4. is going to apply
5. is going to fill out 6. is going to talk
7. is going to advise 8. is going to take
9. is going to read 10. is going to bring

C. Negatives
1. He's not going to 2. He's not going to 3. She's not going to 4. She's not going to 5. He's not going to 6. She's not going to 7. She's not going to
8. He's not going to 9. They're not going to 10. He's not going to

D. Questions and Yes/No Answers
1. Yes, she is. 2. Yes, he is. 3. No, he isn't. 4. No, she isn't. 5. No, she isn't.
6. No, she isn't. 7. No, he isn't.
8. Yes, she is.

E. Short Answers
1. Sasha and Elena. 2. Social work.
3. He's a painter. 4. She's a cashier.
5. To the Unemployment Office. 6. Fill out an application. 7. Two babies.

8. A few more weeks. 9. A Medicare application. 10. Vouchers for baby supplies.

F. Question Words: Review
1. Who 2. Where 3. Who 4. What
5. Where 6. What 7. What 8. When
9. How 10. Who

G. *How often?*
1. How often 2. How often 3. How often 4. How often 5. How often
6. How often 7. How often 8. How often

H. Adverbs of Frequency
1. always 2. usually 3. always
4. sometimes 5. always 6. never
7. rarely 8. sometimes 9. usually
10. always

I. Questions: *How long?* and *How far?*
1. How long 2. How far 3. How far
4. How long 5. How long 6. How far
7. How long 8. How long 9. How far
10. How far

J. *Too* and *Enough*
1. too 2. enough 3. too 4. too
5. enough

K. *If* Clauses: Advice
1. benefits 2. money 3. job 4. buy
5. balance 6. busy 7. free 8. plumber

L. Dialogue: Help is on the way.
1. a-e-c-b-f-d 2. a-e-c-b-f-d
3. a-c-e-d-b

M. Real People...Real Language
1. a. No, but I know people who have.
b. Yes c. Yes
2. a. Yes b. Yes/my husband's aunt
c. Yes/a boy d. No e. Yes/a childhood
friend
3. a. No b. Yes c. Yes
4. a. Hispanic b. softball c. once a
year d. alcoholism

Word List:
Health, Home, and Community

a
a few
a little
a lot
ache
acupuncture
addict
addiction
adoption
afternoon
again
alcohol
alcoholic
allergy
alternative
always
American
and
answer
answering
    machine
any
apartment
application
apply
appointment
April
are
arm
aspirin
ATM
August
baby food
back

bald
bank
bank account
bank card
basement
bathroom
be
beard
bedroom
beer
benefits
better
bicycle
bike
billion
bleach
blind
blond
blood pressure
blood test
blow
bookkeeping
breakfast
bus
but
bye
call
can
can't
cancel
capsule
care
carrot
cash

cashier
cat
ceiling
center
chair
change
cheap
checkup
cheese
chest
child
Chinese
chiropractor
class
clean
cleaner
clinic
cold
commands
community
comparative
conjunctions
continuous
copayment
copy
cough
coughing
cough syrup
could
couldn't
counter
credit card
crime
day

deaf
December
degree
describe
diaper
diet
different
dime
dining room
dinner
directions
dirty
disabled
dish soap
dizzy
do
doctor
does
doesn't
dog
dollar
Dominican
don't
dress
dresser
drink
drip
drive
drugs
drugstore
each
ear
earache
eight

eighteen	future	how often	March
eighty	garlic	hundred	massage
elbow	gas	hurts	May
electrician	get	husband	may
eleven	give	I	Medicaid
employment	glasses	in	Medicare
engineer	go	infection	medicine
enjoy	good-bye	information	meditation
enough	gown	inhale	meetings
evening	grab	international	Mexican
every	group therapy	invite	might
examine	gym	iron	milk
exercise	had	is	million
expensive	hair	it	minerals
extension cord	hand	its	Monday
eye	happen	jacket	money
faint	hard	January	months
fan	has	jeans	movie
far	hat	jog	much
fast	have	July	mugged
faucet	have to	June	mugging
February	he	kitchen	my
fever	head	knee	nausea
few	headache	lab	nauseous
fifteen	health	lamp	near
fifty	heart	landlord	neck
fill	heavy	large	needles
fill out	height	later	negative
fingers	hello	layoff	neighborhood
finish	her	leak	never
fire	hers	leg	new
five	hi	let's	nickel
fix	high school	license	night
floor	him	lift	nine
food	his	light	nineteen
foot	home	lightbulb	ninety
forget	homeless	liquid	no
forty	homeopathic	list	nose
four	hospital	live	November
fourteen	hours	living room	nurse
frequency	house	lock	o'clock
Friday	how	look	October
funny	how many	lungs	of
furnace	how much	many	offer

office	pronoun	simple	tall
officer	pulse	sit	tattoo
often	quarter	six	teacher
oil	question	sixteen	telephone
old	radiator	sixty	tell
once	rarely	slow	temperature
one	ready	small	ten
onion	refrigerator	smell	tense
or	relax	smoke	that
order	relaxes	sneakers	theft
our	remember	sneezing	their
out	rep	social services	there
outlet	repair	social worker	they
paintbrush	report	sofa	thirteen
painter	rest	soft	thirty
pan	restaurant	some	this
pants	results	sometimes	thousand
paper	roller	sore throat	three
past	run	speak	throat
pasta	Russian	sponge	Thursday
paycheck	safe	station	tile
penny	safety	stay	time
people	salt	steal	to
pepper	same	stitches	today
pharmacist	Saturday	stolen	toes
pharmacy	school	stomach	toilet
phrase	see	stop	token
piece	seldom	stove	tomorrow
plug	September	strange	tonsils
plumber	serious	stress	too
plural	service	subject	toothpaste
poisoning	seven	subway	towel
police	seventeen	suit	train
polish	seventy	Sunday	T-shirt
possessives	shampoo	superlative	tub
pot	she	supermarket	Tuesday
practice	shirt	supplies	TV
pregnancy	shoes	sweater	twelve
pregnant	shop	symptoms	twenty
preposition	short	table	twice
prescription	should	tablet	twins
present	shoulder	tai chi	two
pretty	sick	Take care.	ugly
products	sign	talk	unhealthy

urine test	waiting room	wheelchair	won't
usually	waitress	when	would
vapor	wall	where	write
VCR	wallet	which	year
vegetarian	wash	who	yes
verb	water	whom	yoga
video	we	why	you
visit	wear	wife	your
vitamins	Wednesday	will	yours
volunteers	week	window	
vomiting	weight	wine	
voucher	well	wisdom teeth	

Audio Script: Health, Home, and Community

Unit 1: Going to the Doctor

Visiting the Doctor

Listen and repeat.

1. appointment

2. blood pressure

3. blood test

4. doctor

5. exam

6. fever

7. gown

8. headache

9. height

10. laboratory

11. nausea

12. nurse

13. office

14. pulse

15. results

16. temperature

17. urine test

18. vomiting

19. waiting room

20. weight

Parts of the Body

Listen and repeat.

1. arm

2. ear

3. elbow

4. eye

5. finger

6. foot

7. hand

8. knee

9. leg

10. lung

11. shoulder

12. toe

Verbs: *To Be*

Listen and repeat.

1. I am

2. you are

3. he is

4. she is

5. it is

6. we are

7. you are

8. they are

Sentences

Make a sentence from these words.

First, listen to the examples:

Simon/tall	Simon is tall.
Sasha/Russian	Sasha is Russian.

Now it's your turn.

1. Simon/tall   Simon is tall.

2. Sasha/Russian   Sasha is Russian.

3. I/nurse   I am a nurse.

4. you/doctor   You are a doctor.

5. They/paramedics   They are paramedics.

6. It/broken   It is broken.

Nationalities

Make a sentence from these words.

First, listen to the example:

Simon/America   Simon is American.

Now it's your turn.

1. Simon/America   Simon is American.

2. he/Japan   He is Japanese.

3. they/Nigeria   They are Nigerian.

4. we/Korea   We are Korean.

5. I/Central America   I am Central American.

Negatives: *To Be*

Listen and repeat after the speaker.

1. I'm not   I'm not

2. you're not   you aren't

3. he's not   he isn't

4. she's not   she isn't

5. it's not   it isn't

6. we're not   we aren't

7. you're not   you aren't

8. they're not   they aren't

Negatives: Sentences

Make a sentence from these words.

First, listen to the example:

     Simon/doctor   Simon isn't a doctor.

Now it's your turn.

1. Simon/doctor   Simon isn't a doctor.

2. Sasha/social worker   Sasha isn't a social worker.

3. Ming/Mexican   Ming isn't Mexican.

4. we/nurses   We aren't nurses.

5. they/doctors   They aren't doctors.

Questions in Present Continuous

Answer these questions.

First, listen to the example:

> Is Raquel going by the clinic?   Yes, she is.

Now it's your turn.

1. Is Raquel going by the clinic?   Yes, she is.

2. Is Elena feeling nauseous?   Yes, she is.

3. Is the nurse taking Raquel's pulse?   No, she isn't.

4. Is Dr. Summers talking to Jorge?   No, he isn't.

Who?

Answer these questions.

First, listen to the example:

> Who is taking Elena's blood pressure?   The nurse is.

Now it's your turn.

1. Who is taking Elena's blood pressure?   The nurse is.

2. Who is waiting at the doctor's office?   Raquel is.

3. Who is giving Elena an exam?   Dr. Summers is.

4. Who is going to the lab for tests?   Elena is.

5. Who is congratulating Elena?   Raquel is.

Where?

Answer these questions.

First, listen to the example:

Where is the doctor? (clinic)   He's at the clinic.

Now it's your turn.

1. Where is the doctor? (clinic)   He's at the clinic.

2. Where is the nurse? (hospital)   She's at the hospital.

3. Where are the paramedics? (ambulance)   They're in the ambulance.

4. Where is the cashier? (store)   She's at the store.

5. Where is the teacher? (school)   He's at the school.

6. Where is the social worker? (center)   She's at the center.

7. Where are we? (reception desk)   We're at the reception desk.

8. Where is the gown? (dressing room)   It's in the dressing room.

Unit 2: Going to the Pharmacy

Ailments

Listen and repeat.

1. allergy

2. backache

3. cold

4. cough

5. earache

6. headache

7. sore throat

8. stomachache

Pharmacy Items

Listen and repeat.

1. conditioner

2. deodorant

3. prescription

4. shampoo

5. soap

6. toothpaste

Instructions

Listen and repeat.

1. once a day

2. twice a day

3. three times a day

4. before meals

5. with meals

6. after meals

Short Answers

Answer these questions.

First, listen to the example:

    Does Jorge take cough medicine for coughs?   Yes, he does.

Now it's your turn.

1. Does Jorge take cough medicine for coughs?   Yes, he does.

2. Does Elena take lozenges for sore throats?   Yes, she does.

3. Does Simon take cold medicine for colds?   Yes, he does.

4. Do you take aspirin for backaches?   Yes, I do.

5. Do they use antibiotics for earaches?   Yes, they do.

Negative Short Answers

Answer these questions.

First, listen to the example:

    Does Jorge take cold medicine for coughs?   No, he doesn't.

Now it's your turn.

1. Does Jorge take cold medicine for coughs?   No, he doesn't.

2. Do you take lozenges for backaches?   No, we don't.

3. Does Ming take cold medicine for coughs?   No, she doesn't.

4.	Does Simon take cough medicine for earaches?	No, he doesn't.
5.	Do I take allergy medicine for stomachaches?	No, you don't.

Questions and Answers

Answer these questions.

First, listen to the example:

What do you use to wash your hair?	I use shampoo.

Now it's your turn.

1.	What do you use to wash your hair?	I use shampoo.
2.	What does Elena use to make her hair soft?	She uses conditioner.
3.	What does Simon use to wash his hands?	He uses soap.
4.	What do we use to clean our teeth?	We use toothpaste.
5.	What does Sasha use to smell good?	He uses deodorant.

Negative Sentences

Make negative sentences with these words.

First, listen to the example:

I/get up/five A.M.	I don't get up at five A.M.

Now it's your turn.

1.	I/get up/five A.M.	I don't get up at five A.M.
2.	Jorge/go to work/at two P.M.	Jorge doesn't go to work at two P.M.
3.	we/eat breakfast/at noon	We don't eat breakfast at noon.
4.	Ming/work/all night	Ming doesn't work all night.
5.	they/stay home/all day	They don't stay home all day.

What Time and When?

Answer these questions.

First, listen to the example:

What time does Raquel go to work? (9:00 A.M.)   She goes to work at 9:00 A.M.

Now it's your turn.

1.	What time does Raquel go to work? (9:00 A.M.)	She goes to work at 9:00 A.M.
2.	What time does Sasha eat lunch? (12:30 P.M.)	He eats lunch at 12:30 P.M.
3.	What time does Elena leave the supermarket? (4:00 P.M.)	She leaves at 4:00 P.M.
4.	When do you eat dinner? (in the evening)	I eat dinner in the evening.
5.	When do they go on vacation? (in the summer)	They go on vacation in the summer.

How Much?

Make questions with these words.

First, listen to the example:

medicine/Jorge/buy	How much medicine does Jorge buy?

Now it's your turn.

1.	medicine/Jorge/buy	How much medicine does Jorge buy?
2.	juice/Simon/drink	How much juice does Simon drink?
3.	money/it/cost	How much money does it cost?
4.	time/Elena/need	How much time does Elena need?
5.	aspirin/you/take	How much aspirin do you take?

How Many?

Make questions with these words.

First, listen to the example:

classes/they/take	How many classes do they take?

Now it's your turn.

1.	classes/they/take	How many classes do they take?
2.	hours/you/work	How many hours do you work?
3.	tablets/Elena/take	How many tablets does Elena take?
4.	cough drops/he/need	How many cough drops does he need?
5.	hours a week/she/work	How many hours a week does she work?

Telling Time

Say the time in a different way.

First, listen to the example:

    It's ten past two.   It's two-ten.

Now it's your turn.

1. It's ten past two.   It's two-ten.
2. It's a quarter past four.   It's four-fifteen.
3. It's half past six.   It's six-thirty.
4. It's twenty to nine.   It's eight-forty.
5. It's five to eleven.   It's ten fifty-five.

Unit 3: Cleaning the Home

Cleaning Vocabulary

Listen and repeat.

1. bleach
2. brush
3. cleaner
4. dish soap
5. dizzy
6. faint
7. fan
8. floor polish
9. inhale
10. oven cleaner
11. paint
12. remover

13. roller

14. sponge

15. tile and tub

16. vapors

House Vocabulary

Listen and repeat.

1. bathroom

2. bathtub

3. bed

4. bedroom

5. dining room

6. dishwasher

7. kitchen

8. living room

9. sink

10. stove

11. toilet

12. window

Future Tense–Short Answers

Answer these questions.

First, listen to the example:

Will Sasha paint the   Yes, he will.
bedroom?

Now it's your turn.

1.	Will Sasha paint the bedroom?	Yes, he will.
2.	Will Elena clean the kitchen?	Yes, she will.
3.	Will Jorge and Elena go home?	Yes, they will.
4.	Will we vacuum the living room?	Yes, we will.
5.	Will it work well?	Yes, it will.

Future Tense–Negative Short Answers

Answer these questions.

First, listen to the example:

Will Jorge paint the dining room?	No, he won't.

Now it's your turn.

1.	Will Jorge paint the dining room?	No, he won't.
2.	Will Ming clean the living room?	No, she won't.
3.	Will they eat dinner at Ming's house?	No, they won't.
4.	Will we clean the bathroom?	No, we won't.
5.	Will it be enough?	No, it won't.

Singular and Plural

Listen to the singular and then say the plural.

First, listen to the example:

fan	fans

Now it's your turn.

1.	fan	fans
2.	room	rooms
3.	sponge	sponges
4.	window	windows
5.	bed	beds
6.	arm	arms
7.	ear	ears
8.	doctor	doctors
9.	cleaner	cleaners

There Is or There Are

Make sentences from these words.

First, listen to the examples:

telephone/bedroom	There is a telephone in the bedroom.
rollers/living room	There are rollers in the living room.

Now it's your turn.

1.	telephone/bedroom	There is a telephone in the bedroom.
2.	rollers/living room	There are rollers in the living room.

3.	fan/kitchen	There is a fan in the kitchen.
4.	windows/dining room	There are windows in the dining room.
5.	floor polish/floors	There is floor polish on the floors.

A *Little* or a Lot

Answer these questions.

First, listen to the examples:

How much paint will Sasha buy? (a lot)	He'll buy a lot of paint.
How much oven cleaner will Elena use? (a little)	She'll use a little oven cleaner.

Now it's your turn.

1.	How much paint will Sasha buy? (a lot)	He'll buy a lot of paint.
2.	How much oven cleaner will Elena use? (a little)	She'll use a little oven cleaner.
3.	How much floor polish will Ming need? (a lot)	She'll need a lot of floor polish.
4.	How much bleach will she get? (a little)	She'll get a little bleach.
5.	How much time do they need to paint? (a lot)	They need a lot of time to paint.

A *Few* or a Lot

Answer these questions.

First, listen to the examples:

How many brushes will Sasha need? (a lot)	A lot of brushes.

How many sponges will Ming buy? (a few)	A few sponges.

Now it's your turn.

1. How many brushes will Sasha need? (a lot) — A lot of brushes.

2. How many sponges will Ming buy? (a few) — A few sponges.

3. How many paper towels will Elena use? (a lot) — A lot of paper towels.

4. How many sandwiches will they eat? (a few) — A few sandwiches.

5. How many hours will we work? (a few) — A few hours.

Money

Listen to the speaker and say the money.

First, listen to the examples:

a dollar, two quarters, and eight pennies	$1.58
five dollars, seven dimes, and three nickels	$5.85

Now it's your turn.

1. a dollar, two quarters, and eight pennies — $1.58

2. five dollars, seven dimes, and three nickels — $5.85

3. ten dollars, three quarters, a dime, and nine pennies — $10.94

4. twenty dollars, four $21.35
    quarters, three dimes, and
    one nickel

5. fifty dollars, one quarter, six $50.65
    nickels, and ten pennies

Unit 4: Alternative Medicine

Health Food

Listen and repeat.

1. diet
2. health food
3. herbs
4. macrobiotic
5. remedy
6. vegetarian

Exercise

Listen and repeat.

1. aerobics
2. gym
3. jogging
4. tai chi
5. training
6. weights

Treatments

Listen and repeat.

1. acupuncture
2. chart
3. massage
4. meditation
5. needles
6. relaxation
7. stress
8. tension
9. therapy
10. yoga

Short Sentences with the Verb *Can*

Make sentences from these words.

First, listen to the example:

Dr. Huang/do acupuncture   Dr. Huang can do acupuncture.

Now it's your turn.

1. Dr. Huang/do acupuncture   Dr. Huang can do acupuncture.
2. Sasha's mother/cook Russian food   Sasha's mother can cook Russian food.
3. Raquel/make Dominican food   Raquel can make Dominican food.
4. Elena/prepare Mexican dishes   Elena can prepare Mexican dishes.

5. You/ride a bicycle   You can ride a bicycle.

6. I/drive a car   I can drive a car.

Negative Sentences with Can't

Make sentences from these words.

First, listen to the example:

Sasha/stop smoking.   Sasha can't stop smoking.

Now it's your turn.

1. Sasha/stop smoking   Sasha can't stop smoking.

2. Simon/lift heavy boxes   Simon can't lift heavy boxes.

3. Dr. Huang/teach yoga   Dr. Huang can't teach yoga.

4. Simon/cook Dominican food   Simon can't cook Dominican food.

5. We/speak Chinese   We can't speak Chinese.

6. They/cook Chinese food   They can't cook Chinese food.

Kind of, Type of, and Sort of

Answer these questions.

First, listen to the example:

What kind of food can Elena cook?   Mexican food.

Now it's your turn.

1. What kind of food can Elena cook?   Mexican food.

2. What type of medicine can Dr. Huang practice?   Alternative medicine.

3. What sort of exercise can Raquel do?   Aerobic exercise.

4. What kind of food can   Russian food.
   Sasha's mother make?

5. What type of classes can   English classes.
   Simon teach?

6. What sort of painting can   House painting.
   Sasha do?

Adjectives

Listen and repeat.

1. cheap
2. clean
3. delicious
4. expensive
5. funny
6. healthy
7. heavy
8. new
9. old
10. relaxed
11. serious
12. unhealthy

Comparative and Superlative

Say the comparative and superlative forms of these adjectives.

First, listen to the example:

    cheap   cheaper   cheapest

Now it's your turn.

1. cheap	cheaper	cheapest
2. new	newer	newest
3. old	older	oldest
4. funny	funnier	funniest
5. healthy	healthier	healthiest
6. heavy	heavier	heaviest

Here's another example:

delicious	more delicious	most delicious

Now it's your turn.

1. delicious	more delicious	most delicious
2. expensive	more expensive	most expensive
3. nutritious	more nutritious	most nutritious
4. relaxed	more relaxed	most relaxed
5. serious	more serious	most serious
6. unhealthy	more unhealthy	most unhealthy

Questions with *Which*

Answer these questions.

First, listen to the example:

Which food is cheaper, fast food or health food?   Fast food is cheaper than health food.

Now it's your turn.

1. Which food is cheaper, fast food or health food?   Fast food is cheaper than health food.

2. Which foods are more nutritious, hot dogs or salads?

Salads are more nutritious than hot dogs.

3. Which medicine is better, herbal medicine or aspirin?

Herbal medicine is better than aspirin.

4. Which person is more relaxed, Raquel or Ming?

Raquel is more relaxed than Ming.

5. Which person's diet is healthier, Simon's or Sasha's?

Simon's diet is healthier than Sasha's diet.

6. Which treatment is more expensive, acupuncture or Western medicine?

Western medicine is more expensive than acupuncture.

Unit 5: Reporting a Crime

Descriptions

Listen and repeat.

1. bald
2. heavy
3. old
4. short
5. tall
6. tattoo
7. thin
8. young

Clothing

Listen and repeat.

1. dress
2. hat
3. jacket
4. jeans
5. pants
6. shirt
7. shoes
8. sneakers
9. suit
10. T-shirt

At the Station

Listen and repeat.

1. bank card
2. cash
3. credit card
4. license
5. mugged
6. officer
7. paycheck
8. police
9. report
10. sign
11. station

12. steal

13. subway

14. wallet

Past Tense of Regular Verbs

Listen to the present tense and say the past tense.

The past tense of these verbs ends with the /t/ sound.

First, listen to the example:

ask   asked

Now it's your turn.

1.	ask	asked
2.	cash	cashed
3.	help	helped
4.	look	looked
5.	stop	stopped
6.	talk	talked

The past tense of these verbs ends with the /d/ sound.

7.	describe	described
8.	grab	grabbed
9.	happen	happened
10.	listen	listened
11.	offer	offered
12.	sign	signed

The past tense of these verbs ends with the /ed/ sound.

13. need	needed
14. report	reported
15. wait	waited
16. want	wanted

Questions and Answers

Answer these questions in the past tense.

First, listen to the example:

Did a man grab Jorge's wallet or keys?	He grabbed his wallet.

Now it's your turn.

1. Did a man grab Jorge's wallet or keys?	He grabbed his wallet.
2. Did Jorge ask Simon or Raquel for help?	He asked Raquel for help.
3. Did Jorge report the crime to the police or the mayor?	He reported the crime to the police.
4. Did the officer talk to Raquel or Jorge?	He talked to Jorge.
5. Did Jorge sign the report or the check?	He signed the report.
6. Did Jorge need food or money?	He needed money.

Past Tense of Irregular Verbs

Listen to the present tense and say the past tense.

First, listen to the example:

    drive   drove

Now it's your turn.

1.	drive	drove
2.	feel	felt
3.	find	found
4.	get	got
5.	give	gave
6.	go	went
7.	have	had
8.	run	ran
9.	say	said
10.	see	saw
11.	speak	spoke
12.	steal	stole
13.	take	took
14.	tell	told
15.	wear	wore
16.	write	wrote

Possessives

Substitute the possessive adjective for the noun.

First, listen to the example:

Raquel listened to Jorge's story.	She listened to his story.

Now it's your turn.

1. Raquel listened to Jorge's story.	She listened to his story.
2. They went in Raquel's car.	They went in her car.
3. Jorge looked at the criminals' pictures.	He looked at their pictures.
4. He likes Elena's wallet.	He likes her wallet.

Subjects and Objects

Substitute the noun with the subject or object pronoun.

First, listen to the example:

Jorge found Raquel.	He found her.

Now it's your turn.

1. Jorge found Raquel.	He found her.
2. Raquel drove Jorge to the station.	She drove him to it.
3. The officer listened to Jorge's report.	He listened to it.
4. Raquel lent money to Jorge.	She lent it to him.
5. Jorge and Elena gave the money back.	They gave it back.
6. You and I felt bad for Jorge.	We felt bad for him.

Unit 6: Getting Things Fixed

Vocabulary

Listen and repeat.

1. drip
2. electrician
3. extension cord
4. faucet
5. furnace
6. gas leak
7. heater
8. landlord
9. list
10. outlet
11. plug
12. plumber
13. radiator
14. repairs
15. service rep
16. shower
17. stove
18. strange smell
19. waste
20. water heater

Affirmative Answers with *Could*

Give short answers to the questions.

First, listen to the example:

Could Ming smell the gas leak?	Yes, she could.

Now it's your turn.

1. Could Ming smell the gas leak? — Yes, she could.

2. Could Simon find the telephone number? — Yes, he could.

3. Could Ming call the gas company? — Yes, she could.

4. Could they open all the windows? — Yes, they could.

5. Could Ming make a list of repairs? — Yes, she could.

6. Could Simon help her? — Yes, he could.

7. Could we contact the gas company? — Yes, we could.

Negative Answers with *Couldn't*

Give short answers to the questions.

First, listen to the example:

Could Ming paint her apartment?	No, she couldn't.

Now it's your turn.

1. Could Ming paint her apartment? — No, she couldn't.

2. Could she and her cousin carry all the boxes?

No, they couldn't.

3. Could Simon fix the gas leak?

No, he couldn't.

4. Could Ming repair the faucet?

No, she couldn't.

5. Could she and her cousin fix the outlet?

No, they couldn't.

6. Could the landlord do the repairs?

No, he couldn't.

7. Could it be repaired?

No, it couldn't.

8. Could we help with the repairs?

No, we couldn't.

9. Could I pay for a plumber?

No, I couldn't.

Questions with *Who*

Answer these questions.

First, listen to the example:

Who could smell the gas leak?

Simon and Ming could.

Now it's your turn.

1. Who could smell the gas leak?

Simon and Ming could.

2. Who could find the telephone number?

Simon could.

3. Who could call the company?

Ming could.

4. Who could fix the gas leak?

A service rep could.

5. Who could repair the dripping faucet? — A plumber could.

6. Who could fix the electrical outlet? — An electrician could.

7. Who could pay for the repairs? — The landlord could.

8. Who could enjoy their new apartment? — Ming and her cousin could.

Review of *Can/Can't* and *Could/Couldn't*

Make sentences with these words.

First, listen to the examples:

Sasha/paint houses	Sasha can paint houses.
Simon/fix the shower	Simon couldn't fix the shower.

Now it's your turn.

1. Sasha/paint houses — Sasha can paint houses.

2. Simon/fix the shower — Simon couldn't fix the shower.

3. Jorge/speak Spanish — Jorge can speak Spanish.

4. Elena/clean Ming's oven — Elena couldn't clean Ming's oven.

5. Raquel/lend Jorge money — Raquel could lend Jorge money.

6. Elena/cook Mexican food — Elena can cook Mexican food.

7. Jorge/buy Elena's medicine — Jorge could buy Elena's medicine.

8. Ming's aunt/do acupuncture — Ming's aunt can do acupuncture.

9. Sasha/paint Ming's apartment — Sasha could paint Ming's apartment.

10. Jorge/get his wallet back   Jorge couldn't get his wallet back.

Prepositions of Place

Answer these questions with the correct preposition.

First, listen to the example:

Where's the gas leak? (kitchen)   It's in the kitchen.

Now it's your turn.

1. Where's the gas leak? (kitchen)   It's in the kitchen.

2. Where's the telephone book? (table)   It's on the table.

3. Where's the telephone number? (book)   It's in the book.

4. Where's the dripping shower? (bathroom)   It's in the bathroom.

5. Where's the dripping faucet? (sink)   It's on the sink.

Imperatives

Say the negative form of the imperative.

First, listen to the example:

Call the gas company.   Don't call the gas company.

Now it's your turn.

1. Call the gas company.   Don't call the gas company.

2. Open the windows.   Don't open the windows.

3. Wait for the service rep.   Don't wait for the service rep.

4. Tell your landlord.   Don't tell your landlord.

5. Repair the door.   Don't repair the door.

6. Use the outlet.   Don't use the outlet.

7. Fix the faucet.   Don't fix the faucet.

8. Leave your house.   Don't leave your house.

Unit 7: Social Services

Social Services Vocabulary

Listen and repeat.

1. alcoholic

2. application

3. approve

4. benefits

5. blind

6. deaf

7. disabled

8. drugs

9. groups

10. homeless

11. illness

12. laid off

13. options

14. reject

15. shelters

16. teenagers

17. therapy

18. unemployed

19. Unemployment Office

20. Yellow Pages

Maternity Vocabulary

Listen and repeat.

1. baby food

2. diapers

3. discount

4. Medicare

5. postnatal care

6. prenatal care

7. twins

8. vouchers

Affirmative Sentences

Make a sentence from these words.

First, listen to the example:

Sasha/go to/Unemployment Office	Sasha's going to go to the Unemployment Office.

Now it's your turn.

1. Sasha/go to/Unemployment Office	Sasha's going to go to the Unemployment Office.
2. He/fill out an application	He's going to fill out an application.
3. They/approve his application	They're going to approve his application.

455

4.	He/get money from the government	He's going to get money from the government.
5.	Elena/have twins	Elena's going to have twins.

Negative Sentences

Make a sentence from these words.

First, listen to the example:

Raquel/have a baby	Raquel isn't going to have a baby.

Now it's your turn.

1.	Raquel/have a baby	Raquel isn't going to have a baby.
2.	Sasha/be a father	Sasha isn't going to be a father.
3.	Elena/work much longer	Elena isn't going to work much longer.
4.	Jorge/make enough money	Jorge isn't going to make enough money.
5.	They/pay doctor's bills	They aren't going to pay doctor's bills.

Short Answers

Answer these questions.

First, listen to the example:

Are Sasha and Elena going to talk to Raquel?	Yes, they are.

Now it's your turn.

1.	Are Sasha and Elena going to talk to Raquel?	Yes, they are.

2. Is Raquel going to give them advice?

Yes, she is.

3. Is Simon going to receive unemployment benefits?

No, he isn't.

4. Is Sasha going to find another job?

Yes, he is.

5. Is Jorge going to stay home with the babies?

No, he isn't.

Questions

Answer these questions.

First, listen to the example:

Who is Raquel going to talk to?

She's going to talk to Sasha and Elena.

Now it's your turn.

1. Who is Raquel going to talk to?

She's going to talk to Sasha and Elena.

2. Where is Sasha going to go?

He's going to go to the Unemployment Office.

3. What is he going to do?

He's going to fill out an application.

4. When is Elena going to stop working?

She's going to stop working in a few weeks.

5. How is Jorge going to support his family?

He's going to support his family by working hard.

How Long or How Often?

Ask a question with "How long?" or "How often?"

First, listen to the example:

Sasha is going to get a check every two weeks.	How often is Sasha going to get a check?

Now it's your turn.

1. Sasha is going to get a check every two weeks.

   How often is Sasha going to get a check?

2. He is going to call his old boss every month.

   How often is he going to call his old boss?

3. Elena is going to work for three more weeks.

   How long is Elena going to work?

4. She is going to receive vouchers every month.

   How often is she going to receive vouchers?

5. She is going to stay home with the babies for a few years.

   How long is she going to stay home with the babies?

Adverbs of Frequency

Put the adverb of frequency in the sentence.

First, listen to the example:

Simon works in the summer. (never)	Simon never works in the summer.

Now it's your turn.

1. Simon works in the summer. (never)

   Simon never works in the summer.

2. Raquel cooks Dominican food. (usually)

   Raquel usually cooks Dominican food.

3. Ming works on weekends. (sometimes)

Ming sometimes works on weekends.

4. Elena is tired. (often)

Elena is often tired.

5. The babies are sick. (rarely)

The babies are rarely sick.

Too and *Enough*

Finish these sentences.

First, listen to the example:

Ming couldn't lift the boxes (heavy)

because they were too heavy.

Now it's your turn.

1. Ming couldn't lift the boxes (heavy)

because they were too heavy.

2. Jorge couldn't pay for baby supplies (expensive)

because they were too expensive.

3. Elena couldn't take the babies outside (cold)

because it was too cold.

Here's another example:

Ming couldn't lift the boxes (strong)

because she wasn't strong enough.

Now it's your turn.

4. Ming couldn't lift the boxes (strong)

because she wasn't strong enough.

5. Jorge couldn't pay for the baby supplies (rich)

because he wasn't rich enough.

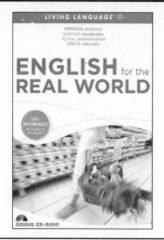

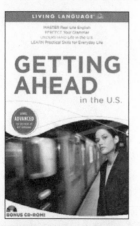